THEATRE /ARCHAEOLOGY

What is the connection between site-specific performance and interpretation of the past?

How and why can the documentation of contemporary performance be related to ancient performative practices, such as Greek warfare?

Theatre/Archaeology is a brilliant and provocative challenge to disciplinary practice and intellectual boundaries. It brings together radical proposals in both archaeological and performance theory to generate a startlingly original and intriguing methodological framework. It facilitates a new way of investigating landscape and cityscape, and notions of physicality, encounter, site and context.

The book takes scholarly innovation to new levels. It is the result of a long-term, unique collaboration between a renowned archaeological theorist and a leading theatre artist. The result is vibrant dialogic writing that bridges the scholarly/poetic divide.

In its unique integration of theory, narrative and autobiography, *Theatre/Archaeology* brings a new dimension to two burgeoning fields of enquiry.

Mike Pearson is Professor of Performance Studies at the University of Wales Aberystwyth. For thirty years he has pioneered innovative approaches in the practice, theory, pedagogy and documentation of performance. From 1981 to 1997 he was an artistic director of the theatre company Brith Gof.

Michael Shanks is Professor of Classics and of Cultural Anthropology at Stanford University. He is one of the world's foremost archaeological thinkers, and author of many works including *Reconstructing Archaeology* (1992), *Experiencing the Past* (1992), *Classical Archaeology of Greece* (1996) and *Art and the Greek City State* (1999).

THEATRE /ARCHAEOLOGY

MIKE PEARSON   MICHAEL SHANKS

London and New York

First published 2001 by Routledge
11 New Fetter Lane, London EC4 4EE

Simultaneously published in the USA and Canada by Routledge
29 West 35th Street, New York, NY 10001

Routledge is an imprint of the Taylor & Francis Group

Designed by Sutchinda Rangsi Thompson
Typeset in Helvetica, Frutiger and Joanna
Printed and bound in Great Britain by T J International Ltd, Padstow, Cornwall

British Library Cataloguing in Publication Data
A catalogue record for this book is available from the British Library

Library of Congress Cataloging in Publication Data
Pearson, Mike, 1949-
     Theatre/archaeology : disciplinary dialogues / Mike Pearson and Michael Shanks.
          p. cm.
     Includes bibliographical references and index.
     1. Theatre–Philosophy. 2. Archaeology–Philosophy. 3. Theatre and society. 4. Social
     archaeology. 5. Historical reenactments. I. Shanks, Michael. II. Title.
     PN2039 .P375 2001
     792'.01–dc21   00-045791

ISBN 0–415–19458–X (pbk)
ISBN 0–415–19457–1 (hbk)

CONTENTS

vi

FIGURES

R: Ruin **S:** Space **A:** Architecture **B:** Body **O:** Object **M:** Monument **E:** Everyday

Pages 20–1

B.1 Brith Gof: *Gododdin*. Photo: André Lützen
M.1 Mike Pearson/Peter Brötzmann: *Der Gefesselte*. Photo: André Lützen
A.1 Brith Gof: *Camlann*. Photo: Jens Koch
E.1 Museum of Welsh Life, St Fagans, Cardiff 1995. Photo: Michael Shanks
O.1 Brith Gof: *Los Angeles*. Photo: Nia Percy
R.1 Mike Pearson: *Der Gefesselte*. Photo: André Lützen
S.1 Brith Gof: *Camlann*. Photo: Jens Koch

Pages 34–5

B.2 Brith Gof: *Gododdin*. Photo: Pete Telfer
M.2 Brith Gof: *Cusanu Esgyrn*. Photo: Pete Telfer
E.2 Museum of Welsh Life, St Fagans, Cardiff 1995. Photo: Michael Shanks
A.2 Brith Gof: *Arturius Rex*. Photo: Pete Telfer
O.2 Brith Gof: *Cusanu Esgyrn*. Photo: Pete Telfer

Pages 134–5

ix

Pages 156–7

PREFACE

This volume traces an evolving dialogue between – and the gradual convergence and co-mingling of – two discrete projects: in performance and in archaeology.

It has its origins in a somewhat unlikely place. At the beginning of the 1990s a centre of archaeological theory was located in a small market town in west Wales, at the University of Wales, Lampeter. It was there that a series of encounters between performance and archaeology began. In their meetings and discussions, prehistorian Julian Thomas, classicist Michael Shanks and Mike Pearson, then artistic director of Welsh theatre company Brith Gof (translated – faint recollections), rapidly found mutualities of interest and approach. The initial talk was of archaeological excavation as performance event; of the dramatisation of the past within heritage re-enactments; of the sensualities of place; of the articulation of space, body and action in bounded contexts; of the problems of presentation and representation; of performance and the past as generative of, and constituted by, multiple and conflicting narratives. Above all, both disciplines acknowleged their functioning as modes of cultural production, involving the recontextualisation of material rather than its reconstruction.

In structure, this volume chronicles the development of the collaboration between Michael Shanks and Mike Pearson in their theoretical and practical endeavours, commencing with their interdisciplinary borrowing of certain notions and procedures to help expand and illuminate particular disciplinary perceptions and stances, and culminating in the joint elaboration of a **blurred genre**, a mixture of narration and scientific practices, an integrated approach to recording, writing and illustrating the material past.

Given the profligate adoption in cultural and critical theory and discourse of terms such as 'performance' and 'the performative' (and indeed 'archaeology' *pace* Foucault 1989) to describe notions of social affirmation, utterance and action – from Erving Goffman to Judith Butler – it was Julian Thomas who first suggested that the use of the term 'theatre' might help signal a specific focus on artistic practice and the aesthetic event and dispel any initial confusion about the situating of the discussants. The almost immediate and contrary use of 'performance' in place of 'theatre' in this text serves to indicate a particular concern with those genres of theatre that, by and large, are not reliant upon the exposition of dramatic literature and that 'stage the subject in process' (Reinelt forthcoming) rather than the 'character' and that attend to 'the making and fashioning of certain materials, especially the body and the exploration of the limits of representation-ability' (ibid.). This is what we term 'performance'. And the 'performative' used herein, at least initially, has a rhetorical dimension.

Given the idiosyncratic and personal nature of two converging projects, it was inevitable that this volume should tend towards the (auto)biographical. But, as Walter Benjamin said (1992: 91), 'thus the traces of the storyteller cling to the story the way the handprints of the potter cling to the clay vessel'. From time to time, the book also relies heavily on others, for their thoughts have often led not merely to further intellectual reflection but to embodiment as tenets of practice or positions to be held, their origins obscured by what they have inspired. And here as Walter Benjamin said (ibid.: 107):

> it is granted to him to reach back to a whole lifetime (a life, incidentally, that comprises not only his own experience but no little of the experience of others; what the storyteller knows from hearsay is added to his own). His gift is the ability to relate his life; his distinction, to be able to tell his entire life. The storyteller: he is the man who could let the wick of his life be consumed completely by the gentle flame of his story.

To help the reader, therefore, and to give credit where due, the Afterword and acknowledgements are quite detailed.

In this way the book necessarily has more than one voice. The typefaces change to indicate the personal voices of each of the authors, and also where they join, though the degree to which we have learned from each other makes this a crude device.

It begins in the present, with reflections on contemporary conditions.   **MP + MS**

A project in performance

As I write this book, we are launching an undergraduate course in performance studies in the Department of Theatre, Film and Television Studies in the University of Wales Aberystwyth (Pearson *et al.* 1999). Our aim is to devise distinctive pedagogical approaches, both practical and theoretical, that utilise the particular – and not, I stress, parochial – cultural and geographical resources of Aberystwyth, its landscape, language and history; that employ the particular material assets of the location, its architecture and social fabric, as a creative stimulus (working in the specific architectures of chapels, the particular social arrangement of cattle markets and in the barely accessible depths of forests, with objects drawn from the local farmers' co-operative and the county museum); that draw upon those traditions of experimental theatre-making that have proposed alternative approaches to the forms, preoccupations, functions and placement of theatre in Wales and that have acknowledged 'the close link between culture, subjectivity and place without reverting to nostalgia, new age mysticism or an aggressive "native soil" ideology' (Roms 1997: 80); that conspicuously foreground those particular histories, personalities and practices that have revealed 'the complex relationship between ourselves, our bodies and our environment, [between] our physical and sensual experience of a place, and . . . the impact a particular location can have on our lives' (ibid.). All this constitutes for us a kind of intellectual ecology, a challenge to notions of **centre/periphery**.

Whilst the course may involve the study of the **aesthetic event** of conventional theatre (as a social encounter and as a mode of cultural production rather than merely the staging of a play), we state our explicit interest in devised performance, physical theatre, site-specific work and performance art – those genres where dramatic literature does not necessarily play a central organising role – as they are manifest historically, ethnically and experimentally. Our simple desire is to find useful ways of understanding and describing what is, or was, going on in the phenomenon we call performance and then to encourage practical initiatives in its conception. If Schechner's definition of performance as 'organised human behaviour presented before witnesses' still holds, then the pertinent questions will be: How is it organised? What constitutes behaviour? How is it presented? What is the relationship with witnesses? We aim to develop a series of 'principles of practice' – approaches to conception, design, rehearsal and manifestation, a continuum of strategies and procedures which attend, with varying degrees of rigour, to questions of real-time presentation and representation.

As performance has grown in importance – particularly within the social sciences – as a means of exploring the myriad ways in which meaning is created and social life is shaped, it is essential to include different histories, genealogies, geographies and politics in the fabric of the academic discipline. It is also crucial to embrace the scrutiny of the widest spectrum of performative practices as they occur in our artistic and social life: in activities and arenas where image manipulation and management is implicated, and in those hybrid artistic genres that electronic communication begins to conspire. Performance studies also employs performance as an optic through which to examine the performative phenomena that constitute our contemporary experience – from theme park to internet, from Brit-art to Jerry Springer, from drag to rap – thereby widening understanding of performance as both a vital artistic practice and as a means to understand historical, social and cultural processes. (http://www.nyu.edu/pages/psi)

How do we constitute the particular accent of our discourse? It is, of necessity, **site-specific**. It assumes, of desire, a deliberate erasure of the finely etched line between the academic and the artistic. Out here, on the edges, off the beaten track, people who speak the same language literally and metaphorically are few enough. Our colleagues from Welsh literature studies can direct us to the performative nature of bardic poetry. But there are others – archaeologists, human geographers, earth scientists, social historians, cultural politicians – who pose familiar questions about place and identity, as well as institutions increasingly charged with responsibility for the representation of notions of cultural and national identity – the media, museums, environmental and heritage agencies. We feel as much affinity with them as with the sociological biases of extant models of performance studies. They can help orient us, revealing new ways of looking and telling. Our approaches then will be diverse, context-dependent and inter-disciplinary. We want to accommodate the broadest range of potential approaches without distilling them into a 'party line'. We espouse pragmatism and flexibility: we acknowledge the anecdotal. We doubt that our 'take' on performance studies has well-defined disciplinary boundaries.

We seem to be operating within a triangular field of attention which includes at its apexes the terms '**practice**', '**context**' and '**analysis**'. Practice because several of us are professional performance practitioners and because we want to make things – performances, knowledges – as much as we want to reflect on things. Context because we are interested in the ramifications of social, cultural, political and historical context upon the nature, form and function of performance, as operational in our particular set of circumstances, and because we are equally concerned with the effect of the performance environment – location, site, architecture, scenography – upon dramaturgy and techniques of exposition. Analysis because we desire to develop appropriate means to describe, document and ultimately legitimise performance practices. Within and upon this field there are a multitude of available stances and viewpoints. And it is always possible to shift position. Each one of us in our work may stand from time to time closer to one apex than the others, whilst still holding the others in view. So whilst we may be considering an analysis of practice (or a practice of analysis), context still claims our attention ('What does this mean . . . here?'). And the folklorist, the archaeologist, the geographer are most welcome to come and stand in our field. We do not simply want to appropriate their methodologies. We want them to look, and to enable us to look through them, at performance: it is already in the nature of their discourses to favour the local, the particular. Their analytical approaches must surely be instructive; at least, they are not forever searching for a universal revelation of the human condition. Finally, we want to reclaim and re-articulate the notion of 'event-ness' in performance studies – practice, context, theory.   **MP**

An archaeological project

As I write this book we are setting our hopes and designs upon a new Archaeology Center at Stanford University, California. It will cut across several departments – of Classics, History, Anthropological Sciences, Cultural and Social Anthropology, Earth Sciences, of Art History. While archaeology has always been this interdisciplinary field, divisions and rifts have been the norm, frequently focusing on that familiar and disabling cultural divide between science and the humanities. We intend something different – a creative intermingling, where the boundaries of the discipline are deliberately blurred, held suspended. Archaeology – truly interdisciplinary. For me this is the culmination of a twenty-year argument about the character of what we call archaeology. For me, archaeology is not a discipline but a cultural field. It means to work upon understanding archaeological things – material traces and material cultures, understanding the creative event that is the construction of archaeological knowledge, and the historical context of such an archaeological project.

This may all seem a little strange and oblique to those unfamiliar with archaeology. Let me explain, and to do so I will need to anticipate some of the arguments of the book. I consider this is excusable, for a preface is, after all, the place where we read of the circumstances under which a book has come to be written. And the topic is a significant one – disciplinary connections, the boundaries of the academy, and the shape of creative practices.

The origins of contemporary archaeology are to be found with the emergence of industrial modernity and Enlightenment thought in the eighteenth century. A reorientation of attitudes towards the material past was central to the new ideologies of classicism (the sanctity of a Graeco-Roman rather than merely Roman past), Hellenism (classical Greece as the childhood of civilisation and Europe) and Romanticism (redefinitions of the political and creative individual) (Shanks 1996). The nation-states of Europe competed for the material relics of ancient civilisations, cultural capital to witness their own membership of a civilised elite. Archaeology simultaneously provided tangible manifestations of national and local ancestry, material continuities justifying territorial ownership. And while the traces of Celtic Gaul or the megaliths of British prehistory might be attached to a sense of enduring identity, the ruin of the shattered archaeological past and its melancholic loss attests as well to the distance and indeed the difference of the past – the past is both here and now, but also lost and distant in its ruin.

The experiences of antiquarians, travellers and Enlightenment scholars of the Mediterranean were central to the emergence of archaeology and this particular form that it took. There were new notions of visiting rooted in the picturesque and sublime, new views of the past in the landscape – topographical interests of the like of aristocratic traveller and collector Choiseul-Gouffier, William Gell writing his itineraries for Greece, military man William Martin Leake locating sites mentioned in ancient history books. New relationships of inspiration between past and present, arts and architectures developed. For example: neo-classicism and the Greek revival, typified by the architectural work of members of the British Society of Dilettanti, Stuart and Revett. The Mediterranean and Near East became a theatre for ostentatious and self-conscious programmes of research and the manipulation of the past in the present – from conservation and restoration programmes in the planning of the new metropolis, to the work of the foreign institutes of learning set up by imperial powers across the world.

From the nineteenth century archaeology was significantly influenced by German scientific history, *Altertumswissenschaft*, developing increasingly rigorous methods and procedures. But it was only in the 1970s that the British archaeologist David Clarke felt able to report a new critical awareness in the discipline. He termed this a 'loss of innocence' (Clarke 1973). An introspective approach began to emerge, which focused upon methods and theories along with a more mature view outwards, which questioned archaeology's place within the humanities and social sciences, and society as a whole. Since then archaeology has come to be seen as much an anthropological as an historical discipline, with artefacts conceived not merely as temporal indices and cultural markers, supplying date, sequence and ethnic identity to an archaeological culture history, but also as means to understand past society. Most importantly, artefacts and material environments are now conceived as *active* in society and history, partners with human subjects in making society and history what they are rather than merely illustrating a logic or momentum established elsewhere.

In the 1980s social archaeologies further stressed the importance of context: that any artefact – a work of art, for example – must be set in the context of the society that produced it, rather than allowed to simply stand on its own and speak for itself. And this context includes also the past in the present. So the enormous growth of interest in what has been termed 'heritage' or 'patrimony' has accompanied a realisation of the vital part played by material culture, and particularly the archaeological past, in contemporary constructions of social identity. At the same time various issues of cultural politics have conspicuously highlighted the same point about the embeddedness of the past in the present – the return of cultural treasures from foreign museums to their origins and the sacredness of human remains and attempted pro-scriptions on their archaeological study by some Native American groups – are two such cases.

A few words of clarification are necessary here, in parenthesis, with regard to the concept of heritage. Defined generally as inherited cultural material and goods, the word always has connotations of conservative political and cultural agendas, nostalgic, consoling and reactionary programmes of the conservation and promotion of a high cultural canon. Heritage: great achievements bequeathed to us from the past, central to our identity, often nationalist identity, as members of worthy nation-states and educated social classes. But the term is also used in a more neutral sense: archaeological heritage management in the UK is the close equivalent of cultural resource management in the US . . . well, arguably. And this is the point – the term is slippery and contested (Shanks 1992a). What is not in doubt is that the culture industry that includes the heritage industry (Hewison 1987) is a vast and growing cultural and economic sector, covering salvage and rescue archaeology, development and planning, the art market, cultural tourism, museums, book and magazine publishing, mass media 'edutainment', as well as academics and their work.

I take a particular stand in respect of the changes in archaeology described here. I have indicated how I ally myself with those who would have of archaeology a powerful interdisciplinary mix. It is not coincidental that here in the heart of Silicon Valley Stanford archaeologists are looking to find just such a new reconciliation of science and humanities, arts and academia, rich cultural textures allied with new communicative media. A premise for making this work is that we have to be sophisticated in our theory and practice. We also embrace open experiment.

For example, and as we will argue in this book, the social needs to be understood as an *embodied* field: society is felt, enjoyed and suffered, as well as rationally thought. The statistical analysis of social science is not enough. Archaeologists, like many others in the humanities, are now attending to the phenomenological qualities of things and places, what it means to experience architectural space and landscape, the significance of different experiences. Megaliths not simply as tombs, but as sculptures in ritual landscapes of vista and social perspective. Weapons not merely as the functional accoutrements of warfare, the compositions of their metals analysed for evidence of ancient metallurgy, but also as appendages to different experiences and techniques of the body. A house not merely as scene of the domestic economy, its refuse analysed for evidence of butchery practices and cropping regimes, but also as the quality or texture of local space.

Here archaeology's intimate connection of the global and the local is relevant. Widely appealing as a subject, archaeology works upon the details of local pasts. Archaeological remains are now so often a main component in regional as well as national planning. And rather

xvi

than treat them as representatives of a past gone and now fragmented, to be conserved or preserved according to some calculation of value to the present, I stress that temporality be described as *actuality*, the return of the past in the present, but in different guise. Something once inconsequential may turn out to be heavily charged with cultural significance for later people. So conspicuously in old places layered in archaeological traces, an artefact, building or ruin from the past does not hold comfortably some point in a linear flow of time from past through to present. It is not just a dated event in the past. Instead the past bubbles around us. This is the life of things in the present, the life-cycle of artefacts and buildings, enfolded in a multitemporal mix which is the fundamental texture of our human social experience.

This is what I mean when I refer to the need to work upon understanding archaeological things and the creative event that is the construction of archaeological knowledge. It is to think about the very character of the social fabric, its materiality and temporality. It is to cut across disciplines and explode the boundaries of academia. It means that archaeologists have much to talk about and work upon with geographers and material scientists, philosophers of science and geneticists, with those who work upon and think about that field of social practice we call performance.

This is actually a brief sketch of some elements of what has come to be termed 'interpretive archaeology' (Hodder *et al.* 1995), and this is my archaeological project, my contribution to our plans at Stanford. The term has grown out of what was called 'postprocessual' archaeology (explained in Shanks and Hodder 1995). It designates a set of approaches to the ruined material past which foreground interpretation, the ongoing process of making sense of what never was firm or certain. This archaeology entertains no final and definitive account of the past as it was, but fosters multivocal and multiple accounts: a creative but none the less critical attention and response to the interests, needs and desires of different constituencies (those people, groups or communities who have or express interest in the material past).   **MS**

A joint project

Our particular archaeological and performance projects came together initially as we met through the work of an arts company – Brith Gof, founded by one of us (**MP**) some twenty-five years ago and which the other (**MS**) joined as a company director more recently. This book is in some ways a document of certain aspects of the work of Brith Gof; we include many illustrations of company work and an appendix listing some performed pieces. But we hope that we have begun to make clear that we stress the deeper structural features of our common project: an interdisciplinary and hybrid focus on the textures of social and cultural experience; the means and materials of forging cultural ecologies or milieux which attend to that contemporary tension between the global and the local; how we model the event of this cultural production, the weaving of connections through such indeterminate times and places.

It is worth saying that, in some ways, this places our project within cultural studies, as it has emerged from Britain (Turner 1996) and as it is has been related to performance studies (Diamond 1996). Our reference here is to located and interventionist work, provocative, challenging orthodox canons of method and objects of interest (juxtaposing Greek art and street shoes in Copenhagen), challenging foundational discourses (such as dramatic literature), stressing the connection between cultural production and its contexts. **MP + MS**

THEATRE /ARCHAEOLOGY

INTRODUCTION

Less and less frequently do we encounter people with the ability to tell a tale properly.

(Benjamin 1992: 83)

Like turning on a tap when the water is under high pressure, a flood of reminiscences comes to me, if I give it a chance.

(Williams 1987: 17)

This is not a book about ruined auditoria, though it could be. Nor does it examine archaic theatre forms, though it might do. It concerns moments so particular that we sometimes suspect it has arisen solely from the chance intersection of two peculiar biographies, from an unlikely convergence of the theories and practices of archaeology and performance.

Whilst this encounter inevitably involves interdisciplinary borrowing and appropriation – performance apprehended through such archaeological notions as 'stratigraphy', 'assemblage' and 'sensorium', archaeological interpretation constituted through performative means – discussion centres primarily on tropes, notions, themes and concepts of mutual interest. These include the body (and its dilation in performance, warfare, death); space and place (site, locale, field); architecture (monument, enclosure, ruin); time; object; trace; memory; the everyday; the document . . .

The convergence of the two biographies/projects/discourses is elaborated in this volume in three main chapters: Theatre Archaeology, Theatre and Archaeology and Theatre/Archaeology.

In **Theatre Archaeology**, the statement of particular stances in performance theory is paralleled by an expanded account of archaeological fieldwork. This serves to identify potentially transferable concepts and to indicate the role of documentation as a core topic of concern. The chapter entitled **Theatre and Archaeology** involves the entwining of two themes: that of historical re-enactment within heritage contexts – and its radical alternatives in site-specific performance – and the use of performance theory to discern and describe (albeit essentially dramatic) historical practices and behaviours, with the Greek hoplite warrior as cyborg, the neolithic tomb as performance arena. The concluding section, **Theatre/Archaeology**, involves a complex interpenetration of the two discourses in an account of projects which begin to fuse performance and archaeology in the dynamic interpretation of the material past.

The themes and approaches in this volume reflect what we might term the 'forensic cast' in contemporary society. The popularity of crime novels and true-crime television programmes – with accounts of detection and pathology – is apparent enough. This may indicate a persistent morbidity in our human condition. But it may also attest to our fascination with, and increasing reliance upon, scientifically verified evidence as representing fact, verisimilitude, truth, and upon reconstruction, informed by surveillance, as helping us understand criminal method and motive, and narrative: to seek clues, to create an authentic account of the lost event is the prime objective. Such matters have long been in the critical realm of both archaeology and performance.

So we begin again. At the outset, two voices are held apart reflecting upon the nature of personal disciplinary experiences and histories, but beginning to signal potential topics of conversation.

A photograph, in black and white

For me, it begins with a photograph . . .

It is January, 1970 in a common room of University College, Cardiff. The padded benches are pulled back, a black cloth hung over the noticeboard, though not quite enough to hide a hand-drawn poster for a 'Teatrical Experience', the missing 'h' added unselfconsciously above. The wall clock shows 8.15. I'm dressed in jeans and black T-shirt, a student in the Department of Archaeology. I'm barefoot, as are my seven colleagues, all exiles from the official student drama society. We are performing a version of Homer's *Odyssey*, without words. At centre Odysseus forms his ship's prow, the strength of the waves in the bend of his knees. To the right, the whirlpool Charybdis eddies. To the left, three of us portray the monstrous Scylla. The naïveté of the work moves me deeply. Here is the art of the beginner: untainted, optimistic, hopeful of great happenings. Here I am before the cuts and bruises of RAT Theatre, before the physical control which came with my training in Noh theatre in Japan, before the deafness which resulted from performing with too many loud soundtracks. There are nine other photographs in the set. They are all that survive of *Odyssey* – they and the memories they evoke for performers and spectators alike.   **MP**

Figure 1
Theatre-in-Transit:
Odyssey.

A technical drawing

For me, it begins with a technical drawing . . .

It is of the Black Gate, part of the new castle of Newcastle upon Tyne, in the north of England, 'newly' built from 1280. I had completed in 1980 a new survey of the well-preserved remains of this many-times altered building (Shanks 1981). I was accurate, no more than a centimetre lost over fifty metres. Or so I thought, until I realised that the drafting paper I was using was highly susceptible to stretch and shrink in the damp January weather and by my gas fire in the garage, used as office, under the railway arches. I was measuring and drawing walls and stonework, marking the edges. The history of the building was well known to me. My fellow archaeologists had excavated the town rubbish dumped into the neighbouring ditches over a couple of centuries. I had dug its dungeon basement (a few scraps of pottery). I now have framed on my wall a sketch of the gate made in 1829 and a photograph of the shacks built against the back and still there in the late nineteenth century, before conservation values and restoration measures removed them. But in this historical density – the black gateway to seven hundred years of life – my record was curiously, if inevitably transparent. Ink lines on tracing film.

It was a career in archaeological fieldwork and excavation, over almost before it began. I was too much disturbed by the attenuation of the past. The past recorded in archaeological drawings? Of course not. I wanted more. Or at least somehow to fill in the gaps between the lines.

MS

A video

For me, it continues with a video . . .

Suspended from the ceiling in the Westwerk Art Gallery in Hamburg in 1994, here I am in black overcoat, one shoe, performing *Angelus*, a production inspired by Walter Benjamin's meditation on Paul Klee's painting *The Angel of the Twentieth Century* (Benjamin 1992: 249) – whom Laurie Anderson sings of as being 'blown backwards into the future' – and by Heiner Müller's meditation (Müller 1990: 99) on Walter Benjamin's meditation. And I'm still not saying much. There would be little point, as I'm accompanied by the great square head and torso of German saxophonist Peter Brötzmann. His very stance supports the enormous power of his heart and lungs; the fearsome intensity of his playing is etched in the swollen veins of his neck. The suspension harness makes my head loll, as if my neck has snapped. I seem to have remained loose-limbed, even though I cracked my kneecap, twisted my ribcage, when working, tied up, with Peter on *Der Gefesselte/The Bound Man* two years previously. But am I flying or dying? After the performance, a spectator shouted and swore at me. She thought I was portraying the latter, I the former.

And these are the things that remain: a few photographs, the odd contact sheet,

Figure 2
Mike Pearson/Peter Brötzmann: *Angelus* © Matthew Partridge

fragments of video, scribbled drawings on scraps of paper, indecipherable notebooks, diaries, reviews, injuries, scars, half-remembered experiences, faint recollections, awakened nostalgias . . .   **MP**

A memory

For me, it continues with a memory . . .

I am at the Department of Archaeology, University of Reading, maybe 1990. Another seminar. It was about a perfume jar again, Greek, found in Sicily. I used the same jar so many times, in talks and writings. It was never the same twice. My notes for talks at this time were flow charts and diagrams attempting to cope with the intersection of ideas, thoughts, facts, materials. Incomplete notes; memory was vital then, and is virtually all that is left. No text to be read. Improvised talks with staged gaps in the argument and between the components of the topic, to allow those listening to be part of the process. Of making sense of something so ordinary, a ceramic laid down with someone who died some two and a half thousand years ago. I wanted to communicate the utter indeterminacy of this tiny but exquisite artefact. I was saying so much (how it had interested nineteenth-century classical antiquarians!), yet so little of times gone by, witnessed now only by the crumbling remnants and our attempts to make good the loss. How it exploded in a cacophony of meanings and significances surrounding its design, manufacture and use.

It was about how the pot connects people and things together in its *life-cycle* (raw material – design – production – distribution – consumption – discard – discovery). What did it connect? I talked of clay and potter, painter and brushes (for miniature work). Its figurative painted designs of animals, warriors, monsters, violence, flowers, special artefacts. Of perfume, oil (perfumed) and the body (illustrated and anointed). Travel away from Korinth (its place of making) to the grave where it was found in Sicily. The ships, the corpse and cemetery. How the perfume jar helped constitute the nineteenth-century art museum (albeit in a small way). This pot has been mobilised many times in defining the discipline of classical archaeology. And I extended this life-cycle to include myself and those listening to me in a seminar room in Reading University.

I talked in fractured juxtapositions, marshalling illustrations and statistics on the overhead projector. And when I looked at my watch, the spiralling associations I had so enthusiastically followed had turned my forty-five minutes into more than ninety. Sue had anxiously watched me so casually handling, as 'visual aid', a similar jar she had taken from the museum case for me. The audience smiled politely. **MS**

Performance

For thirty years, between photograph and video, and beyond, I have been involved in devising performances that are not primarily reliant upon the exposition of dramatic literature, upon the staging of plays. In a succession of companies – RAT Theatre, Cardiff Laboratory Theatre, Brith Gof, Pearson/Brookes – I have helped create works of theatre which have been described variously as 'physical', 'experimental', 'devised', 'site-specific', 'time-based art', forms and genres which are now commonly grouped together as 'performance'. These have often been uneasy with text, occasionally non-verbal, communally composed, dependent variously upon the physical and vocal capacities of performers, the articulation of dramatic material through compositional procedures of structuring and ordering, and the elaboration of scenic and technical devices of manifestation. And if they have survived, it is as the anecdotes and **analects** of shared experiences and as collective memories within an oral culture.

From the outset, mine was a work of synthesis, a drawing together of impressions, influences and fragments of technique. I well remember trying to emulate the contortions of Ryszard Cieslak in the photographs in Grotowski's *Towards a Poor Theatre* (1969) on the mouldy carpet of our student flat. We were influenced by the work of American groups such as the Living Theatre (Rostagno with Beck and Malina 1970; Biner 1972), the Open Theater (Pasolli 1970; Chaikin 1972) and Richard Schechner's Performance Group (Waldman 1972), by the first generation of British fringe companies including Freehold, the People Show and the Pip Simmons Group (Time Out 1971; Hammond 1973) and by peer groups in the universities of York and Keele. All offered alternatives to conventional practice and seemed to align theatre with the aspirations of the radical politics and the burgeoning youth culture of that period. We were also taken with the work of Erving Goffman and the rearticulation of some of his sociological notions of '**front**' and '**region**', themselves drawn from theatrical models (Goffman 1971a). The influence of R.D. Laing's psychoanalytical work (1965, 1971) now seems less easy to admit. Haltingly we began to make theatre; on some impulse we worked silently. We concocted a training regime from the exercises of the Royal Canadian Air Force training manual, from Viola Spolin's *Improvisations for the Theater* (1983), and from what we gleaned from those visiting directors who were beginning to use workshop practice as part of their rehearsal procedure. And thus we created *Odyssey*. Upon graduation, I left archaeology for a life in theatre.

For an equal amount of time I've been trying to find useful ways of understanding and describing what is, or was, going on in performance. And this has always been a political project to justify and authenticate pursuits which have none of the seemliness or common sense of presenting plays in playhouses, pursuits which are easily ignored as invisible or dismissed as ephemeral, illiterate, not serious and ultimately disposable by a critical discourse and by an academy which has favoured the literary analysis of the dramatic text. Only in recent years has performance been recognised as a subject worthy of scholarly investigation. And whilst any record of such performance might help fuel an academic industry hungry for course innovation, it must surely also legitimise lives lived, careers spent, in the creation of such transitory occurrences. **MP**

Archaeological theory

For twenty years I have been promoting archaeology with an attitude. Some people call this 'archaeological theory', though that term needs careful qualification. Some, and not always in criticism, even use the term 'theoretical archaeology', as if it were a kind of spiritual conjuring trick; needless to say, this is not what I do.

I was caught by the wave of interest in theory which swept through the social sciences and humanities from the 1970s. The immediacy of archaeology had attracted me to the subject – taking up what remains of the past. But, after a flush of enthusiasm for digging, I was left profoundly disappointed by a discipline that seemed simply obsessed with a set of techniques (and not particularly good ones) for supposedly recovering the past. Basic questions of how archaeologists might understand and reconstruct societies and cultures in the past seemed, astonishingly, marginal. This is where theory offered a way forward.

The 1960s and 1970s were undoubtedly a time of liberation in archaeological thinking. Those who called themselves *new* archaeologists in the sixties presented a suitably critical stand. Methodology and rigour were put on the agenda. And archaeology was to be holistic, social and explanatory, an anthropological science. My time at Cambridge at the end of the seventies was one of direct contact with an optimism for rethinking the discipline. Seminar groups were devouring the growing number of publications that dealt with theory. From American anthropologies, predominantly functionalist and cultural materialist (Steward 1955; White 1959; Harris 1968; Binford 1972), we moved through structuralist anthropology (Lévi-Strauss of course – see Leach 1976; Sahlins 1976; and Tilley 1990a), structural

Marxism (Godelier 1973, 1977), Meillassoux, Terray (on these see Seddon 1978 and Kahn and Llobera 1981; Hindess and Hirst 1975; Friedmann and Rowlands 1978; the journal *Critique of Anthropology*) to Anglo-American social theory (Gouldner 1973, 1976; Giddens 1979, 1984; Harré 1979), to French thought (Bourdieu, Barthes, Foucault, Derrida (for archaeology see Bapty and Yates 1990; Tilley 1990b)). British cultural studies (publications of the Centre for Contemporary Cultural Studies at the University of Birmingham, Hall et al. 1980, for example, and the journal *Cultural Studies*), literary theory (neatly summarised in Eagleton 1983), and a revitalised Marxist thought) Ollman 1971; Larraine 1979, 1983; and the debates around Althusser 1971, 1977 (see also Althuser and Etienne 1970 (for example, Thompson 1978 and Anderson 1980)) lay behind much of this renaissance of grand and not so grand theorising (Skinner 1985) about the character of society, culture and history. Critical theory (Laclau and Mouffe 1985; Habermas and earlier members of the Frankfurt Institute; Marcuse 1955; and many works particularly by Adorno and Benjamin (see Connerton 1976; Arato and Gebhardt 1978; Held 1980)) offered insights into the sociology of knowledge and the role of the writer or cultural critic. A dizzying experience.

In all, this academic encounter was fostered by publishers like Macmillan, Hutchinson and New Left Books/Verso (now Blackwell Polity, Routledge, MIT and many others), with a flood, ever increasing, of books and new journals. And, more cynically, there were those who saw theory as a suitable career move, responding to the pressure to contribute to the cycle of academic debate, to provide a supposedly original academic approach – hence, for them, the posture of proposing a new theory.

From the 1970s to the 1980s the 'linguistic turn' and the textual metaphor took hold in archaeology – that material culture, as communicative medium, may be structured and read in a way analogous to a text. Agency, the theoretical place of the individual in society, was fore-grounded, with the contention that if we wish a social archaeology we should incorporate in theory the acknowledgement that it is people who make society. Most importantly came an interest in the relation between present interests (social, cultural and political) and archaeo-logical explanations or interpretations of the past – the central focus of critical theory in the construction of knowledge. This began mechanistically (present ideologies shown to be expressed in archaeology, the concerns of the American middle class conditioning their explanation of the past), but soon came a more sophisticated appreciation, in some quarters, of the unity of the present-past (rather than a separate past being distorted by a biased present).

The agenda was twofold – to help forge an intellectual tool-kit for an archaeology seriously interested in understanding societies through their material culture and to consider the rela-tionship between the past and the present embodied in the archaeological project of taking up ruins and remains. The fortunes of the cultural left are relevant, because, for many, archaeo-logical theory has been a way of introducing themes of political and cultural relevance into what has been argued to be a fundamentally reactionary archaeological orthodoxy (Shanks and Tilley 1987: Chapter 7).

My response was two books written with Chris Tilley – *ReConstructing Archaeology* (1992, first edition 1987), and *Social Theory and Archaeology* (1987), polemical and rhetorical texts. Our aim was to raise the level of debate in archaeology. In essays on museum display and prehistoric tombs, grand theory and the design of beer cans, we attempted to address the question of what archaeologists should be doing, other than relaxing in a comforting pastime of digging up ancient relics.

Archaeology with an attitude? I connect this with the question which concerns many students new to archaeology or those who look from outside. They ask: Why theory, why the polemic, why not just get on with digging up the past?

One answer is the need for critical self-consciousness. To be constantly open to alternatives, to hold dear the aim of acting thoughtfully. An academic, professional and enlightenment ideal perhaps. And it has to be said that, for some, theory has become an end in itself. Some do seem to let their enthusiasm for intellectual fashions show a little too much, with slogans and sound-bites, postures and superficiality (on this issue in archaeology see Shanks 1990; Shanks and Mackenzie 1994).

Hence for me it is an issue of attitude. Suspicion of easy answers, of neat schemes for partitioning the world which put things in their place, grand all-encompassing theories which purport to explain everything. A suspicion of comforting familiarity. The attitude is about debunking, retaining a sense of humility, constantly reflecting on what we do as archaeologists. This is that all-important relation of the past in the present, for there is no end to working upon what is left of the past. Archaeological theory for me is less about a body of theory than it is about this attitude. To think critically. **MS**

These are the things that remain

Early in 1992, I was invited by the Centre for Performance Research in Cardiff to give a presentation at The Meeting Ground, a series of weekly gatherings for local artists. I decided to reconstruct, in some way, RAT Theatre's notorious 1972 performance *Blindfold*, in which I performed and for which there is no extant written scenario and no video record. The evening included the showing of slides of performance; readings from production notes, publicity leaflets, press releases and reviews; a demonstration of training exercises, by younger colleagues, retrieved from personal notebooks; the revelation of physical scars and the relating of anecdotes concerning their origin; the memories and reminiscences of performers and audience members alike, inevitably coloured by nostalgia and hindsight; and a question-and-answer session between those present at the original performance and the contemporary audience.

> If you look closely you can still see the stitch marks. Pounding a wooden crutch on the floor, it flew from my hand and hit me in the eye. Spent the rest of the performance dripping blood, which was, of course, what the audience had paid to see. Ironically, fellow performers didn't realise it had happened, as they were all wearing blindfolds!
>
> (Pearson 1998a: 35)

Figure 3
RAT Theatre: *Blindfold*
© Steve Allison

Thus a variety of forms of exposition addressed an incident in the past, standing in for, in place of, an absence. Partly structured, partly rambling nostalgia, this was an event in the present, a source of pleasure in and of itself. Slightly less structure and it would have been a reunion party; slightly more and it could have resembled a performance about a performance, what we might term a 'second-order performance'. Half jokingly, I referred to this as a work of theatre archaeology. Yet it seemed more than an attractive metaphor for the retrieval and reconstitution of ephemeral events. The **traces** left behind by performance are perhaps more susceptible to the approaches of contemporary archaeology than methods taken from textual analysis: the documentation of unwritten happening, attested through material trace, is an archaeological project. For certain, performance is inevitably in the past and ultimately enigmatic. It was thus around questions of documenting performance that I was drawn back to archaeology, a discipline intimately concerned with retrieval, recording and reassembling.   **MP**

Experiencing the past

It began with the image and the question of the character of archaeological evidence. Archaeologists do not primarily deal with texts. They deal in words – the books and articles they write; and images – the plans, drawings and photographs. But their evidence is material; their subject-matter events, environments, and the traces left behind. In my work on ancient Greek art I was confronted with the task of writing and picturing a world of the early city and state in the Mediterranean, a subject heavily overlain with standard narratives – two centuries old and so familiar – of the genius of the ancient Greeks (Shanks 1996: Chapter 2). I was in search of what I saw as an authentic alternative, to represent the indeterminacy of history. I wanted to explore the ways we document social experience. And I first decided to look at the ways we picture the past.

But the book which was to be called *Picturing the Past* evolved into something broader, ultimately an investigation into what I have come to see as some root metaphors of modernity. *Experiencing the Past* (Shanks 1992a) is about how fragments are left behind and pieced together. It is about the indeterminacy of events and how we deal with this, from memory to scientific reconstruction to legal adjudication to the interpretive practices of an archaeological detective. Archaeology, I proposed, is about some very basic and mundane things: grubbing around in decayed garbage, recovering traces of things and processes which go largely unnoticed today – what happens to broken bits of pot, to things that get lost, abandoned buildings, rotted fences, microbial action. A creeping, mouldering underside of things. Archaeology is thus intimately linked to processes of decay, ruin, putrefaction and of ageing, erosion, wearing – and what wears more quickly than memory? The proposition is that archaeology is not merely a disciplinary field but an aspect of our social fabric. The archaeological refers to social and cultural entropy, loss and ruin. Perhaps unexpectedly, given archaeology's affiliation with history, its temporality is not primarily *linear*, from past to present, but *turbulent*, past and present percolating in the building of ways of life.

In the book I considered a field of metaphors surrounding archaeology: layering and the authenticity of depth – digging deep, detective work looking to the significant detail, cleaning and restoring damaged pasts, reading signs in traces of things that have gone before, collecting items we value. The argument was implied, though not historically documented, that the development of archaeology from the seventeenth century was as much to do with the growing significance of these ways of thinking as it was to do with the formalisation of theory and method and the great archaeological discoveries which began with Pompeii. Archaeology, again perhaps paradoxically, is intimately modern.

The archaeological involves an explicit focus upon the materiality of society, with social experiences rooted in all the cognitive and emotional faculties and senses of the human body. Social experience is materially embodied – society felt and suffered as well as rationally thought and understood – perhaps fundamentally ineffable. The term '**sensorium**', a culturally located array of the senses, was coined to try to deal with this embodiment, under a proposition that a task of the humanities is to ground social reconstruction and understanding in sensoria, cultural arrays of the intellect and senses embodied in social practice (cf. Stoller 1989; Corbin 1995). I was taking up the old challenge to find ways of understanding and representing, how to record and write what is at root ineffable – social experience. And I presented in *Experiencing the Past* several narratives, with drawings and photographs, about castles and stately homes, megaliths and Greek ceramics. In these experiments I was part of a growing interest in the traces of ceremonial and funerary rituals; in the discernment of the body orientations and actions of knowledgeable individuals and of performative behaviours in (pre)history; in transient occurrences and ephemeral events; in the significance of 'place'; in all that which has conventionally been regarded as, at best, tangential to cultural evolution and technological progress and, at worst, unknowable or irrelevant.

Concomitantly *Experiencing the Past* argued for a performative model of the construction of archaeological knowledge. The past is not somehow 'discovered' in its remains, for what would it be? Gone is the notion of a singular material record bequeathed to us from the past and from which meaning can be 'read off'. Instead archaeology is to regard itself as a practice of cultural production, a contemporary material practice which works on and with the traces of the past and within which the archaeologist is implicated as an active agent of interpretation. What archaeologists do is work with material traces, with evidence, in order to create some-thing – a meaning, a narrative, an image – which stands for the past in the present. Archaeologists craft the past (Shanks and McGuire 1996). Rather than being a reconstruction of the past from its surviving remains, this is a recontextualisation.

Archaeology then is the relationship we maintain with the past: it consists of a work of mediation with the past. In a sense, archaeology is something that each of us routinely does. This we might call the archaeological imagination. Archaeological knowledge has to be produced and interpretation is always informed by present interests and values. It is contem-porary interest which takes the archaeologist to the material past. Nor is there a single way to do archaeology: different things can be made from the same traces and fragments. People may work on the same material and produce different outcomes. The past 'as it was' or 'as it happened' is an illusionary category, neither stable nor homogeneous. For instance, the pre-historic monument we call Stonehenge has no single, essential meaning: it has been reworked, reconstructed, reinterpreted since building began (Chippindale 1994). The site continues to be used as it always has been: people experience material things, appropriate them and produce a meaning for themselves, be they archaeologists, new age travellers, foreign tourists or latter-day Druids (Chippindale *et al.* 1990). And thus it becomes a place of contention, of conflicting interpretation, of power relationships and contested ownership (Bender 1998).

I was allying myself with contemporary critical approaches in archaeology. These aim at defamiliarising what is taken as given, revealing the equivocality of experiences and of things; they are practices sensual, located and phenomenological; they involve that attitude suspicious of orthodoxy mentioned already and which acknowledges the impossibility of any final account of things in making sense of that which was never certain or sure in the first place. Such polyvocal approaches have also been collectively labelled 'interpretive' (Hodder *et al.* 1995).

The active process of interpretation is to clarify or explain the meaning and significance of something, deciphering and translating the past in the present. In prophesy to interpret is to read significance and infer courses of action. Interpretation is also about the performance of a work – acting out something to give it an intelligible life. This is an *active apprehension* – making a past work a present presence. When you act out a dramatic work you choose to pick on some meanings and not others. You make an explicit or inexplicit critique of other interpretations. So such interpretation is simultaneously analytic and critical.

Located practice. From the 1980s gender issues came firmly on the archaeological agenda, both in terms of women in prehistory and also gendered ways of doing archaeology (after Gero and Conkey 1991). Questions were raised of the possibility of local archaeological knowledges, that is, not belonging to an academic discourse dominated by white Anglo-Saxon middle-class and western males. How do particular communities relate to the material past around them? This is the wider matter of archaeology in society, and one which has been theorised as globalist and postcolonial (Gosden 2000; Shanks 2000a, 2000b). In a more abstract vein global concepts of reason, rationality and a final truth located in an objective past have been questioned.

Embodied experience, the documentation of social practices, retrieving pasts, piecing together fragments, performative models of knowledge – the ground was set for a dialogue.

MS

1 THEATRE ARCHAEOLOGY

I want to say 'He remembered'. But this was not 'joined up' thinking. Images, visions, half-thoughts swirled out of the snow exploding off one another like the blinding charges with which they tried to free the 'Discovery'. Others just flashed and faded in the merciful haze of morphia in that land of mirage and optical illusion, of rigour, hallucination, heavenly portents and utter loneliness. And still others flickered faintly like the pictures of Mr. Ponting's cinematograph.

(Pearson/Brookes: *Dead Men's Shoes 1997*)

In the first phase of encounter, what we term 'theatre archaeology', archaeology proves stimulating and suggestive of alternative approaches to both performance documentation and theory, encouraging inscriptions of performance, and their interpretation, which might be fragmentary, partial, subjective, discursive. How do we document a performed event? Archaeological practice indicates not only ways in which we might work with the remains of past performance, creating contemporary meaning in the present, it also enables us to think provocatively about the ways in which we might create the documents of current work. Rather than pretending to be a final and complete account of things, a closure, the performance document, an equivalent of the dramatic text, might be in itself equally fragmentary, partial and encouraging of interpretation.

It may ultimately be more appropriate to discuss performance (particularly **devised performance**) through archaeological rather than literary means, with performance as a kind of prehistory of scripted drama, and to imagine the retrieval and recontextualisation of performance as constituting a theatre archaeology. The essential questions would then focus upon what is retrievable and how, and upon methods of recovery.

As our encounter begins a third time with two personal views of performance and archaeology, we necessarily commence in the first person singular.

Performance

Los Angeles: a memory

I must have moved, shivered, trembled, for in the photograph my left foot shows six toes. Hardly surprising, as we were cold and terrified, naked in performance for the first time, our bodies untrusting, not quite surrendered to the suspension harnesses, uneasy in our skins. And this was the premiere, shot through with excitement, anticipation, nervousness, foreboding, for we had practised so little.

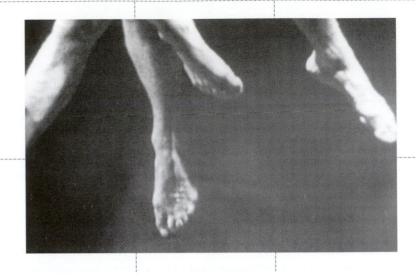

Figure 4
Brith Gof: *Los Angeles*
© Nick Cook

They'd hauled us up to the brewery ceiling on crude ropes and pulleys. The harnesses chaffed wherever they touched: shoulders, groin, back. The spectators had entered, unaware of our presence above them in the smoke. We began to descend, singly, to the pulsing soundtrack. Below us the sawdust circle, blank television screens, the water-tank. At first a certain freedom: to walk in air, to stretch out in all directions, to twist and turn. And then to hang upside-down! Looking down at them looking up at us. Not flying exactly but free of surface, of choreographic imperative, of the need to breathe hard, of sole responsibility for one's physical action, for here we were animated by others. We felt beautiful, weightless, angelic. And then the tank coming towards us. Heating the water with a central heating element had helped little. Mark was first in, shaking, quaking. I followed, frozen fingers desperately trying to unscrew and re-screw the rings that would connect us. Then a huge pull and we rose together linked like a pieta – in intimate contact, with the lightest of touches – without the need to support each other. And then it happened. A D-shaped ring carrying our joint weight turned suddenly from its flat side to a corner. In the air we dropped, about an inch. In our stomachs it felt like a mile, like the gear was collapsing, like death would come rushing up to meet us at any moment. Of course, no one noticed. How would they ever distinguish a mistake in such a new and alien environment? And we kept our composure, showed nothing. But I knew. For that was not only water running down my leg and dripping from my sixth toe!

Apologia

I ought to begin with a definition of performance, to profess allegiance perhaps to an extant theoretical model: 'anthropology' (Schechner 1969, 1973, 1977); 'theatre anthropology' (Barba 1982; Barba and Savarese 1991); 'performativity' (Butler 1990); 'theatricality' (Fischer-Lichte 1995). But performance remains for me elusive, always slightly beyond my grasp, at once a 'doing and a thing done' (Diamond 1996: 1); a special type of behaviour and an event; registers of artfulness (Finnegan 1992: 91–111) and a mode of cultural production; a kind of bodily engagement and a set of interactive contracts; a mode of communication and an encounter; a liminal or 'in between' space (cf. van Gennep 1960; Leach 1976) of contestation and change; a temporary autonomous zone and in our particular set of cultural circumstance, perhaps even a 'third space of enunciation' (Bhabha 1994: 37). Perhaps that's why I do it. Perhaps too that is why my practice is always at the edges, on the outskirts, on the borderlands of professional practice, of technologies, of personal and artistic identity, of conceptual and economic feasibility; on those boundaries where definitions are under constant renegotiation. I work in the slash between performance/everyday, in the space between performer and spectator, in the distinction between ability and disability, in the small print of the transactional conventions, in the brackets that mark off a strip of behaviour as performance. But I must reflect with caution. For as an effective modelling of human action and interaction, performance can appear to embody, and be susceptible to, any number of theoretical or philosophical stances. Look at a particular work and it is possible to perceive Giddens' 'seriality' or Burke's 'sublime' being enacted, or to enact them on the back of it.

Performance for me increasingly constitutes a continuum of practices within which no one set is privileged over another. Artistic and political decisions are then made in response to the project at hand, in response to such questions as 'What is necessary here?', 'What is possible here?', 'What is appropriate . . . or highly inappropriate here?' The single requirement is that I work within the public domain. But it is what I do. It exists for me primarily then as a palette of creative potentials, a discontinuous and interrupted practice of different modes of expression, of varying types and intensities. Theory then arises from, or cleaves to, that series of perceptions, procedures and pragmatics through which I orient my work. Such perceptions are inevitably at ground level, favouring approaches both micrological and phenomenological, and inevitably empirical.

Body: performance and personal engagement (me-performing)

I am nervous. I am aware of being in front of others, of having one chance to get it right. This state of acute self-awareness is characterised by a release of adrenaline which may lead to feelings of 'fight' or 'flight', to shaking, sweating, irrationality, forgetfulness, stage-fright. However, it may also result in heightened energy and lead to impulsive activity, to the achievement of irrevocable acts beyond social norms, to spontaneity, dynamism and ecstatic release in a state of increased physical and perceptual sensitivity without fear of repercussions. I have an ability, a propensity even, to engage in extra-daily activities: to undergo, to tolerate, to endure, to commit, to omit with differing degrees and qualities of energy; to confront and destroy my own cosmetic image; to allow the boundaries of my body to be transgressed; to be other than my socialisation and conditioning might pre-determine; to cast off those behaviours accumulated through habit and heredity which deems what is desirable under what circumstances, to be childlike, undignified, naked in front of strangers; to imagine an alternative body image for myself, increasing the expressive function of its various parts; to be physically composed/ uncomposed, balanced/disbalanced, impulsive/lethargic; to muster my physical and vocal resources at will; to confront those muscular tensions, recurrent postures and obsessive behaviours through which one's fears and repressions – one's attitude – are reflected in the everyday body.

Under scrutiny, I can ensure a continuum of presence, the result of a personal strategy which holds me in the here-and-now and which allows my expressive functioning to be diverse and discontinuous. This is best revealed at thresholds – in the micro-second of engagement, of assembling resources, of the adoption of decorums and demeanours of concentration and application, in 'A deep breath and here I go' – or in moments of accident and injury when, of course, it disappears. I have significance in repose, though I need never acknowledge that I am being watched or modify my behaviour accordingly.

I can articulate my activity, employing rhetorical practices, physical and vocal, in combinations and ratios unusual, unacceptable or even impossible in everyday life. I can invest movements and action with more or less energy over more or less time than is normally required. I can increase and decrease their size, their extension. I can make them tense, repeat them, distort them, reverse them, displace them to another part of my body. I can allow movements to grow and flow from one to another. Or I can do a percentage of them. I can apply such articulations to any gestures without them ever being part of some exclusive stage language. But not all gestures, for certain movements have been selected, simplified and re-energised: my work is characterised by omission. I can order them, arrange them, elide them, juxtapose them, compose them, in relation to plane or surface, standing on the floor, lying on a bed: up, down, out, push from, land upon. Or volume: more difficult to orientate perhaps were I'm suspended, my body twisting, turning in free space, in relation to a rope, to a single line . . . This is enhanced by training and by rehearsal. My ability to achieve such articulation and the nature and quality of the resulting action may be mediated – limited or enhanced – by spatial restriction; by physical restraint; by the climate; by the surface – its texture, its hardness; by topography. There may be a (dramatic) tension between what I am attempting and what I manage to accomplish, between the strategic imperatives of plot and scenario and my tactical engagement. I am not just a neutral vessel of signification: I am experiencing as well as representing. 'My body is that meaningful core which behaves like a general function, and which nevertheless exists, and is susceptible to disease. In it we learn to know that union of essence and existence . . .' (Merleau-Ponty 1962: 147).

I can walk, bend, turn, fall, jump, kneel, spin, crawl, tremble. . .

For him, it is other (see p.182). When he was born, he was not breathing. This caused damage to the motor functioning areas of his brain. He is not mentally disabled and neither – as the small card which he carries round his neck when he goes out says – is he deaf. Ten years ago he would have been called a spastic. Today he is regarded as 'having', or 'suffering from', cerebral palsy. In current parlance he is 'disabled', not 'handicapped'. He cannot stand unaided. Nevertheless, he generates tremendous pull and grip with his arms, and push with his legs. He refuses to use an electrically powered wheelchair, which he feels defines his status of reliance and instead uses a standard manual chair, which he operates by pushing himself backwards with one foot. He cannot turn the wheels with his hands. This is arduous. Yet he achieves a precision of turn, spin, reverse, effectively with one toe. He communicates by laboriously pointing to a given vocabulary of words on a board on his lap or to individual letters to spell out more complex words. He also speaks, in gurgling tones. His voice, with its broken rhythms and swooping articulations – on the breath, against the breath – demands our attention, demands that we listen and interpret. And that we relax, that we accept that there is meaning here. His is a language that one has to learn. As his lungs don't inflate or deflate greatly, the nuances are subtle and there is extreme brevity and clarity in his words. Which is why he likes verbal puns so much.

I stand within an envelope, a three-dimensional space which surrounds my body, its surface at the various furthest points of reach in all directions. This portable territory is my sphere of influence: it is here where I make my gestures, dance my dance, speak my text. The effective volume I can engage and influence will again alter with age – increasing, then decreasing – with environmental conditions and perhaps too with factors such as disability. My capacity to engage its full volume and indeed to enlarge it – stretching, extending, pushing out – may depend upon training, giving greater volume for expressive and inter-active functioning. Any restriction, be it social or legal, I may experience as stress: in performance such conflict may result from scenographic constriction.

For him, it is other. His body is in a kind of rebellion with itself, suddenly jerking into spastic movement or channelling creative impulse into stereotyped gesture. His body is decided. Yet he works with the actions his body wants to make. So pull can become embrace, hold, grip, fight, tear. And push becomes caress, reject, threaten. His work requires a force of enormous will, directly experienced by those of us who hold and touch him in performance, as he organises the effort and imagines his physical goal. Of course, he doesn't make conventional signs, rather a hovering net of gestural hint and suggestion. But we know what he means: we experience him 'as experiencing/as expressing/as signing'. Whilst it may be ambiguous in semiotic terms, it is fascinating and seductive. Occasionally, he can hitch a ride on the randomness, in a fury of physical abandon. At other times, he can achieve an awesome and terrible stillness. However, as we always joke, the one thing he can never do on stage is 'die'. A dance of impulses: intended, random and spasmodic.

The *mise-en-scène* is a set of material conditions where I to go to work. Here the nature of the contracts – body to backdrop, body to object, body to body – and the physical and emotional experiences they conspire may be other than those of everyday life. Beyond questions of representation, the performer's relationship to the *mise-en-scène* is therefore above all ergonomic and phenomenological. And it may indeed be that the constructed environment of performance is active and that environmental conditions, the ecology of this special world – surface, climate, illumination, temperature – are much better or much worse perhaps than in everyday life, changing from moment to moment.

The designed or built environment of performance may greatly increase or decrease ergonomic problems (Dul and Weerdemeester 1993) and these may change from moment to moment, oscillating between acceptable, unacceptable and optimal. It may extend, limit, restrict or compromise four vectors of physical application: clearance – the head-room and leg-room of the body ellipse; reach – the volume of the workspace envelope; posture – the nature and number of connections of body to work space; and strength – the acceptable percentage of maximal strength in output or endurance (Pheasant 1986: 135f.). It may restrict my kinesic, proxemic and haptic abilities, capacities and potentials through increases in hazard, body stress, demand (energy expenditure) and overload (exhaustion): by the closure or limitation of sensory channels – as with blindfolding; the invasion of that personal space which is reserved for more or less exclusive use; by the arrangement of barriers, such as set or furniture. It may cause duress through increasing duration and limiting the potential adjustment of posture and reach. Environmental factors may include noise, which causes annoyance during thinking and communication; illumination with changes in brightness, reflection and shadow; climate changes in the temperature of air and surfaces, air velocity and relative humidity the effects of which may, or may not be mediated by clothing; vibration of whole body or hand–arm through shocks and jolts and the toxicity of liquids, gases, vapours, dusts and solids (Dul and Weerdemeester 1993: 71f.).

Performance might be a difficult, or even dangerous, place to work. Indeed, the substance of performance may be constituted as no more than me dealing with the ergonomic problems of the workspace. You watch my methods and organisation of effort, those planned and those informed by previous experience, my flexibility of response through improvisation and my use of tools, both designed and improvised. You watch the symptoms of my engagement: body and context are intimately linked. Methods of coping may include those planned, those improvised and those informed by previous experience. But I am not solely acted upon. I can alter any environment, any object, in my mind's eye and react accordingly.

For him, it is other. In performance, he is in a state of vulnerable exposure; he cannot give a virtuoso display. His work begins to pose fundamental questions about the nature of physical performance. What is the distinction between ability and disability, for his body can adopt positions, engage in actions which mine never can? What is the purpose and nature of training for the disabled body which will never achieve athleticism? What do notions of timing and dynamic mean, when action is the result of chance and will? And then the difficult questions arise: Does his disability exclude him from self-representation?; In performance, is he asked to 'overcome' his disability, to overcome his biographical body?

Encounter: performance and meeting (we-performing)

We meet. She hurls herself at me and I catch her: perhaps on some instinct, perhaps because that is what we always do, perhaps because we planned to do it, perhaps because we were instructed to do it. We have a history: we have a contract to suspend our social differences; we have an agreement to engage in extra-daily behaviours together, in a particular style, code or sub-code. So we touch and are touched; we operate and are operated upon. We commit without the need for recompense. We build an empathy, a mutuality which only exists as 'the two', as 'we-performing', as an 'interculture'. And this was apparent in our recognition of the mistake and the *faux pas*, with winks and giggles.

Rules, albeit fluid, constantly renegotiated understandings, help to communicate intention. Rules decide what can, and cannot, be done: a balance between freedom and restraint, protecting the weak, restraining the powerful, leading to a tension between confinement and transgression. They require self and group organisation to maximise the effort. I can be obscene, violent, frightening, but I must suffer the consequences. Rules give direction and purpose to the release of energy. Once they are agreed, there can be planning, organisation, strategy, to achieve the desired effect. This can lead to specialisation: the employment of individual skills and the selection of the best person for the job. Rules can also be communicated to watchers who can begin to understand and appreciate the activity. And there may be sequence or pattern – 'I do it, now you do it' – if not plot.

Two spheres collide, interpenetrate, fuse. In social life, our portable territory is demarcated by invisible, though operative zones and boundaries, into which entry is strictly controlled according to kinship, age, gender, status and context. In his contentious study of western intercourse, E. T. Hall (1966) distinguishes several concentric zones within and beyond the envelope which are determined by the characteristics of the sense organs, limb length, cultural conditioning and social relationship with the other. The four zones are intimate, personal, social and public. Entry into different zones permits and enables different modes of physical and verbal discourse: different orders of expression may only be apparent within particular zones; different tones or extensions of voice may only be appropriate in each zone. Inappropriate invasion of a zone – shouting in someone's face – may be experienced as unwanted intrusion leading to unease and stress. But the zones have no sharp divisions. They vary from individual to individual, culture to culture. Transgression may be sanctioned in extreme circumstance or by social convention. And by performance too, always at the interface of the appropriate and the inappropriate. And during meeting, intercourse, physical interaction and exchange, proxemics – interpersonal distance – and haptics – touch of self and others during interpersonal contact, in what contexts and to what degree – become part of the expressive repertoire. We have the propensity to transgress proxemic and haptic boundaries and taboos, without thought for social implications.

For him, it is other. He lives in a sophisticated physical culture which few of us can imagine. He cannot feed himself, wash himself, clothe himself, get out of bed by himself, wipe his arse. He relies on others to lift, carry, position him. In this, he shows immense trust and confidence. He touches and is touched by those with whom he has no ties of kinship: he comes into intimate contact with others in ways which break the everyday conventions of socialisation and conditioning. He is naked with both men and women. He operates and is operated upon. And he communicates desire and intent with the subtlest of gestures and postures: of opening the mouth ready for the spoon; of leaning to one side, arm rigid ready for the coat. I once dropped him. And he fell like a stone. Fortunately his body is tough. But he has no defence, no protective mechanism. To work with him is to know total responsibility. Our working process means the daily breaking of taboos. How do I touch a disabled man? How do I hold him? Will I damage him? It is constituted as a series of sensual experiences, suspensions of personal decorum, patterns of body orientations and chains of altered demeanour. And it is impossible to notate; it resists the document.

Performance resides primarily within a set of contracts and transactional conventions between two orders of participant – watchers and watched; spectators and performers; witnesses and protagonists – and in three sets of relationship: performer to performer, performer to spectator and vice versa, spectator to spectator. Significantly, each and all of these contracts is available for re-assessment and renegotiation. Performance may favour sociopetal arenas (Elam 1980: 64) which throw individuals together and where proxemic and haptic invasion and transgression and changes in status are more likely.

There are at least two orders of participant here – you and us – who have brought to this situation, to this encounter, different knowledges, different expectations, different degrees of preparedness, different strategies of survival. We are usually set apart as protagonists, for we seem to know 'how to go on here': we have facility in this strange environment. The basic encounter of performance resembles the primal scene, a condition of being for the other. The performer bears moral responsibilities well before being given or taking up any concrete responsibility through contract, calculation of interests or enlisting to cause. Yet responsibility for the other is shot through with ambivalence: of simultaneous attraction towards and repulsion from, person or action (Young 1995: 161). It has no obvious limits, nor does it easily translate into practical steps to be taken or refrained from – each such step being pregnant with consequences – fluctuating between complicity and resistance – 'that are notoriously uneasy to predict' – there being no compliance here (Ashcroft, Griffiths and Tiffin 1998: 12–4) – 'and even less easy to evaluate in advance' (Bauman 1995: 2–4).

Scenography: performance and the manipulation of space (place and site)

Imagine a group of people, just standing: they have the status of a crowd. As yet, there is no formal arrangement of performers and spectators, no preordained acting areas –

B.1   M.1   A.1

nothing that resembles a stage, no fixed viewpoints – nothing to focus our attention, no framing devices – no proscenium arch to tell us how to orientate ourselves. There may be interesting things to look at – other people for instance ('look at her!') – but no clues what to watch. The single conditioning factor is of course size. The experience for ten people standing on a bed sheet is somewhat different from that for ten people standing in the desert! What we have is a field within which to place and disperse our activity, our performers and spectators.

Events create spaces. As a fight breaks out the crowd parts, steps back, withdraws to give the action space. Instantly they take up the best position for watching, a circle. It's democratic, everyone is equidistant from the centre, no privileged viewpoints. There may be a struggle to see better but the circle can expand to accommodate those who rush to see what's happening. Or it thickens. A proto-playing area is created, with an inside and outside, constantly redefined by the activity of the combatants, who remain three-dimensional. The crowd may be active, shouting encouragement, pushing in to jostle the combatants, engulfing the area. Or they may constantly withdraw to escape the ferocity of the fight. The size and ambience of the space are conditioning factors. Then just as quickly the incident ends, the space is inundated by the crowd and there are no clues what to watch.

Then suddenly another fight breaks out and the crowd turns, surges forward. And then another breaks out, and the first erupts again. The spectator is faced with choices, for these events may be sequential or simultaneous. If sequential then her attention will change rapidly. She may have to decide whether to move to see better, or indeed to escape. If she stands still she will doubtless see some activity in close-up, some at a distance, some half-hidden, some from behind. If simultaneous, she must choose what to watch, for it is impossible to see everything at the same time. Perhaps she moves towards her favourite happening. But perhaps all the combatants are all doing more or less the same thing, so she stays where she is, sharing similar experiences with fellow spectators elsewhere in the space. If the occurrences differ however, then each spectator will have a fundamentally different experience and interpretation of events. Of course, these events may be other than fights, involving solo protagonist – orator, preacher, drunk – or couples: arguing, dancing, singing.

E.1   0.1   R.1   S.1

The elaboration of ways to be seen and heard may involve raising the performers or the spectators, arrangements temporary and permanent, affecting modes of address: up, down, out. Space may be cleared through the uncompromising nature of the physical activity itself, through the application of crowd control techniques, through the inclusion of dangerous phenomena to be avoided. In such cleared space, there might be intensities of activity, the recurrent, preferred use of certain dispersed locations and the genesis of hierarchies of height and place. And a different experience for each watcher: activity approaching, arriving, passing; activity in close-up, at a distance, in the background; shifting focus; multiple focus; making decisions about what to watch; the proximity and touch of others, both other spectators and performers. Movement up and down, and across.

Performance space may be delineated, cordoned off, set aside: marks, surfaces, structures, both planned and improvised. Activity may be confined to and conditioned by a particular area, volume or architectural feature. Or space may be organised through the displacement of the spectators by arrangements of seating: chairs randomly scattered over the area with the performers moving in and around the spectators; laid out in lines, alleys or even blocks or round the edge of an open square. All of which may mediate the nature and quality of activity.

Such perfecting of space allows a continuity of performing conditions, guaranteeing a similar quality of experience for each audience and of working environment for performers. It allows detailed choreography for known and unchanging dimensions, including speed and dynamism within a small area; the proximity and touch of three-dimensional performers; intimacy; extremes of activity for known surface and the devising of complex and detailed imagery and stage pictures for an unchanging arrangement.

A wall serves to back the activity, cutting out visual irrelevance. It grounds the work, setting it against a certain texture, a certain colour. This arrangement allows the creation of friezes, tableaux and the clarification of movement for inspection. But everything the performers do is now under scrutiny, is assumed by the spectator to be deliberate. They are caught between acting sideways – between each other – and acting out, half-turned, for the spectators. Here, therefore, we witness the genesis of fronts and backs and, with activity close to the wall and some distance in front, also fore-stage/rear-stage, and primary and background activity. If, however, the wall is standing in free space, with an in-front-of and a behind, this then means that we create an off-stage and an on-stage, hidden/revealed and leading to the genesis of at least two different modes of behaviour, performing and not-performing. And in the movement from one to the other, of course, entrances and exits, of suspense and some sort of tension between secrecy and disclosure. Within this two-dimensional picture there may be stratifications in height and depth, layers of activity or information of different intensities and orders in the vertical and horizontal. There may be foreground and background, action travelling back to front and side to side, different actions of different intensity and type happening simultaneously. And with this flat surface behind the performers which can be decorated, so begins the long journey to the employment of backdrops suggestive of other places, illusions of perspective and *trompe l'œil*. The spectators may now be positioned in relation to the wall – close up, far away, at an oblique angle – and their sight-lines organised, with implications for both performance technique used and reception.

Now several walls, an enclosure, a set-aside space, reserved for a particular usage . . . Here there is a mysterious inside and an outside, with thresholds to be crossed, contracts to be made, suspensions of disbelief to be engendered. And within this reserved space there can be an organisation, orchestration and control of theatrical effects, preparation in private, the balance of concealment and revelation, the perfection of a listening and looking place with a fixed delineation and arrangement of stage, seating and technical effects. The stage becomes a place of absolute scrutiny, although it may change its nature, constantly alluding to other times, other places: it might play with notions of hiding and revealing, screening and disclosing, seeing or half seeing.

Site-specific performances are conceived for, mounted within and conditioned by the particulars of found spaces, existing social situations or locations, both used and disused: sites of work, play and worship: cattle-market, chapel, factory, cathedral, railway station. They rely, for their conception and their interpretation, upon the complex coexistence, superimposition and interpenetration of a number of narratives and architectures, historical and contemporary, of two basic orders: that which is of the site, its fixtures and fittings, and that which is brought to the site, the performance and its scenography: of that which pre-exits the work and that which is of the work: of the past and of the present. They are inseparable from their sites, the only contexts within which they are intelligible. Performance recontextualises such sites: it is the latest occupation of a location at which other occupations – their material traces and histories – are still apparent: site is not just an interesting, and disinterested, backdrop. Such performance, in its themes and means of exposition, is not of necessity congruent with its site as when a sixth-century battle is enacted in a car factory. Interpenetrating narratives jostle to create meanings. The multiple meanings and readings of performance and site intermingle, amending and compromising one another (cf. McLucas and Pearson 1996).

The significance of the work of theoretical architect Bernard Tschumi (1990, 1994a) for the apprehension of site-specific performance has been well enough worked over (Kaye 2000); it offers approaches to the linkage, causal or otherwise, of space and event. Yet analysis often concentrates upon his formal devices of architectural deconstruction rather than his notions of *ad-hoc* spatial intervention. He suggests that spaces are qualified by actions just as actions are qualified by spaces: architecture and events constantly transgress each other's rules. It is not a question of knowing which came first, movement or space: they are caught in the same set of relationships, only the 'arrow of power' changes direction. So, events can have an independent existence, rarely are they purely the consequence of their surroundings. In determining whether this relation between action and space is 'symmetrical – opposing two camps (people versus spaces) that affect one another in a comparable way – or asymmetrical, a relation in which one camp, whether space or people, clearly dominates the other' (Tschumi 1994a: 122) – we can see that most relationships stand somewhere in between, vacillating between independence and inter-dependence.

We might assume that within a *mise-en-scène* the relationship between action and space is symmetrical, two camps affecting one another in a comparable way, such is the decorum of normative theatre practice. However, it could equally be asymmetrical – a relationship in which one camp, whether space or people, clearly dominates the other. Tschumi describes the intrusion of the individuals in a controlled, pure architectural space as an act of violence (1994a: 121). They violate the balance of precisely ordered geometry, their bodies rushing against established rules, carving new and unexpected spaces, through fluid and erratic motions. Bodies not only move in, but generate, spaces produced by and through their movements. Movements – of dance, sport, war – are the intrusion of events into architectural spaces. And yet the reverse is always true. Each door implies the movement of someone crossing its frame; each corridor the progression that blocks it; each architectural space the intruding presence that will inhabit it.

In order to examine this complexity, Tschumi devises hypothetical programmes (see, for example, 1990: 103) – sequences of events, usages, activities, incidents – and projects them onto autonomous spatial architectures – frame after frame, room after room, episode after episode – as a form of motivation and suggestive of 'secret maps and impossible fictions'. Most importantly for us perhaps, these programmes fall into three categories: **indifference**, when spaces and events are functionally independent of one another and ignore each other; **reciprocity**, when events and spaces are totally interdependent and fully condition each other's existence, and **conflict** (ibid.: 100–1). There is no implicit hierarchy here and all three can be manifest in sequence or parallel, from time to time, in a given location. Tschumi works mainly theoretically and he is reduced to the drawing and the photograph as representational means, as in *The Manhattan Transcripts* (1994). Yet he craves transformational devices which can apply equally and independently to spaces, events or movements, devices which can permit the extreme formal manipulation of the sequence, formal strategies such as repetition, superposition, distortion, insertion and 'dissolve' in which the content of contiguous frames can be mixed, superimposed, faded in or cut up, suggesting endless relational possibilities.

Tschumi's term 'programme' is akin to the term 'scenario': site-specific performance itself might best manifest the multiple articulations of event and space which he envisages.

Dramaturgy: performance and structure (story and narrative)

We might regard the dramatic structure of devised performance as constituting a kind of **stratigraphy** of layers: of text, physical action, music and/or soundtrack, scenography and/or architecture (and their subordinate moments). Dramatic material can be conceived and manipulated in each of these strata which may carry different themes or orders of material in parallel. From moment to moment such layers may have different relative thicknesses or dramatic significance. The stratigraphy may be susceptible to processes of folding, faulting and erosion which may lead to discontinuities, inversions and disappear-ances and the reassignation of detail, as when we see text visually projected onto the setting or the stamping of a performer's feet constitutes the soundtrack. Any one of these layers may be the starting point in the devising process and any one may from time to time bear principal responsibility for carrying the prime narrative meaning whilst the others are turned down in the composition. Hence the musical soundtrack might carry emotional responsibility, the sung libretto all narrative information and the physical action be released from any story-telling role. Any one layer may also provide a carrier frequency or continuum against which other material is arranged.

[Substituting an analogy based on sound recording procedures for this archaeological model, then material may be developed in different tracks in isolation and then run side by side, relative volumes emphasised, compressed or erased during the editing process (of rehearsal). Whilst we might expect performance to be a homogeneous mixture of elements created minute by minute over time, we might now imagine situations in which tracks are run in parallel, with and against each other, without relative mediation. Or where from time to time performance exists variously as one, two or three tracks only. Material in one track will inevitably mediate material in another: they are read and interpreted onto, into and through each other, whether they have natural affinities or not. Significantly, within such a model the performer is no longer solely responsible for the exposition of dramatic material.]

And within layers there may be the juxtaposition of different varieties of material, stylistic discontinuity and expressive diversity. We can expect the presence of text in the form of poetics, lyrics, in-jokes, quotations, sayings; of vocal delivery as oratory, soliloquy, song, rhetoric, direct address, preaching, communal speaking, solo reflection, thrash-metal singing; of physical action from choreography to task-completion. A collage then carried on simultaneously in different genres, styles and media – from vaudeville to video – without value judgements on their relative worth.

The ordering or patterning within such layers may then, from time to time, resemble three rhetorical figures (themselves resonant of juxtaposition, collage and montage):

❖ *parataxis*, the placing of clauses etc. one after another, without words to indicate co-ordination or subordination or 'cohesion between clauses [or actions] of equivalent rank joined by simple conjunctions, e.g. 'and', 'but' (Melrose 1994: 274), with impli-cations of sequentiality;

❖ *hypotaxis*, the subordination of one clause to another or 'cohesion through dependency of clauses [or actions]' (ibid.), joined by relative pronouns etc., with implications of simultaneity;

❖ *katachresis*, misapplication; originally meaning the use of metaphors for objects for which there is no name, for example, 'the leg of the table'; or in Spivak's usage, a process of reinscription (1991: 70), jarring articulations, with implications of temporal discontinuity.

One is reminded of the Chinese encyclopaedia imagined by Borges and which divides, and juxtaposes, animals into groups such as '(m) having just broke the water pitcher, (n) that from a long way off look like flies' and Foucault's wonderment at the taxonomy, at 'the stark impossibility of thinking that' (Foucault 1989: xv). And Borges's adage (1970: 18) that 'the basic devices of all fantastical literature are only four in number: the work within the work, the contamination of reality by dream, the voyage in time and the double'.

The exposition of performance may be other than the manifestation of a story or dramatic narrative. It may exist as an explicit scenario, game-plan, plot, story-board, shooting-script ('that which is to be attempted') in which different narratives and activities may be sequential or simultaneous, choreographed or improvised. In place of script, its structure might be constituted as anything:

- ❖ from a sequence of images to a musical composition;

- ❖ as a pattern of singular events;

- ❖ as a strategy for action in the form of rules, tasks, instructions, prohibitions or restrictions as opposed to a pattern of dialogue;

- ❖ as a sequence, string, series of discrete occurrences or named sections – divisions of time, plot or musical score, with continuity or diversity of mode, style or technique – poem, song, oration, choreography, random activity, task completion, continuous, discontinuous, fragmented;

- ❖ as a route map of sequential frames or as a chain of stepping stones of choreographed and improvised sections;

- ❖ as a poetic narration against a body of physical action;

- ❖ as phases of bracketed activity or as a 'play-within-the-play', that dramatic parenthesis which may allow the inclusion of material of other orders;

- ❖ as a borrowing or annexation of one set of dramatic conventions to carry another, such as employing the order of a chapel service or conventions of a barn dance as performance structures.

We might also characterise it as an unfolding of a series of **inciting incidents** and their trajectories. These are changes of consequence, crises or innovations and may include sudden shifts in direction, emphasis, orientation. They may be most apparent at thresholds, such as entrances and exits, which are then followed by a period of change, resolution or elaboration. It may also exhibit phenomena such as **irrevocable acts** or irreversible changes, or **decay**, as in the destruction of objects. And **nodes** in which like and unlike phenomena are drawn together into images with complex and equivocal meaning.

Performance is thus far manifest in this model as a stratigraphy of pattern and detail. It also exists in and against axes of time and space, both of which are susceptible to manipulation in the creation of performative meaning. The arrangement of the performance area, the configuration of performers and spectators, architectural and scenographic enclosure and restriction may all affect the nature and quality of the activity and its reception. Different time frames may be manifest by performers during performance, in sequence or in parallel, affecting the expenditure of energy, the application and quality of effort and the dynamic graph of the event: performance may be structured as divisions of time.

Pattern only gains dramatic coherence through a judicious use of **dynamics**, modulations of speed, intensity, rhythm, mounting tension, pushing on and pulling back, energy expenditure, relaxation. Set one level of dynamics, of energy expenditure, at the outset and we may run the risk of alienating the audience, however intense that be. We may need a more subtle graph of speed, exertion, intensity, rhythm. But this might be radically different from everyday life using extremes of energy expenditure and relaxation over extremes of time. And the use of **ruptures** – sudden, unexpected changes in direction, emphasis, rhythm – will serve as a shock, a refocusing. Instructively, current developments in dance music have worked with timbre, texture, rhythm and space rather than the orthodoxies of rock music, that is, lyric (narrative) and persona (character).

Devised performance tends towards hybridity or the heterogeneous. It may be generated as text, action, music, scenography. It exists in space and time as pattern and detail. And it may employ rules, strategies, dynamic trajectories and the manipulation of objects within its elaboration. It is with, and within, these principles, particular practices and axes of manifestation, that rich and complex forms of performance can be generated. It is here that performance employs, manipulates, transgresses, ignores and organises its resources. Creativity can begin anywhere within this matrix. And it is through such principles that description, discourse and analysis might be orientated.

Summary: cultural intervention and social innovation (performance and special world)

Performance is a mode of cultural production that works with material and intellectual resources to create meaning. Performance is a special world set aside from everyday life by contractual arrangements and social suspensions, not entirely hermetically sealed, but a devised world, all the elements of which – site, environment, technology, spatial organisation, form and content, rules and practices – are conceived, organised, controlled and ultimately experienced by its orders of participant. It is a locale of cultural intervention and innovation, a place of experiment, claim, conflict, negotiation, transgression: a place where preconceptions, expectations and critical faculties may be dislocated and confounded; where extra-daily occurrences and experiences and changes in status are possible; a place where things may still be at risk – beliefs, classifications, lives.

Performance tends towards **liminality**: this 'interstitial passage between fixed identifications opens up the possibility of a cultural hybridity that entertains difference without an assumed or imposed hierarchy' (Bhabha 1994: 4); 'the space in which cultural meanings and identities always contain the traces of other meanings and identities' (Ashcroft, Griffiths and Tiffin 1998: 61). It becomes an enacted Third Space where a culture's hybridity is articulated (Bhabha 1994: 37–8). In this it has echoes of Foucault's notion of **heterotopia**:

> There are also, probably in every culture, in every civilisation, real places – places that do exist and that are formed in the very founding of society – which are something like counter-sites, a kind of effectively enacted utopia in which the real sites, all the other real sites than can be found within the culture, are simultaneously represented, contested and inverted. I shall call them, by ways of contrast to utopias, heterotopias.

> (1986a: 24)

Performance is one such heterotopia (and perhaps utopia too). As a forum for examining, challenging and transgressing the relationships, rites and rituals of everyday life, with real changes in status, it is a place where identities may be created, shaped, contested and changed, where new agendas are set.

Performance relies upon the shared competence of all the participants to identify and to mark off a strip of behaviour, this grouping of activities and objects, as being performative. Once they can do this, then they will expect, search for and indeed generate meaning in everything they see. 'Whatever passes the boundary and enters the theatrical space is declared significant' (Roms 1993). However utilitarian, prosaic or banal, nothing will be neutral or simply decorative. Every object, every action, will work simultaneously as the representational, the decorative, the functional and the cognitive, together with the surrogate moments formed from their interaction (Dilnot 1994: 21–32). Meaning is generated relentlessly: performance is a saturated space.

Archaeology

Sicily: an argument

It began with the edge of a trowel. I learned to use one over twenty years ago. A drop-forged mason's trowel, four-inch blade. A British make, WHS, is the best – though the company has been bought up by one of the international conglomerates. In the United States trust is put in the Marshaltown brand; you can order yours on-line, complete with leather holster (some archaeologists do see themselves as the cowboys of science!); for me the shape is wrong. It has to be drop-forged; any other manufacturing technique just isn't strong enough – the leverage exerted in taking up a cobble surface or working through a hard clay floor is enough to snap it. Like many professionals I have a set, for me of five – ranging from a fresh new blade through to one barely an inch long, worn down by use. With these you can, with sufficient experience and expertise, pick up the slightest of distinctions between archaeological deposits, even those invisible to the eye. And this is what I had learned to rely upon. To be understood, what is found by the archaeologist must be connected with its context, whether fine layers of ash deposited over the years of use of a hearth, building rubble left by masons or the accumulated deposits of a town garbage heap. Stratigraphy is a foundation of archaeological analysis and interpretation.

But here in Sicily they were using picks, albeit little ones, and the edges of the trench they were digging were loose and ragged. How could they understand the layering, how could they look to the profile of their excavation and see what they had dug through? It was explained that they thought my experience in the north of Europe was less relevant to sites like this. 'No stratigraphy – only floors and walls', I was told. No need to bother with the subtleties of archaeological contexts. The task for them was to dig down to floors and follow the walls to identify buildings. To me this was like saying that the laws of physics didn't apply in this part of the universe!

Apologia

I could give conventional descriptions and conceptions of archaeology, focus on field and laboratory techniques, perhaps provide a short history of archaeological thought. For many, archaeology is a set of techniques aimed at recovering the past; archaeologists dig up the past. Archaeological thought thus, following from this, deals with what happened in the past, and what archaeologists have said of this. Just look at the many textbooks and popular works on archaeology.

There may be and have been different theories of what happened in the archaeological past, but ultimately, orthodoxy holds, these theories must defer to the remains of the past. As I indicated in the Introduction, critical reflexivity has come to feature significantly in archaeology, especially since the 1960s, as well as in cognate disciplines; this is an extension of theorising to include methodology, philosophy and the practices of archaeology. Here an old debate continues about the extent to which archaeology is a field science, a social science or a branch of the humanities.

There are several good introductions to archaeology which deal with all this, and I do not wish to duplicate them (Renfrew and Bahn 1996 and Thomas 1998 are my favourites). And anyway I wish to challenge some of the basic premises upon which they base their definition of archaeology. For me archaeology is the strangest of cultural spaces. Here I want to delve deeper and set the scene with a sketch of the **political ecology** of archaeology, how it works as a project focused upon the cultural inhabitation of varied locales, from deepest prehistory to the present. The next sections deal with some of the practices and experiences which lie at the heart of the archaeological project.

An archaeological project in Sicily

To the north is a much-visited and quite spectacular ancient site. Segesta – indigeneous settlement contemporary with Greeks and Phoenicians arriving in the 600s BC and after. To the west a fascinating Phoenician island outpost – Mozia. To the south a rich ancient Greek colony – Selinous. But here it was a piece of a perfume jar found broken on an ancient floor that attracted me to the project. Made in Korinth in Greece, the pot was of very distinctive style. I had been studying them for several years. They are treated as art objects and are found in museums the world over. I was keen to move beyond art history to understand their production, distribution and consumption. Yet of the ninety-odd sites I had researched and where have been found these pots, and in spite of two centuries of study, none had the sort of information I really needed to move beyond simple admiration and cataloguing. I wanted to investigate their design and manufacture in Greece. I wanted to understand how they travelled to places like Sicily. I wanted to know where in a house they might belong, with what other articles of daily life, how they ended as dedications to deities, where and in precisely what deposits, where in a settlement they were used and discarded. I also wanted to ask why they have come to be seen as works of art.

And so I joined a large international project excavating a hilltop settlement in Sicily and surveying its region (http://www.stanford.edu/~mshanks). Several universities, government organisations, groups and individuals are involved from northern Europe, the United States and Sicily itself. This is typical of large archaeological projects. There is a broad research design and an aspiration to employ the latest in field techniques. Individual areas of interest, in addition to mine in material culture, include regional economic organisation, and the different cultural groups interacting in the mid- first millennium BC. We rely on different sources of funding to enable the project to happen. Sometimes the different interests work together efficiently, sometimes not, as we debate method, management structures, our different agendas. Is a traditional archaeological approach to culture history really compatible with the aims of others to study the negotiation of cultural identity under a postcolonial agenda? Is an excavation procedure based upon tight control of stratigraphy always to be preferred to a classical archaeological focus upon finds and structures? As will be clear from my discussion here, I am interested in how we mount archaeological expeditions, how the discipline of archaeology operates, the nature of its disciplinary and cultural politics. I want to get into the detective work that is archaeology, and to look at ourselves as archaeologists. Is such an ethnography of the project, locating its interests in a broader intellectual community and landscape, to be pursued or should the site and the past be the focus? Many feel much more comfortable with the latter and feel threatened by the former.

The acquisition and creation of knowledges of the past: issues of research design and project management, even cultural differences between those educated under different intellectual traditions – the rigours of British field science, the pragmatism and finds-orientation of Mediterranean archaeology, the scientific methodology of an American tradition, the humanistic focus of a more theoretically aware archaeology. Debates pervade the project. Mention has been made of the use of trowels and picks (the trowel – the favourite tool of the stratigraphic aficionado). One team is beta-testing a new computer-based surveying and recording environment, GIS software (Geographic Information System) tied to electronic surveying instruments; others see this as an ideal, perhaps unattainable, which needs to be supported by conventional systems of planning and record. Terminologies are debated – should the standard orthodox Greek terms for Mediterranean finds be used (storage jar as a *pithos*; the highest point of a site as the *acropolis*), terms having dubious association with prehistoric Sicily? Or should more neutral and scientific descriptions be found? Rights of access – who can have access to material and information? Issues at the local superintendency of antiquities – conservation of the finds, permissions, negotiations with the forestry commission over the use of earth-moving machinery. Arrivals at the local airport – organising transport and workforce. Photography – digital and conventional, of what and of whom – are the diggers themselves legitimate subjects for record? Recording systems – the design of a database which could encompass different approaches to the site and its finds. Phone lines – ISDN lines and portable cellular phones offering remote access. Water at the dig house – for diggers as well as lab and flotation equipment (to extract botanical remains from the soil). Getting liquid cash to Sicily. Convincing the local commune that we are onto something good – providing a narrative with which they might identify? Cultural differences between some of the locals and some of the excavation team – where to eat and drink and with whom in the local town? The intellectual boundaries of the project – how far should our critical self-consciousness go? Lines of authority and management – who, ultimately, is to reconcile different interests?

An archaeological project? Where is the archaeology? At what is it directed? Of what does it consist? Do science and archaeology refer tightly to the work on site, scrutinising stratigraphy, bagging materials, processing them in a lab and on computer screen? And, if so, what of the rest? Are the permissions to gain access and excavate separate, potentially distracting issues? Is the ethnography of a project, studying its participants and accounting for their interests not part of archaeology, something to do with the *context* of the archaeological study of the past? Is the task of organising efficient earth moving simply the *context* of doing the science of discovery? What of the experiences and practices which are hereby seen not to belong to science, but which are nevertheless part of the project? So much of that mentioned just above.

Relevant here is an orthodox and basic insistence on the distinction between science and its context. It is a fundamental distinction between archaeological science focused upon the past, and management and administration focused upon the present. And involving politics: for our project is highly political, dealing with the articulation of very different interest groups, and with a contemporary search by some for the prehistoric, pre-Greek and pre-Roman origins of Sicily – identities are at stake. I am so used to archaeology being carefully demarcated. This is politics – the permissions, the interest of the local minister of culture, the different and competing interest groups. This is heritage and identity – people claiming their ancestry to lie in a conventional designation of culture historical archaeology, the Elimi culture of the mid-first millennium BC, held to be living in our site at Monte Polizzo. This is entertainment – the party thrown in our honour by the mayor of the local commune. This is interpretation for the community – a display at the local museum. These are archaeological subjects – GIS recording systems, intra-site spatial analysis. These are the objects of archaeological enquiry – structures and finds upon a hilltop.

Instead, I see connections. I wish to take issue with these distinctions, with this sort of insistence upon distinguishing the scientific from the spiritual from the political from the personal. It is, I believe, part of a desire to keep science and society or politics apart, this notion of archaeology and its context. And with this desire I connect a radical separation of the technical and the social, the professional from the political, theory from practice, the past from the present. Also indeed, as will be argued, the non-human from the human in that the tools and materials of the project are usually conceived as means to an end, media, implements in the hands of archaeology's agents or practitioners.

These distinctions are about value, it might be noted (Shanks 1992a: 99–101). A potsherd may invoke an academic interest in ceramic design which is considered quite separate from the value the piece may have to the art market, or to a local antiquarian in a town in Sicily, or to a school child interested in its images of waterbirds. But the different interests are not commensurable, for archaeologists alone are held to speak for the remains of the past, representing them to the present's (epistemological) interest in gaining reliable knowledge of the past.

And the introduction here of value reminds us that these distinctions are often about separating archaeology's *proper* practice from distractions or irrelevant matters. What really matters to some of my colleagues, under this view, is that the project pulled through the summer, in spite of the political/cultural/logistical/practical *difficulties*. I do not see these as trivial interests or values, irrelevancies and difficulties distracting us from the real past, from archaeological methods, ideas and narratives. Instead, I insist that without what is normally kept separate from the field science there could be no field science. Workers need to be transported and fed. Permissions are needed. And, as is commonplace to any researcher, research simply would not happen without the grant applications and awards. All this experience that is a field project is the *concrete life of science*. Agendas and enfoldings. And it is this *ecology* that I call archaeology.

We need to go back to some experiences which constitute (literally, as we shall see) the archaeological. The next two sections deal with two of archaeology's cultural locales and two of its constituting practices. The first is about the museum, collecting and gathering cultural artefacts. The second is about walking the land, travelling and encountering other cultures. In the first the concept of culture will be a pivot; in the second it is landscape.

Material *culture*: people and things

Citing philosopher Krzysztof Pomian (1987), archaeologist and historian Alain Schnapp (1996: 11) associates archaeology with collecting. 'The vital link between the two is the status accorded to an object which has been isolated, conserved, displayed, associated with or distinguished from others as a result of certain traits' (ibid.: 12). Treated as significant and signifying, any object may be collected and subjected to various processes, of which archaeological enquiry is only one. But the association of archaeologist with the collector has been denied since at least the nineteenth century – archaeologists don't want to be seen as successors to tomb robbers of antiquity, medieval traders in religious relics, part of the renaissance *Wunderkammer* mentality. Most wish to oppose the commercial values of our contemporary art and antiques market – in this they would rather be taken for policemen. Nevertheless, they do deal in collections of things, their distinction being they are usually more meticulous, and they are accountable, to state and public institutions. This continuity from (antiquarian) collector to archaeologist is dealt with rather well by Susan Pearce in several books (1992, 1997). She covers the relation of collection to personal identity (1992: Chapter 3), but her primary interest is in the connection between collection and museums. For the museum is one of the primary cultural locales of archaeology.

Most of us will have made a visit to one of the great international museums. Somewhere like the Louvre in Paris. Its galleries display artefacts, mostly old, and many from archaeological sites. They are on display because, by some at least, they are considered worthy of attention. They have exhibition value. Why? It is impossible to dissociate the museum from Art, from artefacts held to represent aesthetic and cultural achievement (Shanks and Tilley 1992, Chapter 4). The finest examples of their kind. Paradigms. For people everywhere to admire, wonder at. And here in an old royal palace in Paris, Walter Benjamin's capital of the nineteenth century.

The Venus de Milo stands ritually encircled by visitors, solitary, punctuating the pattern in the marble floor of the gallery. It was acquired after a scramble on the part of several aristocrats to grab it after it first turned up on a beach of a Greek island. It was an adventure story rivalling those of Indiana Jones (Shanks 1996: 150). Winckelmann, eighteenth-century aesthete and art historian, loved sculpture like this, though he didn't know the piece and was more interested in Roman copies of Greek sculpture. But he epitomises that Romantic shift to a new way of looking and appreciating art, especially the Greek (ibid.: 56–8). In a fundamental re-evaluation of art history and the cultural significance of art works, he re-energised the classical tradition. In lyrical prose he celebrated the aesthetic wonders of fragments left in the Vatican collection. His archaeology was simultaneously historical and transcendent. With Winckelmann we look back to the Greeks and their works, or what is left of them, to experience those human cultural values which escape time itself. We still live with the remains of this cultural ideology of Hellenism (Morris 1994).

And the tension between historical provenance and universal value is there also in works from times other than that of ancient Greece. Islamic and Chinese ceramics may fill galleries too, on the basis of their attestation to the same transcendent cultural values.

Places then of cultural pilgrimage, these museums in the capital cities of the modern nation-state (Horne 1984). Cultural treasure houses built upon the desire to collect and own a transnational heritage, the right to which modern imperial states considered theirs by virtue of global reach and power. So often this heritage has been seen as Graeco-Roman. The nineteenth-century European states competed to acquire the best; their museums are less able to do so now, but the art market remains a determining force in the field of cultural value, dominated by corporate and institutional capital, such as the immense resources of the Getty Foundation.

The art object is one material interface of archaeology and culture. But another Romantic, Herder, and again at the end of the eighteenth century, complained of this association of cultivation with universal human value or progress and western culture, writing instead of *cultures* plural, in an appreciation of the works and values of other societies. This anticipates an anthropological sense of culture as way of life, a definition formalised by Kroeber and Kluckhohn (1952) and probably originating in Tylor's book *Primitive Culture* of 1870, though there it was tied to evolutionary models of human development – from primitive to civilised.

B.2   M.2   E.2

Ethnic or national identity is also found on display in the museum, signified by archaeological artefacts. The Venus de Milo is simultaneously for all humankind, *and* (ancient) Greek.
We find galleries in the Louvre of Roman, Egyptian, Celtic, Assyrian works (of art), alongside
French, Italian, British painting and sculpture. Behind the classification and ordering is the
equation of cultural work and some essential quality of identity.

Not in the Louvre, but in many other museums, we may be able to look upon the works of
peoples categorised according to a more specialised and archaeological meaning of culture.
Gordon Childe is associated with this sense of culture as recurring sets of associated artefacts
or traits held to represent a people or society (discussed by Renfrew and Bahn 1996: 443–5).
It emphasises the expressive or stylistic components of identity over issues of value. In prehistoric
archaeology and in the absence of written sources, these cultures may be named after 'type'
sites, regions or artefacts – the Mousterian culture of the middle palaeolithic period (after the
site of le Moustier); the bronze age Beaker folk (after a type of ceramic vessel); the TRB
(Trichterbecker) culture group (another class of ceramic); the Wessex culture (a region of
southern England). That such 'culture historical' interpretation is now academically discredited
has not been fully accepted. Many archaeologists still orient their work around this concept of
culture. Culture historical classification of archaeological remains, particularly prehistoric, is
still the norm.

Archaeology may make references to art and humanity. It has had, conventionally, an
interest in classical '*civilised*' culture, '*primitive*' other or older cultures. The discipline has
developed its own culture concept uniting material relics with peoples of the past. It has
contributed to anthropological notions of culture. Archaeology has thus been an important
part of the interplay and evolution of the references and meanings of the culture concept.
More generally, it is clear that archaeology and anthropology were central to the cultural
development of the advanced capitalist nation-states of the nineteenth century.

Political revolution (Britain in the seventeenth century, France and the United States at
the end of the eighteenth) and its threat accompanied the forging of a new form of political
unity through the industrial nation-state (Hobsbawm 1990). From the beginning nation-
states have been founded upon a fundamental tension. On the one hand they have invoked,
as unifying force and legitimation, Enlightenment ideas of popular will and sovereignty,
universal human rights. And the form of the nation-state itself has been exported globally

A.2   O.2   R.2   S.2

from its origins in early modern Europe. On the other hand they are all locally circumscribed, each independent of similar polities on the basis of regional, ethnic, linguistic, and/or national identity and history (Turner 1990). Archaeology and anthropology, disciplines formalised at the beginning of the nineteenth century, offered powerful ways of working on these new *cultural* issues.

A crucial factor in ideas of national identity was the imperialist and colonial experience of travel and other cultures (Pratt 1992). Johannes Fabian (1983) has convincingly clarified the dependence of anthropological knowledge upon travel and encounters with other cultures in other lands. This confrontation between western Enlightenment reason and a cultural (and colonial) other was transposed upon time and history – those cultures that help us understand who we are live over there and back then, while we are here and now. Archaeology was another powerful medium in these cultural geographies of the imagination. While ethnography confronted the industrial west with its alternate and provided a foil, difference, against which western nations might understand themselves, archaeology provided material evidence of folk roots of the new state polities, while also attaching the imperial states to the cultural peaks of history measured by artistic values and encapsulated in objects acquired, often from abroad, for the museums. This has been one of the main cultural successes of archaeology – to provide the new nation-states of the eighteenth and nineteenth centuries with histories and origin stories rooted in the *material* remains of the past (Díaz-Andreu and Champion 1996). Myths of ancestry were articulated in new national narratives, stories of belonging and common (civilised) community (the latter particularly identified with Graeco-Roman culture). Both archaeology and anthropology provided specific symbols and evidences used to create exclusive and homogeneous conceptions of identity rooted in national traditions, conceptions of race, ethnicity and language. Moreover, archaeology provided an extraordinary immediacy apparently accessible without academic training – finds which could be displayed to speak for themselves in the new museums, the cultural treasure houses of imperial power, repositories of ancestral remains. Many archaeologies around the world continue to perform this role of providing material correlates for stories and myths of identity and belonging (Trigger 1984; Kohl and Fawcett 1995; see also Olivier and Coudart 1995).

Conceptions of modern identity are still dependent upon the idea of the nation-state and upon the formation of nation-states in the nineteenth century. But recent history shows clearly their instability. They often have no obvious cultural justification in geography, history, race or ethnicity. Nation-states are social constructions (Bhabha 1990a; Anderson 1991). Growing out of the demise of old empires, nation-states have frequently been connected with Enlightenment notions of human rights and rational government (democracy and representation), relying on these to unify people around a common story of their national identity. Such unified history and culture has always failed to cope with diversity. The distinction between nation and nation-state has frequently collapsed into contention, with ideas of self-determination and freedom, identity and unity colliding with the suppression of diversity, domination and exclusion that overrides a genuine egalitarian pluralism (Chatterjee 1993).

The tension between universal political and cultural forms and values, and local cultural textures has shifted emphasis in recent decades. Nation-states now have less power and agency, which is in stark contrast to the ever-increasing influence of structures and movements of corporate and transnational capital. In a period of rapid decolonisation after the Second World War this *globalisation* is about the transformation of imperial power into supra-national operations of capital, communications and culture. This *postcolonial* world is one of societies, including new nation-states, that have escaped the control of the empires and ideological blocs of western and eastern Europe. An ideological unity is engineered through the culture industry, the mass media and mass consumption – a predominantly American culture. And the integrated resources of the global economy lie behind this (Featherstone 1990; Curti and Chambers 1996; Featherstone *et al.* 1995; Spybey 1996).

But with international capital, global telecommunications and world military order, the nation-state continues to be a major structural feature of this postmodern scene. It remains a major focus of regional cultural identity. The postcolonial state is heavily and ironically dependent upon notions of the state and nation developed in Europe, and so too is it dependent upon the same sorts of ideological constructions of national identity developed through history, archaeology and anthropology (Hobsbawm and Ranger 1983). Hence a key tension or contradiction in globalisation involves the fluid free market between nations, epitomised in multinational and corporate capital and based upon ideologies of the free individual operating beyond boundaries of any one polity, and ideologies of difference, ideologies of local identity. Here the nation, nation-state and nationalism remain potent.

And here archaeology remains a vital cultural factor in the context too of ideas of heritage. For the crucial cultural issue is the ways local communities engage with these processes of globalisation. And the ways they do compare with the ways colonised communities dealt with imperial colonial powers; the interpenetration of local and global cultural forces has been a feature of modernity since at least the nineteenth century. It is not simply a one-way process of influence, control, dissemination and hegemony, with an American western homogenised culture taking over and supplanting local identity. It is not just top-down dominance, but a complex interplay of hegemony, domination and empowerment. The key question or issue is the way external and internal forces interact to produce, reproduce and disseminate global culture within local communities. The question is to what extent the global is being transformed by peripheral communities; to what extent, by appropriating strategies of representation, organi-sation and social change through access to global systems, are local communities and interest groups empowering themselves and influencing global systems.

Here then is a broad context for the interface of archaeology and culture. There is the part archaeology plays in the construction of national and cultural identities (Rowlands 1994). A key is an encounter with materiality and regional focus, the ruins of a local past, setting the homogenisation of processes like nationalism, colonisation and imperialism against the peculiarities of history and geography. This is about the relation between local pasts and those global methods, frameworks and master narratives which may suppress, under a disciplinary and cultural uniformity, the rich pluralism and multicultural tapestry of peoples and histories. Questions are raised of whether *genuine* local pasts (Shanks 1992a: 109), implicit in local and distinct identities, are possible, or whether they are always to be understood in relation to abstract categories and the standardised processes of an archaeological science. Archaeology's focus on obdurate remains suggests the possibility of a material resistance to the ideologies of a homogeneous world uniform in its accommodation to the commodity form and principles of the global market.

And all this may happen in the museum – in encounters with collections of things.

Site and locale: walking landscape

The equation between people, their culture and the land they inhabit is central to the time–space systematics of the discipline of archaeology, as just outlined – 'these people were then'. It is an equation crucial to the coherence of the new nation-states of modern Europe. It is encapsulated in the cultural attachment to land so characteristic of Romantic nationalism. For archaeologists it is not enough that their collections of artefacts make cultural sense, whether it is in terms of artistic value or as markers of identity; they must also be linked to a place, a setting. A key term here has become 'landscape' – that distinctive, and aesthetic, set of relationships with the land.

Archaeologists walk the land, observing, recording, drawing, telling. I wish to argue that, in our understanding of archaeology, primacy should be given to this general attention to land. It comes before, and subsumes, *interventions* in the land – excavations, so often considered the defining archaeological activity. To think of archaeology as being about digging up the past is a subtle and ideological distraction. First then let us remember the historical roots of this rela-tionship. We need to recall some antiquaries. (The following section draws upon Schnapp 1996: 139–219.)

In 1586 was published William Camden's *Britannia*, an historical and geographical description of the British Isles. He had been visiting different parts of Britain from 1575, producing local histories. In this work he set a paradigm for future historical cartography. With a precise eye and attention to date and place, he combined literary information with descrip-tions of landscapes, with topographic and toponymic studies. Ultimately in a classical tradition set by Roman travel writer Pausanias, Camden established the antiquarian value of travel and peregrination, an intimate relationship with land and its cultural and historical features. So too in the early seventeenth century Ole Worm and Johan Bure in Scandinavia, Nicolaus Marschalk in Germany were walking in the field. For the first two history located in the land was central to the definition of the two double monarchies of Denmark-Norway and Sweden-Finland. For Marschalk the interest was more in excavation. Antiquaries were leaving their libraries just as the scientists, astronomers, mathematicians and botanists too went out to observe earth and sky. Historian and archaeologist Stuart Piggott (1976: 111) links antiquarianism to the rural world, connecting surveying, precise observation and record in the field, with the culture of landed gentlemen who received their training at the Inns of Court, the English Law schools. He quotes Robert Burton in his *Anatomy of Melancholy*: 'What more pleasing studies can there be than the Mathematicks, Theorick or Practick parts? As to survey land, make mapps, models, dials etc., with which I have ever much delighted myself' (ibid). The earth was coming to reveal its secrets, as peregrination, collection, survey and interpretation were united in the pleasures of education and enquiry.

Ole Worm, a Dane, worked in a Baconian and empirical tradition. Rather than defer to ancient texts and tradition, he started with the remains of monuments, exploration of the land and earth, and only afterwards related them to tradition. He saw no need of Latin or Greek sources, just an enquiring mind, a sharp eye and a taste for drawing. He explicitly asserted local Nordic history over Graeco-Roman tradition, adopting a cross-cultural classification of monuments, setting out clear descriptive methods and relating monuments to the historical record. Worm was reading the landscape and deciphering the signs and inscriptions seen there. The importance of system was foremost – these were not disconnected disparate ciphers in the landscape but pieces of an historical jigsaw.

John Aubrey in Britain, associate of Hobbes and Harvey, colleague of Newton and Locke, brought together philological precision in the interpretation of historical sources with the description and interpretation of landscape (*Monumenta Britannica*, published posthumously). His attitude was one of sensitivity to past in the present:

> that antiquaries are so taken with the sight of old things, not as doting upon the bare forme or matter (though both oftentimes be very notable in old things) but because these visible superviving evidences of Antiquity represent unto their minds former times, with as strong an impression, as if they were actually present, and in sight, as it were.
>
> (Quoted Hunter 1975: 171)

In Scandinavia Olof Rudbeck walked and viewed the landscape with the eye of an anatomist, dissecting the earth in stratigraphical order, producing diagrams, aerial views, plans.

In the eighteenth century Stukeley presented an extension and completion of this paradigm, and again from Britain. Touring and observing ancient sites, gardens, architectures, relying on direct experience, he displayed acute observation and knowledge of landscape in a vision of the earth as a repository of interpretable traces. His pioneering researches on Stonehenge and Avebury, published in 1740 and 1743, are remembered for their field observation and illustration combined with what are now sometimes seen as fantastical ideas about ancient British Druidical religion.

These antiquaries interested in regional archaeology are to be contrasted with those taking in the grand tour of, by the end of the eighteenth century, the Graeco-Roman Mediterranean (Constantine 1984; Stoneman 1987). A whole culture industry of painters serviced the aristocratic tourists (Tsigakou 1981; Stoneman 1998). In sumptuous publications there was often displayed a passion for the picturesque ruin in the landscape – the folios of Choiseul Gouffier and Edward Dodwell, the visionary ruins of David LeRoy. Stuart and Revett famously maintained scrupulous accuracy in their Mediterranean travelogue and studies of Greek architecture (*The Antiquities of Athens* published from 1761). The topographical tradition established by Aubrey and Stukeley continued in Greece with the remarkable work of William Martin Leake, who, from 1805 to 1810, intensively surveyed the Greek countryside to establish the sites of virtually all settlements mentioned by the ancient historians.

So by the nineteenth century I see established a paradigmatic archaeological activity or attitude – intensive attention to traces in the land and earth, the complex articulations of history and place, the milieu of human inhabitation. Walking, observing, scraping, digging, noting, mapping. And much of this has become associated with the concept of landscape.

Landscape is a nexus of inhabitation, place and value. It is a term as complex and ideologically charged as culture. It should not be forgotten that the roots of the term still lie in the notion of an aesthetic cultivation of the view or aspect; a reflexive awareness of the historical roots of the concept itself is important. Landscape painting and architecture improve upon nature according to particular aesthetic or cultural values. This submission of place to reason and imagination imbricates time and history. The landscape genre in the hands of Claude Lorrain and Poussin, myriad landscape painters from the seventeenth and eighteenth centuries, landscape architects like Repton, Uvedale Price and Capability Brown, was always explicitly or implicitly a relationship to history and sensibility to be found in land itself (Andrews 1999; cf. Smiles 1994 for Britain; for literature Williams 1973). History – ancient monuments and ruins, classical, medieval, prehistoric. Sensibility – attitudes to the land which refer back, ultimately, to ideologies of the Roman *campagna* and classical pastoral. History and sensibility – a celebration of the rural, often over the urban and industrial, those scarring features of modernity.

Stephen Daniels (1993), among others, has shown how the aesthetic of landscape has been central to the construction of national identity in Britain and the United States. Powerfully affective, it provides a deep cultural milieu, mapping out values and attachments. Landscape has provided a basis for locating new communities of nationhood in a kind of collective cultural memory of belonging. Monuments and landforms have come to be seen to give history and shape to human communities, nations included. Consider, for example, the legacy of this concept of landscape in Britain. The English countryside is one of interwoven traces and layers of previous inhabitation, punctuated by monuments and the relics of times gone by; a particular cultural ecology of narratives, plants and creatures, geology, language, music, customs, architectures, traces, archaeological sites and finds. It is where the English may be held to belong and find their roots, though others may appreciate its beauties. And note here the articulation of archaeology and natural history, an association embodied in the numerous local natural history societies founded across Britain in the nineteenth century.

Those tensions noted in the concept of culture, between universal human values, the qualities of particular cultures, and the aspiration to cultivated intellectual or artistic activity, are here present also in landscape, and notions of site or monument. So many images of land the world over, photographs and paintings, are now generated from the same aesthetic and pictorial models established by a select elite and culminating at the end of the eighteenth century. Yet narratives of local identity may be considered to lie in the land itself, in an attachment of land, language, culture and people. In spite of social mobility and diaspora, land may still provide a basis for belonging, and the notion of aboriginal folk culture, deeply rooted in place, remains potent.

There is now a sub-discipline of landscape archaeology (for prehistoric archaeology see Wagstaff 1987; Bender 1993; Tilley 1994; Ucko and Layton 1999). There are several defining features. A regional focus is one. Sites and finds are considered in the context of settlement patterns and environments. Mention is frequently made of the early work of Gordon Willey in the 1940s and 1950s in Peru; he considered soiopolitical organisation in the Virú valley through its settlement patterns (Willey 1953). One background, from the 1920s, is aerial photography; another is the distribution map, developed as a summary graphical and interpretive tool only in the 1930s: both are tied to particular ways of seeing the land – distanced and encompassing, detached from walking the earth itself. More recently the analysis of regional settlement patterns has been considerably affected by spatial science which grew out of new archaeology in the 1960s (Clarke 1968 is an early exponent; also Hodder and Orton 1976; Hodder 1978; Clarke 1977). A range of statistical techniques can be used to analyse, essentially, points in a two- or three-dimensional geometric space, the relationships then used in the inference of cultural and social phenomena. Geographical Information Systems, spatially referenced databases, are the latest in this line of tools for spatial analysis. They allow the control of large amounts of data, facilitate statistical analysis, and offer quick and easy ways of displaying information as maps. As well as control and summary visualisation, these systems of regional focus are based upon co-ordinates in a geometric and mathematically defined space.

Landscape archaeology has also been associated with the development of non-invasive survey, that is, survey which does not give primacy to excavation. There are many techniques now available, from surface collection of material found in field walking, through geophysical prospection – ways of seeing into the soil – to remote sensing – the analysis and interpretation of the likes of satellite imagery (Scollar *et al.* 1990; Lillesand and Kiefer 1994). Of particular note is that much landscape archaeology questions the notion of 'site' as a basic unit of study, often being more interested in the likes of field systems and ancient agriculture. Landscape archaeology is often off-site archaeology.

These features connect with that old topographical interest in close observation, local knowledge and empirical description. Leslie Grinsell (1936) walked the fields of England making a comprehensive inventory of prehistoric monuments, every trace, and all measured in Grinsell paces – by the length of his stride.

The reconstruction of ancient environments is undoubtedly another background to landscape archaeology, often connected with a focus upon the way people in the past fed themselves (subsistence strategies, in the jargon) – an interest here in plants and animals, climate and physical geography. Palaeoeconomists in the 1970s and 1980s walked the territories around many ancient settlements, aiming to establish, in this *site catchment analysis*, what it was like in the past, what natural resources there would have been for people to exploit (Higgs 1972, 1975, Jarman, Bailey and Jarman 1982).

The idea of landscape has always been resistant to notions of environmental determinism. After Carl Sauer (Leighly 1963) many have explored the history of human interventions in nature (now Redman 1999), looking at domestication, fire ecology, hydrological engineering, modes of cultivation and agricultural engineering, industry, mineral extraction. The concept of landscape refers to both natural environment and elements of human agency, with environment seen as socially constructed, culturally constituted.

Above all, landscape archaeology is centred upon a concept which seems to offer a unifying perspective, cross-cutting culture and nature, like the concept of 'the body'. It cuts across both time and space too, with continuities and breaks in a temporal line from past to present, in the traces of past in the present, in the geographical shape of lives around us.

We will return again to the idea of landscape, particularly to note its historical tensions. I end the discussion here with the connection I have made between the concept and activities in the land, of looking, walking, digging. The basic point is to recognise that landscape is best conceived as a process and a set of relationships at the heart of the present's historical relationship with the past – and this is how it might help guide our archaeological practice.

A topology of erosions: archaeology and time

I have dealt with what I see as two cultural locales and constituting practices for archaeology – walking the land and museum collections. History was implicated in both. Let me now turn to archaeology and time. Surely, some might think, it is straightforward – archaeologists deal in old things, things from the past. I'm afraid that is not enough. I am going to raise some questions about chronology in archaeology. I wish to emphasise further the interpenetration of space, place and history. To do this I will connect archaeology with photography, introducing another paradigm for modern archaeology (Shanks 1997a, 1997b). An historical link, convergence or homology is implied in the development of photography and the formalisation of archaeology as a discipline from the early nineteenth century. The juxtaposition is also a convenient way of seeing some more features of the archaeological project.

The camera is a clock for making images. Consider some issues on the subject of time, photography and the material artefact. We can begin with three categories of photographic time in archaeology: the moment arrested, captured or frozen; date (attributed to that moment); and a continuity from past through present (the past before us now, embodied in photograph or relic). To these may be added **actuality** – a return of what is no longer the same.

Actuality is the non-arbitrary conjunction of presents: the past's present (in the photograph or relic), the instant of photography, archaeological excavation or discovery and the time of viewing or reading. I argue that actuality is a key concept in understanding photography and archaeology.

Compare the work of the photograph and that of the archaeologist with memory. Memories live on with us, as do found things and photographs, and as we reinterpret memories and incorporate them into new stories of our life, so photographs, archaeological sites and artefacts change. The holiday snapshot becomes a social document or historical source; the stone which was once considered a thunderbolt becomes recognised as a tool and as therefore a trace of a once-lost society. Memories sometimes seem to escape time, in that they stay with us. We may feel too that old artefacts and photographic images sometimes witness or encapsulate that which escapes time, the timeless; this may connect with notions of art or 'human experience'. Or it may be the feelings elicited by fingerprints upon an ancient clay vessel.

The timeless here is not an unbounded infinity, the incomprehensibility of a quarter of a million years, but is convoluted or folded time, a folding or recycling of past moments or experiences. As conjuncture between the person remembering and the past event, memory crosses time (faster than light), just as the place before you now, or the photograph held to be viewed, witnesses lost instants in time past.

Memory is not inventory, but is the act of memorising. This is also the *work* of photography or of archaeology. The past as memory does not exist as it was. The past has to be recalled: memory is the act of recalling from the viewpoint of subsequent time. So too a photograph is meaningless unless lent a past and a future. The captured moment of the photo needs a past and a present to make sense. This is done by the contextualisation that takes place in looking at a photo: we read signs within the photograph (its *mise-en-scène*) and add to these connections made through montage and juxtaposition with text. And just as memories change, so do photographs. This is photowork. An archaeological find is lent a past and a future. The bits of the past need a past and a present to make sense; they need putting in context, either of a collection or with date, provenance, cultural affiliation. This is archaeological work.

To point out the affinities between memory and photography, and to emphasise the temporality of actuality, is not a call for 'relevance', to recognise simply that archaeology happens in the present and that a photograph is a past moment viewed later. Instead we should retain the ambiguity and tension which is actuality; actuality is the *primacy*, but not the *superiority*, of the present over the past. This is to acknowledge that the soluble present is the medium of seeing and knowing the past.

We may add also the idea of rapturous temporality: memory holds on to the past, just as archaeology grabs temporal fragments, potentially missed, now lost. In memory, time stands still: there are no clocks. In the world remembered there is no bottom line, no horizon, no past-as-it-was, no ordained chronology. There are instead enfoldings. We read the signs and connect, to make sense. The photograph snatches and attempts to hold on to the connections. Archaeology shares also this art and science of assemblage.

Let me explain further the process of making connections which is central to making sense of a photograph or an archaeological find. Reconstructions of the archaeological past often aim at photographic verisimilitude – a moment arrested before the viewer, or a reconstruction, *mis-en-scène* ready to be photographed. Consider the number of museum displays which go to considerable expense and use every technological device to do just this.

Here is borrowed the idea of photographic realism. What this means is that a photograph reproduces the familiar space and look of perspective. A photograph acknowledges a disconnected instant, and often, under certain conventions of sharp focus and with certain photographic materials such as fine-grained paper, it provides certainty about that instant, details and textures. This adherence to the appearance of things, a replication of external features, is *naturalism*, to be distinguished from *realism*. These museum reconstructions want to be naturalistic. Photography can do this very well, but may not, thereby, provide a *realistic* picture. A realistic representation is not only or necessarily naturalistic. This is clear from the experience of photographs of ourselves – how often they do not resemble us but only duplicate momentary facets. A photograph of an archaeological deposit may say much about the stones and silts, the particle sizes, shapes, colours perhaps, and it may provide considerable information, but no historical significance. Meaning, it is proposed, comes from making connections and exploring contexts. This is realism – a *process* of making sense, establishing patterns of associations. The construction of narrative is but one aspect or possibility here. In looking at photographs and things found we make stories, relating our looking to our experiences, to connections we see, imagine, establish and research. This is something brought to the photograph by the maker and the viewer, and it may involve considerable deviation – temporal, spatial and conceptual – from the naturalism of the photograph. Uncertainty and doubt are the roots of making sense, and they require their own time for deliberation.

Paul Valéry declared that photography freed the writer from describing, but photographs do not describe in the same way as writing: they do not have the same temporality as text. They have a different duration of interpretation, this process of contextualisation at the heart of making sense. Naturalism may require chronicle: dates and linear chronology. A realistic memory or archaeology may need flashbacks, long-term backgrounds, reflexive reinterpretations of past events. This temporality is the condition of an archaeological method of assemblage, a rigorous attention to things, to the empirical in making connections, following the traces. This, I propose, is an archaeological poetics, the work of poetry.

Let me move on to question the attachment of a singular time or date to the archaeological past. Imagine a photograph of the room in which I sit. The electronic data back on my camera records it as 12 September 1999 14:02:46. But what date or time is this room? There is no one answer: original architectural fabric, dates of structural modifications, dates of manufacture of artefacts, dates of their styles, moment of capture on photographic film, time of reading and interpretation (when it may appear as many different things)?

Archaeology too has a multiple temporality, involving the past, its decay, and the encounter with remains in our future-orientated projects. Photography thus seems so appropriate for the archaeological. Photowork presents us with inventories of mortality, quoting fragments, creating juxtapositions potentially as strange as a fibula, quernstone and ox scapula which may be found together in an archetypal archaeological report. Photographs turn the now into the past, or more grandly, into history, depending upon the rhetoric. Reality is turned antique. Documented triviality is made memorable.

These last points about photographs turning the now into the past, bearing witness to the abrasions of time, bring me to melancholy and the romance of ruin. Most archaeologists ignore these and attempt to use archaeological sources to construct accounts of what happened in the past on the model of a conventional historical or social science – on the model of a, potentially spurious, photographic naturalism. But, for me, this is mistaken. Ruin is of fundamental importance to the way I see archaeology. The archaeological refers to an aspect of materiality and its temporality – a far wider category than the discourse of archaeology. It deals with the gaps between things – the dirt trapped between floor tiles – documented trivia – the results of slow processes of life and death. Archaeology attends to such things and processes, as a pathological materialism or materialist pathology.

Past and present: the political ecology of archaeology

Perfume jars and the ancient Greeks abroad in prehistoric Sicily – let me return to that excavation in Sicily. In all the goings on in and around the commune of Salemi, where is the archaeology? What holds the project together and makes it work – especially given all these splits and distinctions? I propose that these are matters of archaeology's political economy. A broader question is: What holds archaeology's communities together, makes them work? This is a classic question of political philosophy – the nature of social order.

I am going to consider this question in some detail because it raises issues of the interpenetration of people, things and values in, basically, a performative model of cultural activity. I hope also that the discussion of academic discipline will provide some important context for our purpose of working upon interdisciplinary and cultural hybridity.

The conventional answer is that the order and purpose of our project arises from the subject itself, the *discipline* of archaeology. Order lies in the disciplinary paradigms and practices. It is not that order of this sort arises from a common interest in the material past. For this would bring incompatible and potentially conflicting practices together – treasure-hunting art collector with dispassionate scientist. Instead of interest, the very term 'discipline' communicates order and unity. Discipline includes accredited methods, systems of qualification for practitioners and codification of archaeology's object. There are systems of entry and rules of belonging to the discipline. Discipline is thus also partly a moral order of duties and responsibilities, according to which one may be an archaeologist.

Power and normative behaviour are closely associated in disciplines. The edges particularly are policed to ensure the quality of what is taken for normal, accredited practice and belief – archaeologists are indeed often policemen. Cranks and charlatans need to be kept out. Respectability needs to be ensured. When there is doubt, for example in contentious issues, there are systems of arbitration and appeal. These are located in a public sphere of discipline members, the community of archaeology. Reference may be made to peers of professionals or particular authorities for arbitration or judgement. Of course general debate also takes place in this same public sphere, through the systems of peer review and publication. The public sphere of a discipline is usually held in high regard, considered to be the fundamental basis of the rational establishment and progress of knowledge. I also hope it is clear how notions of academic collegiality and freedom of speech fit into such a sketch of a 'disciplinary' community.

However, I propose that this conventional answer to the question of social order in archaeology – discipline – does not adequately answer the question of what holds everything together in a field project such as ours in Sicily. For there still are emphasised the boundaries between what is archaeological and what is not, and for our purposes here, the distinction between matters appropriate to science and those appropriate to culture and politics, between archaeological science and its context or application. And remember that I wish to break down these distinctions.

In this political economy of archaeology let me now introduce the concept of *constitution*. A constitution may lie behind the establishment of social or political order. A constitution determines who shall be a social subject, a social agent and empowered member of a society; it governs the distribution of competencies in a community, decides the rights and duties of subjects. Forms of representation are central to constitutional arrangements, according to which it is decided who may speak and for whom. In legal terms this is also a matter of the reliability of different kinds of speech and witnessing, being about to whom we listen and pay heed.

Again, the archaeological constitution is to do with the discipline and its regulation. Archaeologists are the empowered subjects, representing, or speaking on behalf of, usually, the past, through its testimony, the remains of the past. Archaeologists are obliged to do this fairly and without avoidable bias.

An immediate constitutional question is that of the strength or validity of the arrangement. What makes people believe in archaeology? What makes the archaeological constitution robust? Confidence may reside in the guarantees of quality built into the discipline as a profession – the systems of qualification and regulation. But these can only claim to guarantee a certain kind of relationship with the past on the part of archaeologists. This relationship is one that, it is argued, delivers the most secure knowledge of the past; it is built on epistemological links related to the reality of the past. It seems to me that we believe in archaeology because we believe that the past happened and that its evidence or testimony, the real and material remains of past times, may be fairly represented by an archaeologist working under this particular discipline.

I am going to question some of the assumptions made in this archaeological constitution, particularly the *legal* arrangement between the past, its material remains and their fair representation by archaeologists. I will do this through an historical interlude and a story about modernity and the political economy of natural science. I need to go back again to the seventeenth century.

Archaeology shares its constitution with many other academic disciplines. Like other political constitutions, it took its present form some time ago as part of the Enlightenment's reassessment of people's place in the world. Let me introduce now Robert Boyle, seventeenth-century chemist and natural philosopher, an acknowledged father of modern science. He conducted experiments on air, vacuums, combustion and respiration, developed a new theory of matter and researched various chemical elements. Steven Shapin and Simon Schaffer have written about his arguments for the empirical method in science, the method that is the basis of all modern scientific enquiry, archaeology included (Shapin and Schaffer 1985; Shapin 1994; I rely heavily on the reading of Bruno Latour 1993: 13–43).

Boyle was critical of the science, or rather 'natural philosophy' of his time. And instead of grounding his criticisms and new ideas in the traditional way, in logic, mathematics or rhetoric, Boyle adopted a different system of argument and enquiry. He argued that scientific experimentation, based upon direct experience, is the best way of acquiring factual knowledge of the world. A bird suffocates in a vacuum pump in a scientist's laboratory. This is witnessed by the scientist and his gentlemen associates. It is held to display the existence of air. How is the fact to be disseminated and believed?

Boyle modelled his answer to this issue of reliability on a legal and religious system of witnessing: witnesses gathered at the scene of the event can attest to the existence of a fact, the matter of fact, even indeed if they do not know its true nature (air essential to respiration). Boyle and his colleagues abandoned the certainties of apodeictic reasoning through logic and mathematics in favour of direct experience, the testimony of witnesses, and opinion; he chose a method of argument that was held in contempt by the oldest scholastic tradition.

Juridical witnessing carries the danger of insecure testimony. But Boyle's witnesses are not the fickle masses with their raving imaginations; they are gentlemen – independent of the state, credible, trustworthy, well-to-do. So experimental philosophy emerged partly through the purposeful re-allocation of the conventions, codes and values of gentlemanly conduct and conversation into the domain of natural philosophy.

There is a crucial difference to the practice of courts – the nature and agency of the events, their significance and the witnesses. In experimental science trials were now to deal with affairs concerning the behaviour of inert materials and bodies – the world of natural phenomena. These are not of the human world, but they are endowed with meaning and, indeed, will – showing, signing, and scribbling on laboratory instruments before trustworthy witnesses. And though they do not have souls to lose through perjury, they are nevertheless the source of testimony even more reliable than that of mortals, to whom will is attributed but who lack the capacity to indicate phenomena in a reliable way. The bird suffocates in a vacuum and attests to a natural phenomenon. We will return to the relationship between people and things or non-humans.

This is also the problem of the relationship between direct experience and its report or representation. Proper science is seen as a culture which rejects reliance upon authority and others, and seeks direct experience. But not everyone had a vacuum pump in the seventeenth century; it was a piece of laboratory equipment perhaps as advanced as a fusion reactor today. And the juridical model of credibility and argument has a new mechanism for winning the support of one's peers – the marshalling of the opinion of as many trustworthy 'gentlemen' as possible, whether this opinion is expressed directly or through footnote in a scientific paper.

The broader argument here is that in securing knowledge we rely upon others. This reliance is a moral relationship of trust; crucial to knowledge is knowing who or what to trust – knowledge of things depends upon knowledge of others. Hence Boyle's translation of gentlemanly conduct into scientific practice. What we know of the chemistry of air, or atoms, or indeed the past *irreducibly* contains what we know of the people who speak for and about these things (just as what we know about people irreducibly depends upon what they say about the world). Essential therefore to the spread of science is machinery, the laboratory instruments capable of inscribing the witnessing, trust in the freedom of action and virtue of gentlemanly conduct, and a network or community of science ensuring the consistency of instrumentation and communication between its members.

Central to this experimental life is the *conduct* of the experimenter. For Boyle is not only creating a scientific discourse. He is creating a political discourse from which politics is to be excluded. Gentlemen proclaim the right to have an independent opinion, in a closed space – the laboratory – over which the state has no control. Reliability thus hinges on freedom – political freedom. This involves an absolute dichotomy between science as the production of knowledge of facts, and politics as the realm of state and sovereign.

Nevertheless, the empirical method is based upon a juridical and indeed political metaphor of representation, agency and competency. Machines and instruments in the laboratory or in the field produce costly and hard-to-reproduce facts witnessed by only a few, and yet these facts are taken to be nature as it is, directly experienced, believed ultimately by the majority. The machines and witnesses are believed to be reliable, fairly *representing* the facts to others. The key term uniting science and politics is 'representation'. Consider two fundamental and homologous questions of science and politics. Who is speaking when the scientist speaks? Who or what is signing when the dial on the instrument moves? Who speaks when the political representative speaks? It is proposed that this homology makes it possible to speak of the conjoined invention of scientific facts and modern citizenship, dependent as it is upon representation and democracy, trust in the virtue of the political will of the majority.

This intimate connection between enquiry and politics is denied or found problematical, as I have tried to argue in the case of archaeological field science. It is as if the stability of knowledge of things requires the implicit relations of trust and issues of representation to become invisible, the politics, circumstances, culture, contexts of enquiry to be a problem or embarrassment. For Bruno Latour, Boyle's arguments are archetypical of this parallel strategy or structure of modernity. On the one hand is the creation of extraordinary **hybrids** or translations, like Boyle's joining of law court, moral virtue, the accoutrements of scientific laboratory, the facts of nature and its underlying reality. All in an experimental method which, of course, has been extraordinarily successful. On the other hand, such hybrids are often fervently denied, being based upon a partitioning of experience and practice. Latour (1993: 5-8, 35-37) calls this the modern critical stance – a radical separation of science, society, politics and religion, the human world of people and culture divorced from the natural world of things.

Let me summarise and pull together the main points of this digression into the history of science.

- ❖ Scientific credibility, rooted in empirical and experimental method, has a moral history as well as an epistemological structure.

- ❖ The history of modern science, archaeology included, is not about the emergence of 'proper' scientific practice out of pre-scientific superstition. This is not just the case of Boyle. Historical studies have repeatedly shown how the progress of science does not depend upon some force of truth operating in favour of better science; it is not about the achievement of closer epistemological approximations to truth or reality (see Fuller 1997 for summary and bibliography).

- ❖ We are encouraged to see scientific disciplines as communities and moral orders inseparable from the construction of knowledge. Indeed, people and their politics and morality are the medium for the construction of knowledge. We should be suspicious of the sort of splits I have claimed are endemic to a discipline like archaeology – the separation, for example, of method from political significance, from culture or context.

- ❖ We are encouraged to consider science as an irreducible hybrid of heterogeneous cultural and natural elements. The corollary is that society too is so composed. Concepts applicable to both are representation and constitution.

- ❖ This all points towards scientific knowledge being understood as a social achievement. This is a *performative* model of reasoning and the building of knowledge, a position associated with a growing body of science studies (Pickering 1992; Collins and Pinch 1993; Fuller 1993, 1997; Knorr-Cetina 1999).

This digression was to illustrate the relevance of the concept of constitution in an analysis of the activities of the discipline of archaeology. What I have described as archaeology's current constitution is only one limited schema of apportioning rights, responsibilities, competencies, agencies and pertinences. For this is what constitutions do. And more: as a mode of constructing knowledge of the past, archaeology is rooted in a metaphysics of reality, past, present, subject, subjectivity, object, objectivity. For every constitution determines who counts, who, or what, is subject to the will, desire, scrutiny and use of its social agents. And on what basis: for example, complex notions of subjectivity and objectivity, or personal bias and distanced

A.3 M.3 B.3 E.3

fair-mindedness, are considered important for judging the words and actions of one who is representing another.

This constitutional issue involves the past itself, which is represented, in its remains, by the archaeologist and is deemed subject to their competency and responsibility as an accredited member of the archaeological profession or community. Let me deal a little further with this political issue of representation.

Representation may be more or less direct. The strongest position in this political economy is often considered to be one where the role of representation is apparently minimised or absent, where emphasis is thrown upon the past itself. The ideal is thus to let the past speak for itself, an ideal found in those notions of archaeology as primarily a field practice which *discovers* the past. This throws suspicion on the activity of interpretation, on the representative, and refers us to the grounds upon which adequate representation may be considered to have been made. Whom do we believe when they talk of the ruined past? The matter is sharpened by the difficulty, indeed frequent unfeasibility, of corroborating witnesses, of questioning again the represented interest, the ruined past, because the past is partly or wholly destroyed in its excavation, in the act of questioning. We cannot pose the question again, re-excavate a site, so we must assess the trustworthiness of the archaeologist, the representative. Professional accreditation becomes all the more important.

It should be noted that such a disciplinary constitution involves apportioning rights to inanimate objects – the remains of the past. We are not used to thinking in terms of such *political rights*. Nor are we used to crediting agency to such things as instruments of examination and measurement like laboratory equipment, yet this is the implication of histories such as that of Boyle and the early days of the Royal Society. Seeing archaeology in terms of its constitution reconnects archaeologists and the past that is their interest.

Anthropological and historical studies of science have shown again and again how they are so little about abstract method or epistemology. Every practising scientist knows the importance of the committees, institutions and funding agencies. Alongside Latour's familiar critical stance of science and its objects radically separated from a context of society, history, religion and metaphysics, we find *networks* of fundamentally *political* connection running through archaeological and other scientific projects. Like Boyle, they may connect laboratories with field locations with instruments, with new insights into real homologies between scientific and

R.3 0.3 S.3

cultural practice. I am picking up here that point above about the hybridity of Boyle's scientific innovation. The hybridity of these networks of association, these social orders, makes my argument less about political economy and more an ecology of practices and knowledge, a *political ecology*. For the systems of translation that are archaeology may connect a trowel with a computer database with a debate about cultural ethnicity with a community's aspiration to tap the affluence of a tourist trade, all as I described as our field project in Sicily. The political is not just about people, rights and relationships; it is about things too. This is the main thrust of Latour's fascinating history of modernity, *We Have Never Been Modern* (1993).

So a discipline like archaeology is, I propose, a hybrid process of '*heterogeneous engineering*', to borrow a phrase from the sociologist of technology John Law (1987). Archaeology may connect all sorts of heterogeneous things, ideas, aspirations, values, communities, subcultures, contexts (Shanks 1992a). The things left of the past translated through the cultural and political interests of the present. As Bruno Latour puts it for science (1993: 4): 'it becomes impossible to understand brain peptides without hooking them up with a scientific community, instruments, practices – all impedimenta that bear very little resemblance to rules of method, theories and neurons'.

So how am I proposing to think of archaeology? It is an ecology of mobilising resources, managing, organising, persuading, of practices like collecting, walking and intervening in the land. It is such practice (which developed from models radically reworked in the modern state) that defines the discipline. Archaeology is a *hybrid* and heterogeneous practice. I think this is more useful and indeed more correct than seeing archaeology as beginning with method, excavation and other technical operations, and an epistemological relationship between past and present.

So archaeologists do not happen upon or discover the past. Archaeology is a process in which archaeologists, like many others, take up and make something of what is left of the past. Archaeology may be seen as a mode of cultural production (Shanks and McGuire 1996), moving from source materials or resources to the consumption of an end-product such as a book, excavation report or museum exhibition. This does not necessarily question the validity of the work of archaeologists – it may indeed result in a real advance in our knowledge of the past. But such knowledge is always a social (and political) achievement.

Summary: assemblages (archaeology and cultural poetics)

What are the features of this work of connection or assemblage, this heterogeneous engineering I am also calling an archaeological or cultural poetics?

First note a symmetry or homology. Archaeology is interested in social practices and cultural phenomena in the past, and what is left of them. But archaeology is also itself a set of particular social practices and cultural phenomena. It is not necessarily privileged over what it investigates. The symmetry between past and present is that both archaeology and its object (social practices and cultural phenomena) are these heterogeneous assemblages.

Remember also that investigating the fragments of the past is immediately to represent them. The poetics of forging assemblages is the issue of how to represent natural, social and cultural phenomena. These are very broad issues. Let me simply note some ways that connections may be established. I will focus first upon three processes: quotation, collage and montage.

One of the few historians who has dealt with this character of archaeological or material sources, their actuality, heterogeneity and materiality, is Walter Benjamin, most notably in his uncompleted *Passagenwerk* (*The Arcades Project*) (1999). The title refers to shopping arcades, but the project was far wider than this – Benjamin was intending to write a definitive history of modernity, but one rooted in the particular details of urban life in Paris. Consider the following list, taken from his notebooks for the project, of some of his categories of evidence about nineteenth-century Paris. It is a phantasmagoric collage of fragments, apparently unconnected remains of the life of a city seen through Benjamin's collector's consciousness.

arcades, *magasins de nouveautés,* sales clerks	prostitution, gambling
fashion	the streets of Paris
ancient paris, catacombs, demolitions, decline of Paris	panorama
boredom, eternal return	mirrors
Haussmannisation, barricade fighting	painting, modern style, novelty
iron construction	types of lighting
exhibitions, advertising, Grandville	Saint-Simon, railways
the collector	conspiracies, *compagnonnage*
the interior, the trace	Fourier
Baudelaire	photography
dream city, dream house, dreams of the future, anthropological nihilism, Jung	Marx
dream house, museum, spa	the doll, the automaton
the *flâneur*	social movement
on the theory of knowledge, theory of progress	Daumier

The remains of the *Passagenwerk* are collections of notes, within which Benjamin foregrounds his source materials in direct quotation.

> Method of this project: literary montage. I needn't say anything. Merely show. I shall purloin no valuables, appropriate no ingenious formulations. But the rags, the refuse – these I will not inventory but allow, in the only possible way, to come into their own: by making use of them.
>
> (1999: 460 (N1a,8))

So collage and montage are important elements of quotation. Collage is an extension of an artist's palette or a writer's vocabulary, prose and poetic art to include actual pieces of reality or fragments of what the artist or writer is referring to. It is direct quotation, literal repetition or citation of something taken out of its context and placed in another. Montage is the cutting and reassembling of fragments of meanings, images, things, quotations, borrowings, to create new juxtapositions. When recognised for what it is, collage is a simple questioning of the notion of representation as finding some *correspondence* with an exterior reality. 'Reality' and other bits and pieces are instead brought into the picture; collage may be tangible representation without attempting some sort of an illusion. It represents in terms of change – the shift of borrowings from one context to another, from 'reality' to 'representation', and from represen-tation to representation.

The aim, whether it is recognised or not, is to construct something new out of old, to connect what may appear dissimilar in order to achieve new insights and understanding. This emergence of new meaning depends on the perception of instability, of retaining energies of interruption and disruption – the quotation interrupts the smooth surface or text; it is distracting. The interruption of illusion and distraction by collage sets off allusions through the juxtaposed, montaged elements. So the new understanding comes through contaminated representation rather than pure reference to the depicted subject-matter. The quotations are cut out of context to create new meanings.

Disruption, cutting and juxtaposition make of this poetics or discourse an *unstable* set of links between images, words and concepts and the material world, between signifiers and signifieds. Things and words and images can always be disengaged from their meanings and inlayed into new combinations. This disassembly *should* be constant. The discovery of *new* insight depends on a nervous novelty which avoids the settling of montages into accepted equations and identities. Consider again Benjamin's notebooks and plan for the *Passagenwerk*. A certain degree of shock and jolt are necessary – moving on when the juxtaposition becomes too homely. In doing this, collage maintains an ambiguity of presence and absence, the presence of fragments of absent items being referenced.

Montage and collage may occur along both syntagmatic and paradigmatic axes. Poetics may use syntagmatic or syntactic sequence and narrative of images and words, melodic succession over discursive surface. Paradigmatic connection is like harmonies of association, layers folded within a representation and its reading.

How might links be established between the quoted and juxtaposed elements or fragments? The following are four overlapping kinds of connection and some methods appropriate to their investigation:

❖ Empirical association (as in the original archaeological concept of assemblage); things found together.
   Methods: inductive reasoning, statistical analysis (based upon data definition, collection and classification) – looking for patterns in the material.

❖ Logical links between things.
   Methods: structuralist readings, formal or mathematical analysis of patterning and design – determining an algebra of patterns of association.

❖ Conceptual alignment, causal relationships, narrative emplotment.
   Methods: historical and social interpretation, semiotics, deductive reasoning – forging links in the patterning.

❖ Creative elaboration; further exploration of metaphor, metonymy, synecdoche.
Methods: speculative modelling or abduction (Peirce 1958: 89-164; Shanks 1996: 39-
41) – electro-cultural articulations.

So consider an archaeological artefact. Do not begin with the question 'What is it?' Instead ask 'What does it do?' Enquire of its social work: What does it connect through its design, exchange and consumption? With the artefact understood as assemblage, the task is to establish the relationships which make an artefact what it is, and to make sense of them. As is hopefully clear from the lists of links and methods above, there is nothing mysterious or new about this empirical method of following the tracks leading from a particular artefact. It is about familiar processes of categorisation and classification, analysis and narrative. But we also hope to show how recognition of heterogeneity and the folded temporality of archaeological phenomena can lead to some surprising assemblages.

Let me also note something of the materiality of the archaeological find. I return to the paradigm of photography. A photograph may be given a caption, positioned in relation to other images and text, used as direct quotation. Or it may, through its *mise-en-scène*, suggest and engender connections through what is brought together in the photographed world of people and things. We may read the subject-matter and pictorial structure according to discourse – interpreting sense and reference. However, in its attestation to the infinite detail of materiality, in its unwitting record, a photograph sometimes has its transparency clouded. A detail may intrude and indicate that it is only an item of discourse. Perhaps we know something of someone or something in a photograph which subverts its apparent message. Perhaps an anomaly disturbs the categorisation and genre. The photographed world is rarely ever fully controlled. The heterogeneity of photowork, with all those possible interconnections, may break the predictability of *mise-en-scène*. Roland Barthes (1982) calls this the *punctum* of a photograph. Indeed this is part of the heterogeneity of assemblage: resistances to the order imposed upon the world are endemic. The wider topic here is social order, that classic question of political economy and social theory which I touched on in discussion of the shape and boundaries of the discipline of archaeology.

Theatre archaeology: convergences

Having made our personal introductions of performance and archaeology, we now move to consider how they converge.

A symmetry

Throughout these convergences we highlight a symmetry, indeed a homology: performance and archaeology are social practices, or modes of cultural production, and social practice has performative and archaeological dimensions.

Liminality

The special practice that is performance operates in a liminal space or heterotopia. Archaeology too is at the edge and in the gaps, working on discard and decay, entropy and loss. Its topic of the material and ineffable immediacy of the past has given it a special place in constructions of personal and cultural identity.

Cultural identities

It is in these liminal spaces and with these heterogeneous elements that both archaeology and performance work and negotiate identities, of people and things.

Cultural production

Both performance and archaeology are modes of cultural production which work with resources to create contemporary meaning: a range of phenomena and procedures are made available for manipulation according to current interests. Both are therefore pluralist. All sorts of things may be done with the same resources under different conditions, aspirations, interests.

Social fabric

Both performance and archaeology attend to the discernment and modelling of the actions and practices of knowledgeable agents in bounded spaces. Archaeology's ultimate object is this cultural fabric and its remains. Social practice always involves material culture. Performance is always at least corporeality – the materiality of the performer's body. Indeed social actors are as much artefact as any other material cultural form. Hence it is better to write of the social and cultural '**fabric**'. The object of both performance and archaeology is this social fabric.

So too the social fabric, as corollary, has dimensions or aspects we have termed the 'archaeological' and the 'performative'. The former refers to entropy, loss and trace; the latter, under its broadest definition, to heightened cultural experience.

Sensorium and embodiment

It is not just that there is logic and structure to the social fabric. The social and cultural are lived and felt. They are **embodied** in social actors, people and artefacts. A key concept here is that of **sensorium** – culturally and historically located arrays of the senses and sensibility. We introduce sensorium as a way of working against the dualism of mind and body.

The sites of both performance and archaeology constitute **sensoria**. They are apprehended as a complex manifold of simultaneous impressions – any account will be inevitably embodied, subjective and poetic. For performer and spectator alike the performance event exists as a locus of experiences – spatial, physical and emotional – preserved in the bodies and memories of the varying orders of participants: touch, proximity, texture. For the performer it may exist rather as a chain of physical and emotional orientations and reorientations: as body-to-body and body-to-environment engagement and re-engagement, as a chain of demeanours. But also as a series of physical, sensual and extra-daily experiences, as alterations of perceptions and life strategies which may or may not be made explicit to the spectator, as sequences of tension, relaxation and acceleration, changes of consequence and innovation. Encounters, movements, episodes, passings. All preserved as analect and anecdote, description and incoherent babbling, as a chorus of conflicting voices, as a way of telling.

This connects with the inherent pluralism and multivocality of archaeology and performance.

Ecology and site

Performance and archaeology favour body, object and place, activity and context. It is the ecology of performance – that matrix of environment, people and events and the narratives generated – which may represent its basic descriptive and analytical unit. We have also explored above the ecology of archaeology, both as discourse, and as heterogeneous object of interest.

Ecology may be defined as inhabitation – a broad and inclusive concept (consider Thomas's (1996) Heideggerian archaeology of dwelling). Site, as concept, must be connected with place and locale, as the natural and cultural are entwined in a true ecology which moves beyond these familiar dualisms. So too we emphasise that site is as much a temporal as spatial concept – landscapes are enfolded; scenography works with the multidimensional temporality of memory, event and narrative.

Convoluted temporality

The temporality of performance and the archaeological project is neither linear nor a slice through time; it is convoluted. Memories, pasts, continuities, present aspirations and designs are assembled and recontextualised in the work that is performance and archaeology.

Fragments and assemblage

Both performance and archaeology work with fragment and with trace. Performance and social practice, and their subsequent documentation or representation, through surviving traces and fragments, constitute heterogeneous assemblages.

Archaeologists excavate an indeterminate mess of flows of things and particles in the ground. They discern categories of evidence and compose these fragments in images, diagrams, inventories, collections, reports and writings, forging links to make sense. But these constructions remain as pieces of evidence, stored in museums and libraries, to be reworked, reassembled, recontextualised.

Devised performance, as contrasted with conventional theatre, results from the identification, selection and accumulation of concepts, actions, texts, places and things which are composed and orchestrated in space and time according to a set of governing aesthetics, ideologies, techniques and technologies. It comprises a spectrum of strategies, practices and procedures which attend to questions of real-time presentation and representation. What begins as a series of fragments is arranged in performance: dramaturgy is an act of assemblage. It then immediately falls to pieces as traces and fragments of a different order, ranging from documentary photographs to the memories of its participants: fragments/order/fragments.

A series of modes and methods of affiliation are common to both archaeological and performative assemblage. Within this analytical, interpretive and rhetorical field we have identified:

- ❖ the syntagmatic: parataxis and katachresis
- ❖ the paradigmatic: hypotaxis
- ❖ quotation, montage and collage
- ❖ empirical, logical, conceptual and metaphorical connection.

Heterogeneity

The assemblages at the heart of archaeology and performance are not of one or more homogeneous categories of components: actors and props, texts and stagings, people and things, social structures and natural environments. These very categories are reworked and renegotiated and have no essential properties in the work of performance and archaeology. Thus the assemblage, both practice and representation, is heterogeneous.

Partiality and pluralism

Assemblages – performance and document – are inevitably partial. Rooted in uncertainty, they all require acts of interpretation. And there is no end to what can be said about them, to how they might be interpreted.

The assemblage of performance may be extremely schematic, requiring the spectator to elaborate a mental construct from a limited range of illusionistic or even two-dimensional clues: she may need specific cultural competence to interpret it. It may work with extremely limited material and performative means. Everyday objects may be included, though their placement, ratios and combinations are governed by extra-daily principles. Semiotic economy is an essential feature of performance: it is by nature **synecdochic**. A limited repertoire of sign-vehicles generates a potentially unlimited range of cultural units. It is interpreted according to the expectation, experience and background of the watcher.

Archaeologists may dream of the past perfectly desiccated in the sands of time, life caught preserved at a standstill in earthquake or volcanic eruption. But there are only ever fragments. Virtually everything has been lost. Archaeology's semiotic can only ever be synechdochic – pieces for whole ways of life gone. Uncertainty and the need to connect the pieces, to interpret the absences are endemic. But an archaeological sensibility is also one of hope, a faith in the resurrecting powers of its interventions in the land, its obsessive collection, its reason and constitutive imagination.

And these partial views are also the existential condition of the social and cultural fabric – there is never a complete and definitive picture. This is the hermeneutic ground of any archaeological sensibility (Johansen and Olsen 1992; Shanks and Tilley 1992: 104-110; Shanks and Hodder 1995; Thomas 1996).

Documentation and the ineffable

Assemblage is construction, production, representation and **documentation**. Both archaeology and performance involve the documentation of practices and experiences. Their embodiment in sensoria raises the issue of the representation of phenomena which are, partially at least, ineffable – beyond language.

Detail and texture

Both performance and archaeology attend to detail, focusing tightly but sensitively upon particular conjunctions and instants. Their substance is local, whatever may be done with relationships to more general settings. To put it another way, the cultural production which is archaeology and performance is reflexively dependent upon historical and cultural context.

The particular relation of the archaeological and performative to identity makes of them both important sites of cultural work in the globalist contemporary world. It is in new performative work and strategies, in new constructions of archaeological **heritage** that may be found some of the most radical local and regional receptions of the commodity form and alienated culture associated with the global capitalist market and its political forms.

Documenting the event

What has happened? What survives after the event? How is it remembered and recalled? The issue is the document. We will now outline some features of a project of theatre archaeology.

Theatre archaeology begins with a simple premise: that the description and documentation of devised performance – that matrix of places, objects and activities, of performer and context, worker and workspace, agency and structure – constitute a sort of archaeology, a rescue archaeology of the event. And the wider issue is how to document/represent social and cultural experience. This is the archaeological question – what is to be done with the remains of past lives?

Performance survives as a cluster of narratives, those of the watchers and of the watched, and of all those who facilitate their interaction – technicians, ushers, stage-managers, administrators. The same event is experienced, remembered, characterised in a multitude of different ways, none of which appropriates singular authority. And these may constitute the traces generated by theatre that is not reliant upon the exposition of dramatic literature – the artefacts it leaves behind; these, and plans, drawings, lighting plots, a handful of photographs. From the watched comes the folklore of practice, coloured by aspiration, intention and rationalisation, preserved in memory as anecdote and analect and revealed in discussion and interview and in personal archive as diary and notebook. And from all types of watchers – first-timers, aficionados, critics – springs description, opinion, personal interpretation. Ironically perhaps, performance most often survives in the writings of critics – as reportage, article, thesis – because of their high rate of preservation in libraries and cuttings agencies. By narrative, we simply mean discrete ways of telling, some recognition of the oral nature of performance practice. But if we extend the notion of narrative to cover all orders of information generated by, and around, performance – strategic, operational, observational, critical, speculative – before, during and after the event then we might envisage documentation as requiring an integration or incorporation of these narratives. Performance might then be reconstituted as complex forms of text which integrate image, musical score, technical instructions, dialogue or as second-order performance, or as installation. Just as performance need not resemble the exposition of dramatic literature, the performance document need not resemble the play script. These observations are exemplified in the diagrammatic, choreographic records of Anthony Howell (Kaye 1996: 129f.) and in the boxed set of performance documents edited by Adrian Heathfield (1997), 'a maverick intervention into the debates on the status and imagining of the body in western culture and the historical preservation of transient performances'.

Performance exists in and amongst these narratives. Its record will need to be adequate and appropriate, necessitating creative acts of representation. And it will need to draw upon disciplines, principles, methods and terminologies, other than those of textual analysis, to describe and document itself, approaches taken from sociology and ergonomics, architectural theory and forensic science. Yet we can neither create the authoritative record nor control its reception.

But is it only about aftermath? Documentation is generated before, during and after the event by all orders of participants. As Cliff McLucas puts it (1993: n.p.):

> Those before the event all refer to something that hasn't happened, that doesn't exist. They are utopian in their nature. They unify. They generate effects. They are pro-active. They propose concept, preference, intention. Those after the event are more verifiable, authoritative, though no less utopian in their need to control and construct an authorised history. They are descriptive and political.

Hence the question of aftermath actually throws into doubt the primacy of event and the dependency of document or representation. There are and were only ever assemblages of practices, experiences, tellings, retellings, memories, perceptions. Representation is thus less to do with replication than reworking and recontextualisation. With respect to narrative as a documentary form, archaeologist Julian Thomas (1994: 158) has observed

> that what we are discussing is a particular way of being attuned to performance and its traces, which involves a form of production. That is, the production of narratives which stand for the past, rather than constituting faithful replicas of the past.

The form of the document

What form might the document take? It is, as we have indicated, to focus upon fragment and assemblage: to define the objects of retrieval of performance around notions of site, time, structure and detail, which direct the attention of the narratives.

This will involve discussion:

❖ Of the genesis, delineation and formalisation of performance space and the creation of playing areas through the nature of the action, the placement of the audience and architectural and scenographic demarcation.

❖ Of the effect of spatial restriction and configuration upon the type, nature and quality of the activity and upon the essential contracts of performance – performer to performer, performer to spectator, spectator to spectator.

❖ Of the existence of spatial hierarchies, intensities and stratifications of activity, the reservation of particular locales.

❖ And of the extent, volume and restriction of the spheres of influence of performers and spectators alike which collide and penetrate during interpersonal contact.

And this will require map, plan, section, axonometric projection.

❖ Of the ways in which different time-frames are manifest by performers over time and from time to time in performance, in sequence or in parallel and how they affect the nature of the activity, the expenditure of energy and the application and quality of effort. And the overall dynamic pattern of the event.

And this will require chronologies and time-bases.

❖ Of the explicit structure of performance as set of rules, sequence, route map, montage.

❖ Of the juxtaposition of different orders of material and styles and techniques of performance.

And this will require libretto, list, image, graph.

❖ Of the dramaturgical detail and the equal importance of kinesic, proxemic and haptic signification: of signs, distances and body-to-body contacts (Elam 1980: 56f.). After Mauss (1973), it may be interesting to select a limited range of activities – walking, sitting, falling – and discuss their particular articulation, their stylistic diversification, within this performance, this genre. Equal attention might be given to the nature of meeting and physical contact.

And this will require diagram, drawing, photograph, video.

The object of documentation then is to devise models for the recontextualisation of performance as text and as second-order performance, as a creative process in the present and not as a speculation on past meaning or intention – 'the point is that there is no definitive originary meaning, since what the "original" performance meant will itself have been fragmented, and experienced in many different ways' (Thomas 1994: 143). These models must be adequate and appropriate to the task of representing the sociology of this special world, drawing upon disciplines, principles, methods and terminologies other than those of textual analysis, and encapsulated, we are suggesting, in *archaeology*.

The scene of crime – aftermath

Aftermath – think of the scene of crime as a paradigm for our documentary efforts.

At the scene of crime, a cordoned off, isolated and sealed site, everything is potentially important, as 'every contact leaves a trace'. No thesis is advanced until the chain of evidence is secured. 'Everything that could matter' is recorded according to the experience of scene of crime officers. The site is treated as a totality. The scene is photographed from different perspectives and viewpoints. The general layout and specifics are carefully noted. Detailed descriptions are made of clothing, furniture, weapons, loose articles. Particular objects are tagged as exhibits. 'Physical evidence encompasses any and all objects that can establish that a crime has been committed or can provide a link between a crime and its victim or a crime and its perpetrator' (Saferstein 1998: 36).

On a map of the site, the bodies are marked along with trajectories of blood splattering and ballistics (Saferstein 1998: 37–41). Statements are taken from witnesses, neighbours, suspects, those 'helping us with our enquiries'. Expert testimony will eventually emerge, primarily from the pathologist in a description of wounds and speculation on the time and cause of death. The central aim is to establish a chain of events – a sequence or chronology – for the crime. At site, a series of irrevocable changes such as the stratigraphy of overturned furniture may help establish a relative chronology, as might the decay of site and body and evidence of disturbance. The crime generates dozens of narratives, many of them discursive and tangential.

Such an application of forensic science and police procedure might be instructive to us:

❖ Detail. It might indicate suitable techniques of interrogation. Anything might be relevant. From the watchers and the watched, we need detail, not a summary of the plot. We might think here of the thick description characteristic of some historians of the Annales School. Or of some photographs.

❖ Plurality of event. Many different, sometimes contradictory and divergent, narratives are generated.

❖ Sideways glance. We may need to ask oblique questions ('Tell me about your performance scars?') to reveal useful information.

❖ Orientation. Photographs, plans and initial observations are collated in scene-of-crime books which allow successive investigators to orientate themselves at site and to 'relive' the events.

❖ Symptomatic reading. This interpretation is about reading traces and clues – a semiotics. This is a creative process of speculative modelling which demands no hierarchy between empirical attention, analysis and leaps of the imagination, and whose logical form is abduction.

❖ The scene of crime demands a poetics of absence. Archaeology is all about absences, about writing around what is obstinately not there – which is why archaeology should be poetic. Poetics here involves a labour of production/creation/transformation, but it also means attending to things in an intimate way in following the connections.

But we have heard of forensic archaeology. Archaeologists are brought in to help with police investigation, applying their techniques to the excavation of buried murder victims, lending to the police project their sensitivity to material context. The growth of forensic archaeology as a means of identifying both victim and crime has mirrored late-twentieth-century atrocities and the secret disposal of the anonymous dead in countries such as Argentina, Chile, Bosnia and Rwanda. The speed with which the living becomes the deposit is most poignantly reflected in the photographs of Gilles Peress in his work in Srebrenica and Vukovar (Stover and Peress 1998).

Now while these techniques produce invaluable and exhaustive information about presently existing materials, they say nothing whatsoever about the past. The past is a context within which things had a significance. It is a world which was. To enter this world always requires a leap of interpretation. Let us consider further this paradigm of archaeology. We need to recognise the alliance of scientific technique with a particular archaeological imagination.

We all think we know what crime looks like: blood on the carpet, the chalk outline of the body, the drugs in a plastic bag. Yet scenes of crime are often ordinary, even banal locations. What for instance distinguishes a 'murder site'? It is the event which suddenly turns a dark street, an under-pass, a public toilet into a place of significance: the mundane locales recorded in the photographs of Athne Grayson; the spot near a bus shelter in London where Stephen Lawrence was murdered and which is now marked by a memorial. We remain fascinated with such places long beyond the point at which the physical traces of the event disappear. A whole genre of guided tour, of performed narrative, has appeared which will guide us to the locations of Jack the Ripper's murders. And in his photographic series *Landscapes for the Homeless* (1995), Anthony Hernandez records the ad-hoc shelters and meagre, material traces – a flattened cardboard box, a hanging blanket – of transient populations in Los Angeles.

Think of the things at a scene of crime under this forensic attitude. Anything might be significant. Can we distinguish figure and ground – an event and a setting? That incidental object left behind may witness the absence of an event now passed. Things may not be what they seem – their content cannot be seen. At the scene of crime the object/process distinction must be suspended – objects here are not self-contained. For significance depends upon context, and a sliding temporality from crime past through presence here, as trace or witness, to a future potential at the trial.

Indeed there is a dialectic at the heart of the scene of crime – a surplus and a simultaneous dearth of meaning. Looking at the scene of crime we experience an overwhelming presence of meaning, but a sense also of the evanescent, banal, insubstantial. It might be that hair, or this stain. In their dialectic of presence and absence the commonplace may also be an incarnation of evil. In this, evidence always has a multiple identity. Objects as clues are inherently unstable. The character of this information is, whatever the rhetoric, one of fluid and contradictory fragments. There can be no categorial hygiene in the forensic imagination. This kitchen tool may also be the murder weapon. We have to improvise.

The eye of the investigator at a scene of crime may require a fetishistic interest in material trivia. An obsessive urge to find narrative order in the traumatic chaos may be necessary as it all threatens to fall apart and make no sense. Remember – anything could be relevant at the scene of a crime, and any place could be a scene of crime. In this forensic world every empty space is always littered with debris, traces. There is ubiquitous entropy, even when we have managed to connect. Our occupation is precarious.

What are these spaces? They are urban – the threat of crime in the metropolis. Benjamin connects them, dialectically, with the security of the bourgeois interior. They go with photography, with its haunting sense of time passed, event over, lost, present now only in its absence, wit-nessed by the photograph. Atget compulsively photographed the streets of nineteenth-century Paris. Most of his photographs are empty of people. To Benjamin, he was photographing scenes of crime under a 'scientific' aesthetic, requiring not private contemplation and appreciation, as in the art object, present to the senses, but interpretation and analysis – absence is witnessed, presence is ruptured. We ask: What has happened? The temporality of these spaces is one of aftermath – the traces left behind. Time is fractured as present appearances are haunted by indeterminate pasts, events now gone and evident only in their alienated traces. Here the alienated trace is the precondition of meaning.

And, in seeing places in this way, there is a latent criminality to space. This resides in the temporal relation to practice, in the traces, with the inherent tendency to decay, fall apart, make no sense. This criminality is an aesthetic haunted by degradation. Their architectures always seem so deteriorated. Even when the scene of crime is pristine we are forced to look at the dirt in the gaps.

There is thus here an anxiety at contact with the abject, and we may connect this with a fascination with crime, witnessed by the culture industry of detective fiction and crime reportage. But the fascination with crime is not primarily focused upon evil. The horror is that these are events where ordinary things become special in their proximity to violence, to transgression, to upturned convention and morality. In a terminal linkage, as the hammer becomes exhibit 'a', the paper clip exhibit 'b', we engage in those associative acts so favoured by the surrealist imagination.

What do we do with this anxiety, the urge to make sense of the inherent disorder? The detective investigator adopts an aesthetic of immersion, an improvising and ambulatory strategy of no single viewpoint, an oblique approach to isolate significant traces in the inconsequential and absent details. Looking directly at things and you maybe miss their point, their ambiguity as alienated trace. So the best is a sideways look, and a key, perhaps, is losing one's way.

Stories are told . . . stories are extracted. Stories are constructed in those operations which impose order and reason, of hygiene, empowerment and disempowerment – some believed, some discarded. The documentation of everyday detail in the construction of archives of clues and cases creates a kaleidoscope of hybrid fictions and competing perceptions – a richly sedimented environment of secret lives, lies and stories. The end is not normally the 'truth' of 'what happened'. Many serious crimes go unsolved and, anyway, the juridical verdict is a legal argument. There are miscarriages of justice, and can we ever know the mind of the criminal?

Entropic fragments, traces, terminal associations, aftermath, degradation, the sedimentation of everyday life, haunting absences – this is also, we propose, an archaeological sensibility.

The scene of crime – site report and hypotaxis

The site report is an archaeological genre – the publication of excavation plans and photographs and attendant analyses of finds and evidences. But here is a very different model. This work at scene of crime also generates site reports – compendia of superimposed documents and materials which involve: the formal description of gesture and movement through space; each person's (watchers and watched) fragmented reflections and recollections of experience, tied to location; and evidential fragments pertaining to both. We can imagine such reports being constructed not merely as a re-creation of theatrical performance, but also of historical events (Sarajevo 1914? Moscow 1917?), or in exploraring the hypothetical movements, experiences and rhythms of work within a prehistoric settlement (Thomas 1994: 158).

Both site report and crime account begin to suggest documents, in both archaeology and performance documentation, which combine plan, section, projection, photograph and drawing adjacent to, and overlapping, poem, technical data, musical notation and source material in forms of incorporation, in the non-hierarchical integration of text and image, the inscribed and the remembered, the critical and the poetic, of strategy and operational account. This is hypotaxis.

The scene-of-crime report *Case No. 00–17163* by Diller and Scofidio (1992: 345–60), which integrates time base, autopsy data, interviews, plans and photographs, is an exciting model. And in *The Manhattan Transcripts* (1994b), Bernard Tschumi, in a programme which outlines spaces and indicates the movements of the protagonists, notates a murder. 'Photographs direct the action, plans reveal the alternatively cruel and loving architectural manifestations, diagrams indicate the movements of the main protagonists' (ibid.: 8). He adds that 'The purpose of the tripartite mode of notation (events, movements, spaces) is to introduce the order of experience, the order of time – moments, intervals, sequences – for all inevitably intervene in the reading of the city' (Tschumi 1990: 101).

Could documentation be more a collage of these deep but fragmented observations, rather than 'the big picture'? Collage is unstructured temporally, genealogy is unstructured spatially, but threads a temporal way through the seeming disorder. Two stages of an analysis?

And we might envisage strategic documents within which all the performance elements – text, score, choreography, dynamic shape, sound, lighting and technical instructions – are represented and unfold in parallel across the page as a horizontal stratigraphy of layers or tracks, rather than down the page as a vertical reading, and set against a time-base. They achieve a fascinating stratigraphic hypotaxis in Cliff McLucas's reworking of Brith Gof's performances (forthcoming). 'However, such documents have no fixed and forever relationship with what they propose or describe. They cross swords with other utterance in a quiet and constant battle for the high ground' (McLucas 1993).

The film-maker Peter Greenaway (1997: 10) has suggested that there are ten different aspects of cinema vocabulary: location, light, frame, audience, properties, actors, text, time, scale and illusion. He works simultaneously along all these axes, though often favours one over the others. And this approach informs his installation work, for he often deconstructs these elements and presents them for our contemplation outside the medium of film. His installation *In the Dark – SPELLBOUND ART & FILM* (Haywood Gallery, London, February 1996) included props, sets, actors in glass cases, soundtrack, diagrams, projections and research references as the kind of remains of an imagery film, a film the visitor creates in the imagination. In *100 Objects to Represent the World* (Academy of Fine Arts, Vienna, October 1992), he juxtaposed a stuffed horse with ink, a crashed aircraft with the Willendorf Venus (Greenaway 1992).

In drawing dissimilar objects and live performers-as-exhibits into juxtaposition, Greenaway's curatorial practices and gallery installations serve to challenge conventional orders of classification and display. He has pioneered new approaches to collection and arrangement, including the unexpected and perhaps shocking recontextualisation and juxtaposition of objects, which create new insights and indeed new identities for material. Such exhibitions confound and challenge the five orthodox categories of museum taxonomy: age, authorship, nationality, material and ownership. He quotes Descartes: 'When our first encounter with some object surprises us and we find it novel, or very different from what we formerly knew or from what we supposed it ought to be, this causes us to wonder and astonish at it' (Greenaway 1993).

In *The Physical Self* exhibition (Museum Boymans-van Beuningen, Rotterdam, November 1991; see Greenaway 1991), Greenaway gathered paintings, advertising posters, objects, sculptures and 'living exhibits' – performers in glass cases – into thematic groupings headed 'mother and child, man and woman, hands, age, feet, touch, narcissism'. In the 'hands' section he simply grouped all the museum's gloves together. He even sees the exhibition as a kind of film-set or performance: 'The props are the objects on display. The visitors provide the extras. The plot is the exhibition content. Its architectural organisation is its structure' (Greenaway 1993: section 14). The spectator creates his own time-frames of attention, his own fictions and interpretations from the material, viewed in various orders and with varying degrees of attention.

Christian Boltanski too assembles found objects – a mass of clothing, old photographs, rusting tins – in his memorials for his own youth and for victims of the Holocaust (Semin, Garb and Cuspit 1997). Cornelia Parker exhibits the reassemblage of fragments of purposefully destroyed artefacts, remnants of a shed and its contents blown up by the army (Parker, Medvedow and Ferguson 2000).

Narrative

It is worth singling out narrative as a feature of the cultural work that is both archaeology and performance. It is a common aspiration of much archaeology eventually to construct historical narrative. And these have been of great importance in providing depth and orientation to cultural identity. Consider also how the narratives of performance may intersect with the narrative of personal identity. Audience experiences the performance in a state of preparedness which derives from past experiences and the way in which they have chosen to order them and accord them significance. This is that already mentioned hermeneutic base of assemblage – the audience comes to performance with a grid of pre-understandings which are partly unconscious or non-discursive, but are also contingent upon autobiography. Thus not only is it impossible for the same performance to take place twice, it is also impossible for the audience to experience the same performance twice. Historiographically we may say, and adapting Adorno's aphorism, that nothing ever happens twice, because it has already happened before.

Improvisation

And so in this partiality, with the dramaturgy of cultural assemblage always already located, there is no end, only works in process. Work in progress is endemic improvisation.

Performance may be very familiar with the concept of improvisation, devised performance particularly so in its liberation from the dramatic text. In archaeology we propose a similar attitude to normative and pre-defined methods. Rather than approach archaeological remains with pre-defined categories and a pre-set method, we support a more pragmatic and improvisational style, wherein method arises out of the encounter with subjects of interest (object-orientated method is fully discussed in Shanks and Tilley 1992, and Shanks 1999: Chapter 2).

Deep maps and story-telling

Reflecting eighteenth-century antiquarian approaches to place which included history, folklore, natural history and hearsay, the deep map attempts to record and represent the grain and patina of place through juxtapositions and interpenetrations of the historical and the contemporary, the political and the poetic, the factual and the fictional, the discursive and the sensual; the conflation of oral testimony, anthology, memoir, biography, natural history and everything you might ever want to say about a place. The term was coined in relation to William Least Heat-Moon's *PrairyErth* (1991), an account of Chase County in the American Midwest which conflates oral testimony, history, topographic details, local folklore, travel anthology, geography, journalism, memoir, natural history, autobiography and everything you needed to know about Kansas. This work finds echoes in Luc Sante's *Low Life* (1991), an 'underground' history of New York.

A number of contemporary novels address the depth of place. In *Ulverton* (1998), Adam Thorpe tells the story of an English village from 1650 through specific historical moments which illustrate continuity and change. In works such as *Lights Out for the Territory. 9 Secret Excursions in the Secret History of London* (1997), Iain Sinclair creates a psychic geography in east London where the past is close to the surface. In *Rodinsky's Room* (Lichtenstein and Sinclair 1999), he speculates upon the existence of a David Rodinsky whose possessions and writings were left undisturbed in a room above a synagogue for twenty years. *And When Did You Last See Your Father?* (1993) is Blake Morrison's instigation of a genre of confessional, biographical writing which marries intimate memory, journalese and novelistic reflection. In *The Collected Works of Billy the Kid* (1989) and *Coming through Slaughter* (1984), Michael Ondaatje experiments with deconstructed approaches to historical narrative.

These works take us into the genre of narrative and then story-telling. In *Another Way of Telling* (1982), John Berger and photographer Jean Mohr attempt in a series of photographs and paintings to demonstrate the ways in which memory is partial and repetitive, the ways in which an event is remembered both as details, fleeting moments and as 'the high points', but rarely in toto. In the process of converting narrative, expert and amateur, to text we may need these other ways of telling. In *Blasted Allegories: An Anthology of Writings by Contemporary Artists* (Wallis 1989), visual and performance artists contribute thoughts on their practice as biographic detail, lists, fictive stories, fragments of polemic.

Geographer Allan Pred (1990, 1997) attempts new forms of academic writing which include the diagrammatic, digressive and the poetic. A context is the 'time geography' of the Lund school (Pred 1977). This considers 'the choreography of everyday life' by establishing a notation which traces through time the paths traced by individuals moving between places. Notoriously, such an approach tends toward a formal and schematic view of the world: it tells one nothing about how living through time and space *feels* (Gregory 1989). What one might suggest, however, is that we should consider these life-paths as the raw stuff of narratives (Thomas 1994: 158). The search for new forms of writing is continued in the work of archaeologist Mark Edmonds. His *Ancestral Geographies of the Neolithic* (1999) has chapters on themed aspects of landscape and monu- mentality in the prehistory of northern Europe interspersed with fragments of fictional narrative, acting as provocative counterpoint. A similar attempt to catch the intimacy of the quotidian is that of Janet Spector's archaeology of a Lakota village, 'What This Awl Means' (1991).

From the outset, performance-about-performance, second-order performance, has presented potentials for the reintegration of surviving fragments. These may take the form of re-enactment, revival, lecture, demonstration, audio-visual presentation, story-telling. It may be that the notion of second-order performance may be of considerable significance to archaeology as well as performance studies. It may be in this area that a practice which is helpful for both disciplines will emerge. For if a language and a notation is devised which allows us to talk about sequences of actions taking place within defined locations, this may provide us with the basis for a broader discourse on the deployment of human bodies in significant space.

In a series of linked performances entitled *From Memory* (1991) Mike Pearson explored modes and techniques of solo exposition – autobiography, reminiscence, impersonation, family history, geological data, improvised asides – which subsequently informed approaches to the site of Esgair Fraith (p. 163). Such story-telling mixes useful information with the pleasure of the telling. We are used to people talking and the sudden shifts in technique and material they make. The solo narrative can include truth and fiction, lying and appropriation – the fragmentary, the digressive, the ambiguous. There are no hierarchies of information, no correct procedures.

Rhetoric and the performed lecture

The lecture is a basic form of archaeological exposition. What better than to hear an archaeologist talking about her own work, particularly with slide illustration? There is usually a strategy or script but frequent digression and verbal improvisation, to include anecdotes provoked by the slides, to answer questions, to provide provenance for artefacts appearing on slide. Such improvisation often results from sensing the tenor of the audience. There are many orders of narrative – data, reminiscence, jokes – and even the manual demonstration of artefacts ('We think it was used like this!'). We might take such extant forms, regard them as performed events and further theatricalise them with an extended range of heightened performance techniques – oratorical devices, gestural engagements – and technologies – multi-screen projection, video, soundtrack. We might conceive of forms of exposition appropriate to the complexity of performance. This might include a central narration with attendant rhetorical techniques, audio-visual presentation (video and slides projection, soundtrack), activity 'in parenthesis' (re-enactment of past events), exposition of 'data' (reviews, documentary records, plans), discussion ('question-and-answer'), examination of objects and speculations on past activities around the structural components of site. Of the past and the present. With time-frames, different orders of information and material, different analytical approaches assigned to different media . . . or not! Of course, this may be equally site-specific in its direct engagement with another space – museum, gallery, auditorium. And it may involve a slippage in the exclusive notions of performance and installation, and the inclusion of artefacts in new narratives, new stories of fights, murders, death, games, copulations . . .

Other modes of presentation might include replication and demonstration. Iben Nagel Rasmussen of Odin Teatret has devised a demonstration which includes her (former) training practices, the (chronological) re-enactment/recontextualisation of characters she has created and a script which includes autobiographical biographical details, description of creative processes and analect. And dancer Wendy Houston can demonstrate the sort of training she was engaged in, the sort of choreography she was presenting, in every year of her career.

Here the rhetorical origin of our techniques of assemblage (parataxis, katachresis, hypotaxis, etc.) is to be noted. We have widened out to include the whole field, coincident indeed with a theory of discourse, its generation, form and delivery.

Theatre archaeology: summary

In the first rush of enthusiasm for theatre archaeology it was possible to envisage performance as a contemporary experimental practice in understanding the processes of cultural transformation, as 'an experimental archaeology of events'. A theatre archaeology has then the following intentions:

❖ to find appropriate and useful ways of describing and documenting what is, or was, going on in performance, with performance as a totality of context, strategy and operation, and not simply the record of the words or choreography of performers;

❖ to regard performance as generative of materials produced before, during and after the event, not only as technical information but as personal experience;

❖ to attempt a synthesis of the narratives of the watchers and watched in non-hierarchical integrations of the written and the remembered.

The key features of theatre archaeology are:

❖ process – there is always more to collect and say;

❖ pluralism – there are different ways of describing and representing;

❖ multiplicity – reality itself is plural;

❖ assemblage – documentation works as dreamwork – forging and following connections in an indefinite network;

❖ indefinite series – social practice (performance) generates further social practices, and ultimately there is no priority such as primary event and secondary response;

❖ absence and uncertainty – the space between materials, documents and narratives generates authentic insight. This is the place of interpretation – interpretive work done on happening and event, and the purpose of documentation is to open this creative space;

❖ critique – theatre archaeology is implicit critique of narrower approaches to the documentation of performance and practice.

2 THEATRE AND ARCHAEOLOGY

It is as if something that seemed inalienable to us, the securest among our possessions,
were taken from us: the ability to exchange experiences.

(Benjamin 1992: 83)

In the second phase of encounter, what we have termed 'Theatre and archaeology', attention
moves to two issues of mutual interest: the re-enactment and representation of the past at
interpretive centres and heritage sites and the detection of ancient performative practices.

First, re-enactment. It may be that the archaeological imagination constitutes a kind of
dramaturgy. The archaeologist may resemble writer, choreographer, director in organising, in
meaningful ways, the motives, behaviours and actions of anonymous, indeed fictional, individuals
within bounded analytical spaces, be they site ground-plans or landscapes. A metaphor too far
perhaps but certainly as soon as archaeologists and cultural resource managers begin to replicate,
reconstruct, represent and restage the past, then they invariably employ the scenographic devices
and dramatic techniques of theatrical practice. And for some of us at least these are not unprob-
lematic. Consider some sites of English Heritage or those like the outdoor museum of prehistoric
life at Lejre in Denmark or the historical reconstructions at Colonial Williamsburg in the United
States. They use interpretive agents, actors, normative techniques such as characterisation,
impersonation and plot to re-create supposedly authentic images of the past. Are their fictions
created any more truthful than 'the creation of industrial man and woman by Prometheus,
Hephaestus and Frankenstein' at the disued British Coal Foundry in Tredegar in Brith Gof's site-
specific work *Haearn*? (McLucas and Pearson 1996: 220ff.) Surely the only distinction between
nominated heritage sites and such semi-derelict industrial buildings is one of definition. But the
techniques developed in such apparently valueless places may serve to suggest animations of
historical locations which can juxtapose varying orders of dramatic material, contemporary and
historical, documentary and fictive, without monopolising interpretation, without suggesting 'this
is exactly how it was'.

Second, performance in the past. One of the principal ambitions of interdisciplinary approaches
to performance and the past must surely be the discernment of performed behaviours in antiquity.
Encouragingly, archaeologists, particularly of prehistory, are beginning to employ the terminology
of theatre – staging, backdrop, audience – in other than metaphorical terms ('social actors'
(Giddens 1984: 281–5); 'academic audience') and to identify those occasions and locales where
performance is more or less likely. Consider, for instance, architectures such as the stone and
timber avenues, circles and chambered tombs of neolithic and bronze age Britain (Barrett 1994:

17–18). Barrett comments that 'the history of southern British mortuary rituals could now be seen as progressive attempts to make some of these rituals increasingly effective media for display. This would have demanded more than the simple use of exotica for burial with the corpse, requiring instead a more public staging of the ritual process' (ibid.: 186). Thomas comes closer to distinguishing performative activities in his examination of early Bronze Age funerals, suggesting that 'the intended reading of the dead person was made by the audience within the temporarily restricted conditions of the funeral' with 'the large pit acting as a stage for its display' (Thomas 1991a: 34). Both Barrett and Thomas employ the term 'display', a notion close to that of showing or *ostension*, 'the most basic instance of performance' (Eco 1977: 110 cited in Elam 1980: 29–30). Both imply the presence of two orders of participant, the watchers and the (albeit dead) watched, orders fundamental to the contract of performance. If we accept these initial perceptions, then an examination of contemporary performance theory and practice might reveal a number of attributes to further extend and elaborate the description of prehistoric funerary procedures. We do this in this chapter.

There are two further premises. The first is that performance is not restricted to any such social or cultural locale as a theatre or ritual. The performative is a dimension of social practice. This takes us on from the field of theatre anthropology which has defined cross-culturally the range and variety of performed practices. Relevant also is the theory of performativity (most frequently associated with the work of Judith Butler; see e.g. 1990, 1994, 1997), that performative behaviour or utterance is not primarily about an extra-linguistic or underlying reality, but enacts that to which it refers. In such anti-essentialism, gender, for example, can be described as performance, as both a 'doing and a thing done' (Diamond 1996: 1); the ego or 'I' has no core identity, yet enunciates and acts as itself. Performance both affirms and denies this evacuation of core substance and identity in the coexisting reality and pretence. The concept of performance, under this broad definition, can be used to help understand past societies and contemporary archaeological practices.

The second premise is that archaeology is more than the recovery and examination of the material remains of societies and cultures. The archaeological is held to be a dimension of social practice, referring to the articulation of people and things and the material processes they undergo and witness. In particular the archaeological concerns the material presence of the past.

This chapter deals with the articulation of these two concepts or conditions – the performative and the archaeological. Its trajectory (overly) concentrates upon violence, warfare and death because the traces these phenomena leave – material, physical, psychological – are (overly) explicit.

The cyborg from archaic Greece to postmodernity: dramaturgies of sovereignty

Cyborgs

A fusion of flesh and mechanism, person and artefact combined. Genetic modifications, implants, microtechnologies; utopias and dystopias; the ethics of changing selves, of self-creation; avatar and other: the figure of the cyborg has come to haunt us.

In this section I turn to an ancient Greek perfume jar as a way of approaching some past and contemporary performative behaviours, and then to raise questions of the articulation of performer and their accoutrements, of the status and character of the social actor. The subject is ultimately the social fabric.

Figures upon an ancient perfume jar laid down with the dead

Consider the *aryballos*, the perfume jar in Figure 5. It is from Brindisi in southern Italy , though made in Korinth in Greece in the seventh century BC, a time of experiments in political forms, expansion of that Greek polity, the city-state. This *polis* was at the forefront of changes, with new architectures, new cityscapes, redefinitions of public and private spaces, representational arts (as here); new forms of regularised warfare accompanied a shift from kin-based community to what became in some places a civil society of the state citizen.

Korinthian pots depict the new phalanx of men (Salmon 1977), the hoplite citizenry of the *polis*, featured in a rich figurative art of stylised animal and human bodies and vegetal and floral forms. Perfume jars and soldiery travelled abroad: men as mercenaries, the hoplite phalanx as efficient military technology, the *aryballoi* to be laid down with the dead or to be dedicated to divinities in the new public sanctuaries.

Here in a painted scene two heavily armed and armoured soldiers, the new hoplites, do battle, face to face. Their coupling is mirrored in a lion attacking a deer, a phallic and naked male assaulting a robed female figure, and two monsters, eastern sphinxes of male and female

Figure 5
A seventh-century
Korinthian *aryballos*
from Brindisi

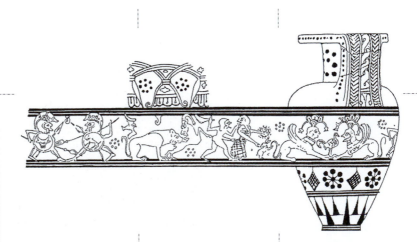

sex. All this is beneath a field of stylised flowers, eastern lotus and palmette. The shape of the jar mirrors the canopic jars of Egypt, vessels containing the innards of embalmed dead.

Iron Man and Bodyhammer

Tetsuo: two movies by Shinya Tsukamoto (Kaijyu Theatre/Toshiba EMI 1989 and 1991). They are violent and surreal fantasies of body transformations.

Tetsuo 1: Iron Man, is a broken narrative and collage about the confrontation and ultimate merging of a metal fetishist and a businessman. It begins with a bleak industrial wasteland and the fetishist – in a scrap metal hideaway he inserts a steel bar into his thigh. After accidentally knocking down the fetishist with his car (and with flashbacks of some guilty sexual encounter), the businessman is infected by his electric shaver. Pursued by a metal-mutating female, he is forced to react to the threat and becomes metal himself. Hard and unfeeling, through dreams of homosexual rape and an amazon mutant woman, he destroys his wife in a bizarre and machinic sexual encounter. The dénouement is a homoerotic merging of the businessman with the fetishist, who has turned out to be the businessman's *alter ego*; together they become a monster, part machine, part inert material, part organism.

Tetsuo 2: Bodyhammer, is a reiteration of the same themes. A respectable businessman takes on an underground sect of muscle and metal fetishists who are experimenting with body mutation, body sculpture, and have threatened his secure nuclear family. The businessman's *alter ego* this time is a charismatic, semi-divine figure in touch with a world of otherness, who turns men to metal through injected infection. Their encounter is one of bodies turned into explosive weapons and gunnery, blowing holes through armoured bodies.

Full Metal Jacket

Full Metal Jacket: a film by Stanley Kubrick and Warner Bothers (1987), after the novel *The Short-timers* by Gustav Hasford. It sounds like armour, but the title is in fact a reference to the live ammunition round of a US Marine. The theme is the initiation of American youth into Vietnam. But this is no formulaic treatment. As in some of his other films, such as *Clockwork*

Figure 6
Tetsuo

Orange (1971), *The Shining* (1979), *Dr Strangelove* (1963), Kubrick continues his exploration of the monstrous alliance of psychic independence and excess.

The first half is set in the recruit depot and follows eight weeks of standard training. The film opens with hair cutting – this is to be about the body. The Senior Drill Instructor (not an actor but a professional soldier who started out as adviser to the film) meets the recruits. He is hard, he tells them. They are ladies, filthy, low-life, worms, nothing, puke, amphibian, shit, slime.

'If you ladies leave my island, if you survive recruit training . . . you will be a weapon, you will be a minister of death, praying for war. But until that day you are pukes! You're the lowest form of life on Earth. You are not even human fucking beings! You are nothing but unorganised grabasstic pieces of amphibian shit!'

Lawrence Leonard is Private Pile. He can't learn. He can't change into what he is supposed to become. He is too soft and too fat. He brings down the squad, the collective group of recruits. He slips and falls in the mud on the assault course. They beat him up with towels and soap in the night.

Private Pile gets serious. He becomes Section Eight – a nutcase, compartmentalised, mad. He is born-again hard. He shoots the Drill Instructor, showing that *he* is not hard after all. Then he shoots himself, in the latrines: 'I am in a world of shit.'

The recruits are now soldiers. Their weapons are their girls. They keep them clean. The recruits are married to the iron and the wood, ready to eat their own guts. They are off to Vietnam, a foreign and exotic locale. They meet with violence and prostitutes, war and women.

The life is one of horrifying violence. Bodies and minds explode. Cornered by a sniper, the marines break out and sneak up to find they were being shot by a young girl, an amazon Vietcong. Joker and Animal Mother stand over the wounded sniper, debating what to do. She asks to be shot. Joker looks into her eyes and jerks the trigger.

Figure 7
Full Metal Jacket

Figure 8
Archaic Korinthian helmet from Olympia

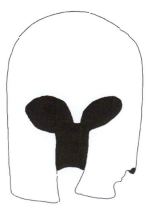

THEATRE/ARCHAEOLOGY

Eyes upon a helmet

Let us turn again to two of the figures upon the perfume jar and their archaic Greek world of citizen soldiers – *hoplites*. Heavily armed, they fought for their community in formation. What was this warfare about?

We begin with an oblique view – the eyes of a helmet. A late-eighth-century BC grave found in Argos, excavated in 1971, contained a bronze helmet, typical accoutrement of the soldier. Those soldiers upon the perfume jar are looking at each other through their helmets. This helmet from Argos has two extra eyes embossed on the forehead (Deilaki 1973: 97–9 and Plate 95e). The returned gaze of the opponent is an experience of close battle. Phalanx formations clashing in combat involve a particular perception of individual and group. The hoplite is one of a formation phalanx, moving and fighting with fellow hoplites. Individual urges and actions are dominated and transformed by the needs of the phalanx to keep together and push forward; the individual becomes one of the group. Anonymous within helmet and armour, the hoplite in phalanx achieves human and direct contact with the enemy through the eyes; the moment of individual contact is that of the returned gaze of the enemy over the top of shields locked with fellow hoplites.

More generally let us say that the gaze returned mirror-like is also a confirmation of the self of the viewer, a self defined in terms of the world looking back (Lacan 1977 on the 'mirror phase'). And if we might wish to belong with that world, then the eyes are those of desire, another experience of the returned gaze.

Violence, desire and sexuality

'Eyes meet, and the soldier is confronted with the seducer who has tempted him so long. The enemy surfaces as a momentary apparition of the soldier's own mirror image', Theweleit writes in his discussion of the psychology of the warrior male in inter-war Germany (1989: 195). The returned gaze is also erotic.

For Greece in the ninth-century days of Homer, Vernant (1991c: 100) draws attention to the description in the *Iliad* (22.373–4) of Hektor's dead body, stripped of armour. It was *malakoteros amphaphaasthai* (softer to handle) – *malakos* (soft or limp) refers to the feminine or the effeminate. Vernant relates the image to a series of terms found in early Greek literature which associate combat to the death with the erotic embrace: for example, in Homer *meignumi*, sexual union, also means joining in battle (see also Vermeule 1979: 101f.).

René Girard has presented an analysis of violence and desire in Greek literature. Violence may be rooted in rivalry based upon opponents sharing a desire for something (1977: 145). An association between sexuality and violence also exists through their respective dual characters and through notions of exchange and sacrifice. So violence is both terrifying *and* seductive (ibid.: 151). When purified through ritual, violence expends itself upon a victim whose death provokes no reprisals, no bloodfeud. It is as in the ritual violence of sacrifice, an exchange (of a slaughtered victim) to achieve order (between mortality and divinity). Such good violence is contained and ordered; distinctions between self and other, differences within and between social groups are established and maintained. This is generative violence, directed against an other who may be a scapegoat, a surrogate victim, expelled in a return to differentiated harmony. Bad impure violence, in contrast, is that which results from a crisis of distinctions, as in fraternal enmity; it is a sacrificial crisis, when purity is ignored or not possible (ibid.: 43, 51). The dangers of sexuality are incest and seduction which confuse the distinctions and order of (legal) sexual association, involving impurity and mixture. Marriage, in contrast, is a legal exchange of women which serves the reproduction of social order. In the terminology of Deleuze and Guattari (1988) which we will introduce again later, the contrasts are between molar and molecular fields of order and contagion.

The perfume of panthers

> *then the rage tripled and took hold of him, just like a lion.*
>
> (Homer, *Iliad* 5.136)

Violence, warfare and violent animals are a major feature of the new representational and figurative ceramic art, like this perfume jar in Figure 9. Martial themes of fighting hoplites accompany animal friezes of stylised lions – boars, bulls, goats, deer – mixed with monstrous recombinations of animal parts – sphinxes, griffons and the like. In the works of Homer, a favourite metaphor of the soldier hero is the lion.

In these scenes the creatures and men run in rings around vessels and look at each other, following a line of sight across the surface of the pot. Only panthers and gorgon heads look out from the painted friezes of perfume jars.

Detienne (1979: 38f.) has noted that panthers were later thought to be animals which hunt with cunning and through their scent or perfume which attracts their prey. Deceit and seduction are thus related. Perfumes and spices are of the order of the gods, belonging with sacrifice (the scent of burning meat), and so heat. As aphrodisiacs, perfumes arouse and heat the seduced, their sexuality and excess threatening the order of marriage (ibid.: 60f., 127f.).

Figure 9
A panther upon an *aryballos*

Figure 10
Gorgo, from a black
figure *dinos*

The face, death and personal identity

Here then is an **assemblage** of cultural forms, scenarios and meanings which takes us from battle and the gaze through faces, panthers, violence, seduction, marriage, social order and disorder, and recognition of what the viewer may be and become. What, now, of those other faces, gorgon heads? An immediate connection is that they appear upon pots and as shield devices, but it goes much further. Vernant (1991b), following literary references, shows associations between gorgon heads and martial themes, in these strange gorgon worlds beyond the everyday there are horses, brilliant gazes, death, infernal sounds. Grimacing, human yet inhuman, the gorgoneion is a mixture, revealing the alterity of human and animal. It was associated with marginal states such as death, sleep, exertion, drinking and music (Frontisi-Ducroux 1984). Gorgo was also, of course, female. When you stared into the eyes of the gorgon you turned to stone. Disquieting mixture and disorder,

> the face of Gorgo is the other, your double. It is the strange . . . both less and more than yourself . . . It represents in its grimace the terrifying horror of a radical otherness with which you yourself will be identified as you are turned to stone.
>
> (Vernant 1991b: 138)

Deleuze and Guattari (1988: 168f.) have made an interesting distinction between the head and the face. The head, not necessarily a face, is connected to the body, is coded by the body in that it completes the organism. In contrast, a face is when a head ceases to be part of an organic body; the face 'removes the head from the stratum of the organism, human or animal, and connects it to other strata, such as signification and subjectification' (ibid.: 172). Faces, or rather the process of facialisation, do away with corporeal co-ordinates to replace them with a system of plane and holes – the face and expression, just as in a bronze helmet. 'The face is not universal' (ibid.: 176), but depends on an *abstract* system or 'machine' of screen and holes, and which signifies, goes with the idea of, a subject to and behind the face, and forms a different medium of expression. In contrast, the head belongs with the body, corporeality and *animality*. This contrast between animal head and abstract face makes it possible for Deleuze and Guattari to write 'the inhuman in the human: that is what the face is from the start' (ibid.: 171). The face provides an overarching layer of identity or expression, and in so doing makes reference beyond that which is the human or animal.

We mention again the context of physical violence in Greek battle: the individual apparently anonymous in standardised armour, bronze protecting his soft vitals, presenting a formalised head of bronze sheet pierced by eye sockets and slashed down across the mouth.

Do we see the other in the eyes? Face to face across the tops of wide round shields, threatening with spear tip. A drilled, disciplined and armoured body was the hoplite's protection. The hoplite is held together by the talismans of his identity, the armour and weaponry, which makes him the same as the others. Identity is found in stylisation, in the phalanx as multi-bodied individual: the unity of the group. It is challenged in the threats, real and conceptual, to the integrity of the body. But think of the aftermath; finding the dead after the battle. Spear thrusts were made below the shield: facial injury across shield top was common, and bodies were bloated from being left after battle, disfigured, cooked in bronze armour by the heat of Greek summer sun. How would you find your son?

Korshak (1987) has collected and examined examples of frontal faces in archaic Attic vase painting, from a little later than this *aryballos* from seventh-century Korinth. The subjects who gaze out from the vases are satyrs, gorgons, dancers and partying *symposiasts*, fighters defeated or dying, athletes, centaurs. All are predominantly masculine; and female examples occur only later. Masculinity is hereby related with sexuality and animality (the satyrs), death, the body and lifestyle, through faciality. Korshak associates satyrs, gorgons and *symposiasts* via masks (in drama), eastern and exotic god Dionysos as patron of drama and wine, and she makes a further association between masks and helmets. In summary, these all represent 'the coming together of opposites in frontality', that is, occasions 'when governance of the self is relinquished and nature takes hold' (ibid.: 23–4). Vernant and Frontisi-Ducroux (1983) have also noted connections between masks, the gorgoneion, Dionysos, drink and states of 'otherness', adding also references to virgin huntress Artemis and the animal world.

In sum so far: the face breaks the easy order of human and animal, mediating and pointing beyond to identity, death and desire, states of 'otherness'. In all there is a tension between securely categorised identity and an uneasiness associated with marginal states. Looking at the panther draws in animality, violence and warfare. And in hoplite warfare are associated the face, the helmet, the individual in the group, an armoured individual overcoded by the phalanx-group and the system of heavy armour. This is a gendered field, and one of power and violence.

Some dimensions of a culture of war: an aesthetics of risk taken and death faced

Let me widen out from these aspects of the facial encounter in hoplite battle.

> Glaukos, why is it that you and I are honoured before the others,
> with pride of place, with choice meats and the wine-cups of Lykia
> filled to the brim, and all men look on us as if we were immortal? . . .
> It is our duty to take our stand in the front line of the Lykians,
> to bear our part of the blazing of battle, so that a Lykian man,
> fighting close-armoured with us, may say:
> 'Indeed, these are noble men [kleos], these lords of Lykia,
> these kings of ours . . . – there is strength and valour in them,
> since they fight in the front line of the Lykians'
>
> (Homer, *Iliad* 12.310–21)

For Homer, the god-like fighting aristocrat, the *agathos*, owed his position and its accoutrement to prowess in battle. And this meant that success mattered, action not intention: good intentions matter not to the dead soldier. The compensation for the risk of the front line was *kudos*, success and its glory, the prestige and authority of the victor, and *kleos*, fame. This makes the culture of the hero a public one of shame and results, not inward intention and guilt. The Homeric conception of man is one where man and action are identical, and there are no hidden depths to the person; the hero is what others see and say of him. With no boundaries between feeling and corporeal existence and action,

> he does not confront an outside world with a different inner selfhood, but is interpenetrated by the whole, just as he on his part by his action and indeed by his suffering penetrates the whole event . . . Even what a man does to others is part of himself.
>
> (Fränkel 1975: 80, 85)

The hero clearly enjoys physical pleasures – food, wine, sex, sleep and festivity, even melancholy (*Iliad* 13.636–9; *Odyssey* 4.102–3). But in such an external selfhood the meaning of the act, indeed existence, lies in death and its confrontation. When fame and existence depend upon being talked about (and having deeds done sung in poetry), real death is silence, obscurity and amnesia. So the hero risks his life in the front ranks; 'life for him has no other horizon than death in combat

> . . . In a beautiful death, excellence no longer has to be measured indefinitely against others and keep proving itself in confrontation; it is realised at one stroke and forever in the exploit that puts an end to the life of the hero.'
>
> (Vernant 1991c: 85)

And the heroes in Homer do not have lingering deaths.

Vernant (1991a) establishes links in this system of archaic values between excellence achieved, a beautiful death, and imperishable glory through the song which remembers and celebrates the death, in a sort of collective memory. The beautiful death is also an escape from the death associated with ageing. Old age, evil and death are contrasted by seventh-century poet Mimnermos with love and pleasure, the 'flowers of youth' (West 1992: 1). Ageing only brings decay, a loss of the *kratos* or power that allows the hero to dominate an opponent, misery and an ignoble death. So at the moment of *euklees thanatos*, the glorious death, the hero guarantees his immortal and heroic youth. The *hebes anthos*, flower of youth, is not so much a chronological age, but an attribute of the glorious death; the hero's *hebe* goes with his position and standing, his *aristeia*, and an heroic death is always youthful.

> it is disgraceful this – an old man falling
> in the front line while the young hold back,
> his head already white, grizzled beard,
> gasping out his valiant breath in the dust,
> his bloodied genitals in hand–
> this is shameful (aischra) to the eyes, scandalous to see,
> his skin stripped bare.
> But for the young man, still in the lovely flower of youth (hebes anthos),
> it is all brilliant, this –
> alive he draws men's eyes and women's hearts,
> beautiful – felled in the front line.
>
> (Tyrtaios (West 1992: 10.21–30); see also Iliad 22.71–6)

Here Tyrtaios, another seventh-century writer, describes the awful and disgraceful (*aischra*) death of an old man. Yet this would have been glorious and beautiful for a young man. There is an aesthetics to the death of the hero (Loraux 1975, 1986; Vernant 1991a).

The beautiful death, as well as being contrasted with that of the old man, is marred by various things (Vernant 1991a: 67f.). This is *aikia* (disgrace) – dirt, disfigurement, dismemberment, the dogs, birds and fish, worms and rot which eat and spoil the corpse, deprive it of its wholeness, integrity, beauty. These all threaten the proper securing of the beautiful death: the purifying funeral pyre which sends the *hebes anthos* off to eternity, retaining the corpse's unity and beauty, and the burial mound raised in his memory.

The work of Victor Hanson and others (Hanson 1990, 1991; after Keegan 1976), presenting a phenomenology of ancient war, reminds us of the most simple fact, that archaic Greek warfare was based upon a particular conception of battle as direct and formal confrontation, face to face with long thrusting spears in a short decisive encounter, with risk of bloody wounding and death across the tops and below the rims of the round hoplite shield – the faces we have discussed, and the old man in Tyrtaios. War was not about drawn out, cowardly 'terrorism' or guerrilla tactics at a distance. Risk was heightened and blood proliferated, at least in the front ranks. (Alternative experiences of war and battle are neatly summarised in Keegan 1993.)

And what more of hoplite battle? There is the aesthetics of heroic death; there was an aesthetics to the art of hoplite war.

In short, anyone who paid attention to the poetry of Sparta . . . and examined the marching rhythms they used when going against the enemy to pipe accompaniment, would decide that Terpander and Pindar were quite right to associate valour with music. The former says of Sparta:

There the spear of young men blooms and flourishes and the clear-voiced Muse and Justice (Dike) too, that helper in fine deeds, who walks in the wide streets.

(Plutarch Lykourgos 21.4s; Terpander Bergk 6, Diehl 4 in Campbell 1982–93)

War, display and the body

There is the display of armour, crests and shields. Vernant (1982) has written of the ceremonial, ritualised, performative character of early hoplite warfare (see also Connor 1988). The fighting formation moved rhythmically. Pipers accompanied phalanxes: this is known from illustration upon Korinthian pots. Henderson (1994: 109–10) has connected war and dance in his interpretation of a Tyrrhenian neck amphora of the early–mid-sixth century.

The Korinthian helmet, a favourite design, had particular effect upon the look and experience of its wearer (Figure 8). We have already discussed eyes and the gaze of the enemy. Consider also body armour. Muscled bronze torsos harden the hoplite against the spilling of blood and intestines, but follow the contours of the human body (however idealised). A widespread convention of Greek art is furthered when the hoplites appear naked apart from their armour and weapons. Other figures too are drawn naked. Why is this, if not because war and violence are a function of the **body** of these men, its aesthetic and politics?

Let him fight toe to toe and shield against shield hard-driven rest aginst crest and helmet on helmet, chest against chest.

(Tyrtaios (West 1992)11.31-3)

to fall to work upon the paunch, to hurl belly against belly, thighs to thighs.

(Archilochos (West 1992) 119)

And Archilochos is writing about sex.

Fighting in formation in this warfare required discipline, rhythmic movement, trained manipulation of weaponry – the cultivation of distinctive techniques of the body. These techniques of the body and the bodily lifeworld of archaic violence are clear also in early lyric poetry. There is much reference to discipline and posture:

You, young men, keep together, hold the line.

(Tyrtaios (West 1992) 10.15, translation West 1993)

Make your hearts strong, for you are the race of the never-defeated Herakles – and Zeus does not stand with his neck held askew.

(Tyrtaios (West 1992: 11.1–2))

Figure 11
Argos cuirass

Figure 12
An archaic Greek *kouros*

The hoplite stands upright and straight in the line. Contrast the death of a monster:

> *Herakles shoots three-bodied Geryones in the head with an arrow:*
> *it stained with darkening blood*
> *his cuirass and gory limbs.*
> *Geryones bent his neck to one side*
> *just as a poppy spoiling its delicate structure*
> *suddenly lets drop its petals.*
>
> (Steisichoros (Davies 1991) S15ii.12–17)

An image from Archilochos is another reference to neck and bearing:

> *hair cut short, off the shoulder*
>
> (Archilochos (West 1992: 217))

Consider now early Greek sculpture: stone *kouroi,* male figures (Figure 12) (Richter 1970; Stewart 1990: 109–13, 122–6). These were set up as dedications to divinities and are found associated with graves. The *kouroi* are all in stiff poses. Why? It is clear that they are the desired appearance of the ideal male. And they are naked. But there is no experiment with bodily form. This artistic conservatism (Snodgrass 1980: 185) is a social requirement – there was no desire to sculpt *animated* naked males. They are made upright and hard, representing the valuation of a posture belonging with new and expressive techniques of the self and body. Simonides, a little later, has the *agathos,* the man of *arete* (virtue) hand and foot alike, and in understanding cut foursquare (*tetragonon*), fashioned without flaw (Page 1962: 542.1–3).

Tetragonon (foursquare) is reference to *tetractys*, a Pythagorean term of excellence and justice, root of harmony and *arete* (Fränkel 1975: 276–7, 308). *Tetragonon* may also be connected to technique of manufacture: the method of sculpting *kouroi* is clear — separate views were sketched on the four faces of a block of stone prior to taking it down to the final form.

The relationship of these sculptures to aristocratic ideologies has been well covered by art historians. Stewart associates these expensive artistic commissions with the aristocracy and its ideals (Stewart 1986; also Zinserling 1975). As grave markers they were monuments to aristocratic excellence (*kalokagathia*) in the flower of youth (*hebes anthos*). Hurwitt puts it like this: 'The kouros and kore (female) forms were perpetuating symbols of the physical prowess, moral authority, goodness and beauty that aristocrats (naturally) considered innately aristocratic' (Hurwitt 1985: 198–9).

Further connections can be made between the anatomical detailing of *kouroi* and bronze armour (Kenfield 1973). Courbin noted (1957: 353 and Figure 37) a similar schematic of muscle on a famous bronze cuirass found in an eighth-century warrior's grave at Argos as on the Argive statue of Polymedes at the sanctuary of Apollo at Delphi. Kunze's study of archaic greaves at the pan-Hellenic sanctuary at Olympia (1991) shows clearly their 'artistic' credentials; they are not simply functional items. The detailing of the knee joint is common to both greaves and *kouroi* (Snodgrass 1991).

Movement, travel and the consumption of goods

Soldiers travelled. There is, for example, the famous graffiti scratched by some Greek mercenaries on the left leg of a colossal statue of Rameses II at Abu Simbel, 700 miles up the Nile. They were on an expedition in 591 BC (Austin and Vidal-Naquet 1977: 209). Korinthian pots, like the perfume jar in Figure 5, are found in graves and sanctuaries across the Mediterranean Greek world. The major archaeological provenance of archaic armour and weaponry is the sanctuaries of Greece. Recently much has been made of the factor of mobility in the archaic Mediterranean: mercenaries, traders, slaves and materials were moving (Purcell 1990; Sherratt and Sherratt 1991, 1993).

For archaeologist and historian De Polignac, religious sanctuaries in these times were rallying points, locales for the exchange of hospitality and alliances, like fairs (Gernet 1968). Games and dedication particularly made of them theatres of ostentation (De Polignac 1994: 17) with individual and inter-state rivalry a function of a loose clan structure. The import of goods, including eastern exotica, is a prominent feature of the mobility represented by sanctuaries, meeting points for local populations and those travelling from further afield. Catherine Morgan mentions the likelihood of itinerant craftsmen (Morgan 1990: 37). Local populations, Greeks and foreigners, sacred and profane goods and activities: the sanctuaries were connective locales for the meeting of different worlds. This may also be seen in the siting of the great pan-Hellenic sanctuaries (Delphi, Olympia, Isthmia and Nemea) in marginal areas between cities and states (Morgan 1993: 31).

The sanctuaries received gifts and pillage, but not all artefacts found in the sanctuaries are votive. There is considerable evidence for sacrifice and burning, cooking and eating from early times onwards. At the Korinthian sanctuary to Poseidon at Isthmia 'the material record indicates that drinking and dining were the principal activities . . . emphasis seems to have been placed on communal dining rather than on the display of wealth, and no investment was made in building' (Morgan 1994: 113). Consensus is that communal dining was a significant part of archaic Greek cult activity (Tomlinson 1980, 1990; Kron 1988; Bergquist 1990).

Here then is a connection of mediation and travel between different worlds, real and meta-physical. So consider that in the already mentioned and famous rich warrior grave (number 45) at Argos, dated to about 710 BC, were found, with the fine aristocratic weaponry and armour, twelve iron cooking spits and two fire dogs in the shape of warships (Courbin 1957: 370–85). Other similar firedogs are known from four warrior graves in Crete and Cyprus (Coldstream 1977: 146). Eating a meal with the dead, smelling the roast, and you see the warships to carry you off on travels.

With respect to consumption and feasting, Mason, in discussing the archaic poet Hesiod's cosmogony and account of the origins of sacrifice (1987), isolates a culinary semantic field (separating mortals and immortals via operations performed upon grain and meat, particularly in sacrificial rites) and connects it with gender and economic distinctions. The fire, smoke and aroma of sacrifice draw perfume too into this culinary field. Vernant more generally relates eating and cuisine to personal identity – what it is to be a person – you are what you consume and how you consume it.

Space, sovereignty and the hoplite

De Polignac (1984, 1994) has connected the establishment of Greek sanctuaries in the eighth and seventh centuries BC to a dynamic of territorial sovereignty. Temples and sanctuary precincts marked out the territory and principal axes of a city. Morris (1987: 189–92) also stresses profound eighth-century BC changes in boundaries between gods, men and the dead, with living space more sharply differentiated from the sacred spaces of the gods and dead – sanctuaries and cemeteries. One of the changes in the city-state of Korinth, origin of the perfume jar, was a shift in the burial of Korinthian dead from around houses and living space to formally designated areas.

For De Polignac the rural sanctuaries in the territory (*chora*) of the *polis* were set up as focal points of mediation; these 'passages between two worlds' (1994: 8) indicate the impor-tance of boundaries. So the sacred landscape, which is the *polis*, centres on frontiers – political borders between neighbouring states, but also boundaries between the sacred and profane (ibid.: 30), mortal and divinity, this world and that beyond. Axes are set out in the *chora* from *astu* (the city) to sanctuary, axes enacted in the sacred calendar with periodic processions and festivals (ibid.: 48–50, 54–6, and 85–92).

The soldier citizenry of the *polis*, the newly regulated or standardised *hoplitai*, would have figured prominently in these rites, processional, dedicatory, culinary. With Antonaccio (1994: 82) and Connor (1988: 16–17), we repeat the vital point here that archaic Greek war was not about territorial acquisition but civic representation, and was often focused upon borders, disputed or liminal territory suitable for a fight of phalanxes.

So we move through warfare to a human geography – locales connected in the conduct, bearing, dress and performative activities of a soldier citizenry, in their goods and accoutrement, in the form of the architectures and spaces through which they moved.

The heterogeneity of Greek warfare

We have tried to give some indication of the embeddedness of archaic Greek warfare. Far from a unitary phenomenon it extends into fields of the erotic, ideas of otherness (mediatory and marginal states), distinctions between 'us' and 'them', mortality and divinity, identity, lifestyle, posture and discipline, travel and the exotic. In this gendered nexus a prominent feature is a will to wholeness threatened by wounding, ageing, death, anonymity.

A prominent branch of anthropology considers war an aspect of aggressive species behaviour, related to group fitness and often occurring in circumstances of environmental stress and/or social competition over subsistence resources (for example, Haas 1990). Such theory is cross-cultural *a posteriori*. Particular social and cultural expressions, forms and meanings are eschewed. Moreover, the ethics of war and violence are irrelevant to this theory. The position we hold here is different. War is here considered a total social fact, socially and culturally embedded, a heterogeneous phenomenon.

In all this there is a theme of power and control. Let us move on now to piece together a dramaturgy of sovereignty.

The sovereignty of the soldier

In an interpretation of popular German military literature of the 1920s and after, Klaus Theweleit (1987, 1989) has provided fascinating insights into the psychology of a soldier 'society', the *Männerbund* of the *Freikorps*. With their militarism, male camaraderie and heroic youth, these were part of the political and intellectual culture of the inter-war period, out of which indeed emerged fascism.

A major contention is that war is not only a restricted field of political authority and physical domination; war is a function of the body. The body is the site of the political ethos of militarism. Theweleit is concerned with the social psychology of male sovereignty and its world which elevates the experience of violence and war, hardship and discipline. The centrality of the body is apparent in techniques of the self which define and are practised by the soldier – bodily drills, group drills and regimes, countenance (those eyes and the helmet), keeping one's bearing and expression correct and upright, training, self-control.

A primary motivation is towards bodily and social unity. This will to wholeness arises because of the perceived threat of its opposite: those wild and disorderly powers which break down barriers, setting off floods and waves of lower and sordid elements; there is fear of dissolution, commingling with these base elements, fear of engulfment. For the member of the German *Freikorps* in the 1920s, this was the threat of engulfment by communism and bolshevism, the lower classes, and their women. In archaic imagery there are hybrid monsters, threats of guts spilled in the front rank, associations with seduction and the female gaze of death – Gorgo. The will to wholeness is a will to power. It is a compulsion to put down that other which threatens the soldier's unity and integrity, to oppress those elements in the body of another, or the body in his own self, bringing to order. The relationship with bodies is one of violence and hierarchy, not commingling with the base and dirty, but establishing the preponderance of self over the other, of man over the monster and animal (within).

So the soldier male's commitment to unity and the whole arises out of his own fear of splitting.

> Think in terms of the whole = don't forget that you are subordinate = don't forget that without us you would have no head, nothing above you. Think in terms of the whole = without us you would die = without us you would lack divinity (masculinity) and would be animals.
>
> (Theweleit 1989: 102)

And the soldier is split if and when those 'lower', suppressed and animal elements demand independence.

Unity is the phalanx, those dangerous and animal elements of the body damned and subdued by the machine-like physique of the soldier, his self displaced into armour and weaponry. Homer has *krateron menos*, the 'conquering energy' of the hero, put on like armour (*Iliad* 17.742–6; also Vernant 1991a: 63 on the shining armour of the hero). In Tyrtaios the *arete* of the soldier hero is achieved through weaponry and death (West 1992: 12). Archilochos, a mercenary-poet of the seventh century BC, identifies the staples of life with his weaponry:

> *By spear is kneaded the bread I eat, by spear my Ismaric*
> *wine is won, which I drink, leaning upon* [keklimenos] *my spear.*
> (Archilochos (West 1992: 2), translation Lattimore (1960))

And *keklimenos* is the word which would be used to refer to reclining upon a dining couch in new and exotic eastern style.

Homer's conception of man is a complex mediation of what Deleuze and Guattari call the '*molecular*' and '*molar*' (1988). He has no words for the soul or indeed body of a living man, who was, as related above, a unity of energies, organs and actions (Fränkel 1975: 76f.). It was only in death that *psyche*, soul, became separated from *soma*, corpse.

> So long as the body is alive, it is seen as a system of organs and limbs animated by their individual impulses; it is a locus for the meeting, and occasional conflict, of impulses or competing forces. At death, when the body is deserted by these, it acquires its formal unity.
>
> (Vernant 1991a: 62)

And becomes *soma*. The fear of the hero is of *aikia*, disgrace done to the corpse, dirt and disgrace spoiling its wholeness and preventing the death from being beautiful. The images quoted above of the old man's death bring in another element: his death was disgraceful, because old and because it was not masculine – the reference to the wound to the genitals (also eaten by dogs and birds (Vernant 1991a: 68)). There is fear too of not receiving proper burial, which preserves the beautiful death, and provides, in the funeral mound raised, a mark which is stable and unchanging – *empedos* (meaning 'intact' or 'immutable') (ibid.: 69, citing *Iliad* 17.432–5). So unity, the molar, is a protection from that molecular death represented by dismemberment, splitting, decay, decomposition, being the food of birds and dogs. Unity is that which is preserved by the *kalos thanatos*, the beautiful death. Perpetual unity comes with the funeral pyre and the mound raised for all to see.

Gregory Nagy (1979, especially 151–61; see also Vernant 1969) has interpreted the poet Hesiod's myth of the five generations of humankind (*Works and Days* 109–201) as representing, in the men of gold, silver, bronze and the demi-gods (those generations preceding the present), this dual character of the heroic ancestor. Particularly interesting is the characterisation of the darker side of the heroic, the men of bronze: they were brazen, *chalkeion*, and made of ash (*ek melian*) (*Works and Days* 144–5) just like the warrior's spear. Hard and violent, they ate no grain (*Works and Days* 146–7) and died by their own hands. Nagy compares this violent and destructive masculinity with that of the warrior associations such as the *Männerbund*, and those violent earth-sprung figures of myth, the Spartoi and Phlegyai, who combine categories of mortality, immortality and the heroic fighter (also Vian 1968).

'People told us that the war was over. That made us laugh. We ourselves are the war. Its flame burns strongly in us. It envelops our whole being' (quoted in Theweleit 1987: x). Fear of that molecular otherness is also seductive and fascinating, and the struggle to retain hard (molar) control is a never-ending one. Battle and actually fighting is a supplement (in Derrida's sense too: Deleuze and Guattari 1988: 417). The warrior caste lives in permanent war. Why fight? For *kleos*, or for city, or for *dike*, justice? It does not really matter. The motivations are easily transferred.

I would as soon fight with you as drink when I'm thirsty Archilochos.

(West 1992: 125)

War is just something that you do; it is even a necessity. Mercenaries appear almost with the beginning of the *polis*, it would seem, and in numbers. Greek historian Herodotos (2.152) records 'brazen men' in Egypt in the seventh century (mentioned above; see, for example, the account by Murray 1993: 223f.). The mercenaries did not need the state. War does not need battles; it is more a war-machine.

In a fascinating and innovative interpretation of seventh-century social turmoil, James McGlew (1993) supplies a vital clue for making sense of this phenomenon of archaic violence. In the actions and discourses of the political radicals, the tyrants, popular leaders who staged *coups d'état* and usurped power in many city-states in these times, McGlew finds a redefinition of political power and sovereignty.

Consider the oracles from the sanctuary of Apollo at Delphi, claimed to foretell the rise of Kypselos, the tyrant of Korinth. In them the tyrant's persona is an agent of justice:

an eagle is pregnant in the rocks and will
bring forth a lion, a mighty hunter of flesh,
who will weaken the knees of many.
Be warned of this, you Korinthians who live
around the fair fountain of Peirene and the heights of Akrokorinthos.

(Herodotos 5.92e.2)

For the oracles, tyranny and social revolution arises from injustice, and this belongs with the city and its leaders, not with the motivations and ambitions of the tyrant. So the oracle quoted here reminds the Korinthians of the coming of tyrant Kypselos, whose rule is likened to a lion exacting punishment on (unjust) Korinthians. The tyrant's persona as a reformer required a conspicuous display of freedom (*eleutheria*), hence the lion.

McGlew notes (1993: 67 note 32) many instances of this use of the lion as a political symbol of heroic power, fearful and irresistible, sometimes image of divinely willed destruction.

In those other political commentators of these times, poet Theognis and statesman Solon, there is a reciprocity between crime and punishment, between the wicked ways of a city's administration and an autocratic tyrant putting things right.

Kyrnos, this city is pregnant – and I fear it may
give birth to someone [aner euthunter] *who will right our wicked ways* [hubris].

(Theognis 39–40)

By claiming and being supported in an unprecedented and unique right to autocracy the tyrant implicitly defined that rule as untransferable. This is the basis of their ambiguity – tyrants were popular leaders, but fiercely resisted. Resistance aimed not to overthrow tyranny so much as to appropriate the freedom (*eleutheria*) of the tyrant for the people. Just as the tyrant's divinely willed *eleutheria* involved the subjection of fellow citizens, so the appropriation of that same freedom by the citizenry involved subjugation – of slaves. After tyranny there was no return to political innocence. The persona as agent of justice (*dike*) was adopted, the treasury and foreign interests assumed, *eleutheria* preserved – those aspects of sovereignty which made the tyrant lord both attractive and dangerous.

So in this seventh-century discourse of power, there were two sides to justice and sovereignty. The hero appears as a lion, but the lion, the animal within the hero, may turn and destroy. The soldier damns up, faces, shares the forces of otherness (whether they are conceived as animal furor or violence, spilled intestines eaten by carrion, or divinity); his armour, posture and actions shared with the group help him in this. This is a gendered field – that powerful otherness. So threatening yet seductive is the feminine.

Sovereignty . . .

The point is that much of the imagery and cultural logic of these works and of war is about (masculine) sovereignty, articulated through techniques of the body in a broad assemblage of social practices, values, artefacts and dispositions. Sovereignty is unrestricted power residing in itself, the autonomy to govern, as of a state or monarch, their territory. It is an autonomy of self. Crucial to its understanding is the notion of otherness or heterogeneity. Sovereignty is articulated with barbarism or heterogeneity.

. . . and heterogeneity

This is to do with the affective, states of aesthetic, erotic and ecstatic excess. Heterogeneous states are those which provoke reactions of both attraction and revulsion: marginal states and substances for anthropologist Mary Douglas, subject to taboo (1966). Think of the three types of animal – personal pets; those speciated, domesticated, classified and named; and the quality of the animal which can never be tamed. This latter is the heterogeneous; it cannot be pinned down. Heterogeneity is 'the horror'. It refers to the raw body within, of blood and guts. It is the violence of the animal, the otherness within, which threatens order and civility.

In the three works considered here, the perfume jar, *Tetsuo* and *Full Metal Jacket*, gender and subjectivities are pictured as struggling with the affective energy of the other, with heterogeneity directed into power and domination, through, among other things, violence and militarism. Heterogeneity poses as an external or internal source or threat of disorder and violence. Animality or primitivism are seen as the origin and location of disorder and violence, to be rooted out or requiring domestication, and thereby providing beneficial purpose through vitality. These narratives are centred on the body and the body-politic (see also Rowlands 1989).

We have thus identified two uses of **heterogeneity**. The first is the sense just defined. The other is to do with our statement that we are treating war as a heterogeneous phenomenon. In this use we are stressing heterogeneity as that which escapes orderly classification. War as a total social fact comprises the assemblage or association of heterogeneous phenomena – from perfume jar to human geography. Heterogeneity is thus to do with hybridity, the fusion or overflowing of classes of things.

This use of heterogeneity will connect directly to our argument that we are dealing with cultural work understood as **assemblage**, and we are also relating this to **dramaturgy**.

A Korinthian perfume jar

Perfumed oil, corpses, armoured torsos, eyes across shield tops, helmeted faces signifying the identity of the individual merged into group and facing the risk of the spear thrust into face or groin, dismembered parts monstrously recombined (sphinxes and other monsters in this strange visual world), exotic motifs – orientalia and flowers from an other society, the heroic fight bringing warrior together with his fellows and with divine heroism, sanctuaries and death. Women are excluded in their contagion – war is not their place and they hardly appear in the visual imagery of the perfume jars. They define the boundaries of this cultural assemblage through their absence. But when they do appear it is as threat, as amazon, as female sphinx, or they are controlled and subject to judgement.

Consider again the design with which we began (Figure 5). Fear of those threatening and dirty base elements leads to a stiffening: control, armour, hard bronze. And, of course, more:

stiffening and hardness are supposed confirmation of manhood. Here a phallic and naked man (hard body bared) assaults with a weapon one of the few likely female figures in this imagery of the new political state. She is dressed in a checked flowing robe (soft, compared with bronze torso), holds a wreath of flowers and pats a hare. The hare touches a sphinx, one of a pair who sit on either side of a bird. One sphinx is bearded, therefore male. Floral devices grow from their heads, associating them with the assaulted female. So from the female extend the otherness of monstrosity, mix of animal lion, avian and human, the dubious sexuality of the sphinxes, the floral and the avian, with eastern associations. The hare was later a gift between lovers (Schnapp 1984). Behind the phallic man a lion jumps upon a goat, and the two hoplites fight a duel. Parallels are suggested: armoured hoplite fight – drill (the hoplites mirror each other, as is proper) – violence and the animal – violent sexuality against the female – hard body, soft clothes – amorous gift – monstrous sexuality. It is not difficult to weave a set of narratives out of these elements of what we have termed the molar and molecular dimensions of sovereignty.

Tetsuo

Tetsuo is reminiscent of Marinetti's futurist fantasies of machinic society, with its violence, fire and speed. There is constant slippage between normality and fantasy worlds (heterogeneity), mediation occurring through industry and metal. The monsters, representatives of the power and fascination of otherness, are part-thing, part-person, part-alterity, part-cultural appendage, as artefacts stick to the Iron Man and merge. *Tetsuo*, this poetics of metal and blood, of mutation, this pyropoetics of forged flesh, is about a collision of artefact and flesh, questioning the boundaries, and is thus about heterogeneity. Sovereignty, and its dual character, is so evident in the finale of *Tetsuo 1* as the businessman merged with fetishistic alter-ego rampages through the city, ending as some great monument to industry and war. In *Tetsuo 2* the businessman's triumph sets loose the explosive violence of his inner self over the gang who threatened his ordered and civilised life. Gender dimensions are present in the female seen as threat and image of familial security, in the homoerotic, heterogeneous mergings and the bonds of shared male experience of violence.

Figure 13
Tetsuo

Full Metal Jacket

The first half: otherness defined, faced and controlled or expelled. Again the duality of sovereignty is evident. Pile apparently becomes the perfect soldier, but in fact he is not hard and disciplined enough. Though at one with the steel and wood of his M-15 rifle, he is still within a world of shit, not a minister of death praying for war and the realisation of selfhood. He is a monster.

Out in Vietnam we witness the confrontation of otherness – foreign locales, devastated cities which ensnare, mind-exploding violence, and the amazon, the Vietcong, epitome of communist threat, girl-soldier who is minister of death to several of the platoon. But their teamwork triumphs and her threatening otherness is destroyed, or rather encompassed in their weapons.

Heterogeneity is here identified with softness, the amphibian, filth, the explosion of the body in violence. It is madness. Heterogeneity is also woman: the recruits themselves, and the angel of death. Heterogeneity threatens. It is held in check by being hard: drill and regimen.

Dramaturgy – the performer as cyborg

I have presented these evocations of war as focused on techniques of the body – the body sculpted, managed, materialised in various ways and with various props, attachments, accoutrements. It is an embodied and expressive field, and we have tried to locate it in **sensoria**, those culturally located arrays of the senses we mentioned in the introduction as an important focus when attempting to understand social and cultural phenomena. We have been exploring particular *cultural assemblages*, and we propose a connection between this concept of assemblage and dramaturgy (for further definition of assemblage see below and Shanks 1999: Chapter 2). In its creation of scenarios and postures, bringing together narratives, personae, props and characters, we have been exploring an expressive dramaturgy of sovereignty.

Dramaturgy, as cultural assemblage, works equally with settings, people, bodies, things, texts, histories, voices, architectures. In these connective networks that are the dramaturgical,

Figure 14
Full Metal Jacket: amazon

it is usual to consider things and people as separate, their conjunction considered after their distinction. We propose instead the inseparability of people and things, values, etc. And in a strong sense – we are not dealing with mixtures of people *and* things, but with *people-things* – the body as artefact, the artefact as constituting the cultural body, conduct and scenario defining the person. This raises immediately the anxiety prompted by the cyborg – that monstrous and hybrid mixture, that heterogeneous merging, as we termed it above.

To encounter this anxiety we will make a diversion into material culture studies and consider how people and things differ, or are indeed two aspects of the same cultural field.

Archaeological cyborgs – the life of things

> Haraway's world is one of tangled networks: part human, part machine; complex hybrids of meat and metal which relegate old fashioned concepts like 'natural' and 'artificial' to the archives. These hybrid networks are the cyborgs, and they don't just surround us – they incorporate us. An automated production line in a factory; an office computer network; dancers lights and sound system in a club – all are cyborg constructions of people and machines.
>
> (Donna Haraway interviewed by Hari Kunzru 1996 (and after Haraway 1991))

Anthropologists and sociologists have begun again to take seriously the things that we live with. There is a clear and popular disciplinary field now concerned with material culture. Included are design studies and design history, cultural studies more broadly, cognitive science and human–computer interaction, anthropologies and sociologies of everyday things, histories and sociologies of technology; and archaeology (Mackenzie and Wajcman 1985; Elliott 1988; Law 1991; Bijker and Law 1992; Collins and Pinch 1998).

We follow a central proposition of interpretive archaeology: that society is inconceivable without artefacts. It is not as if people make society, which happens to include things, goods, artefacts. Material culture actively communicates and helps build society into what it is. Closely connected is the issue of social agency, the power and intentionality in creating society (for a general review in archaeology see Johnson 1989). Goods have come to be seen not as *epiphenomena* (secondary to some essential and non-material dimension of society, representing, for example, economic structures) but as being central to the working of society. Material culture is active. (This actually means the term 'material culture' is tautologous – culture is always already material. We retain the use for convenience.)

How does this activity occur? How does this unite people and things?

Consider something found by an archaeologist, that perfume jar in Figure 5 perhaps. Of what time is this archaeological find? We can attribute a date – it is from the seventh century BC. But the attribution of date does not answer the question of the time of a find, however. Which date or moment or period of time is to be chosen? Normally date is accepted to refer to the time of the making of an artefact, or the time of its incorporation in the archaeological record. But why these two dates, both back then in antiquity? The perfume jar is also of our time in that it has been found quite recently, and published a little later. These dates may also be attributed to the artefact;

museums record dates of accession, and publication dates are often cited. But these are also usually considered to be secondary to those dates which are conceived to belong to the *original context* of the artefact.

All these dates are points upon a temporal continuity. That continuity is the duration of the material find. It is the durability of the perfume jar which allows there to be these different dates which are chosen as significant moments along that continuity. In this respect it is common to refer to the life-cycle of an artefact (for example, Schiffer 1987: 13f.; the classic in anthropology is Appadurai 1986 and especially Kopytoff 1986). Raw material is taken and transformed according to conception of design, an artefact produced, distributed or exchanged, used, consumed and lost or discarded. It may be recycled, given new life. This can be held to end when the artefact enters the physical archaeological record and is buried. But it is quite possible to argue that, found in the archaeological excavation and written into archaeological discourse, an ancient artefact is being recycled again, its life-cycle continuing. The durability of the artefact, its historical continuity, its materiality, holds together these events of its life-cycle. There is a continuity, albeit one with lacunae.

The life of an artefact is accompanied by physical changes and processes. An artefact becomes worn in its use and consumption. Marks upon it attest to events it has witnessed, things that have happened to it. It can deteriorate. The artefact ages.

Here then are our first points of similarity between people and things. People too have life-cycles, display changes and marks of time and experience. Some are gathered in the term 'physiognomy'. People show signs of their experience and ageing. These are the *human* conditions of mortality, physicality and morbidity (Olivier 1994).

Marks of origin and individuality. Marks of ageing, time and use. Discard and disposal. Deterioration and death. The physical processes and changes that occur and accrue to objects and people in their life-cycles are archaeology's very condition of being: archaeology, and of course society, is simply not conceivable without them.

In archaeology they are dealt with in a particular way, most often treated as technical issues or belonging with the natural sciences. Conservators in their laboratory work with chemical and other means of dealing with decay and repair, halting the life-cycle (Plenderleith and Werner 1972; Kuhn 1986; Cronyn 1990). Mortuary analysis, as it is often called in archaeology, is the method-ological means of moving from traces, archaeologically recovered, of the practices focusing upon the dead to 'active' social process or structure (Chapman and Randsborg 1981; O'Shea 1984; Tarlow 1999: Chapters 1 and 2). Middle-range theory, as it has been called in archaeology, is held to be a technical means of moving from the statics of the archaeological record to the dynamics of social process (Binford 1977, 1981, 1983a: Section IV, 1983b; Raab and Goodyear 1984). The way things become part of the archaeological record, the way buildings fall down, rubbish deposits accrue, discarded things settle into layers, the way a cooking hearth looks after two millennia, is called the study of site formation processes (Schiffer 1987). This is again usually treated in a technical way, understanding ruin as something to be overcome in getting back to the past, under-standing formation processes as a means to an end, a means to regain the past.

Hence, and ironically, archaeological mortuary analysis is little concerned with death and the accompanying putrefaction. Grave goods may be connected to social hierarchies, skeletons may be analysed for evidence of disease, for demographic patterns, their genetic material used as a means of tracing population dynamics. Just as the sentiments which surround bereavement are considered unnecessary or contingent to mortuary analysis, so too are the manifold dimensions of the central physical processes – death and rot (but see now Tarlow 1998, 1999).

Consider also what is often called the 'conservation ethic'. That things from the past should be preserved or conserved seems unchallengable. The past should be protected and conserved (Lipe 1977, 1984; Lowenthal and Binney 1981; Cleere 1984; Renfrew and Bahn 1996: 522-33; Carman 1996). It is more than a little sickening to think of the loss of so much of the past due to contemporary development and neglect. The seduction of conservation is one of gratification – ridding the self of this nausea of loss and decay. Associated with loss and decay are dirt, death, illness, those organic properties of the past. They are to be removed. The past is to be purified in a staunching of decay; death held in check. The task is given to science. Science is applied to clean up the wound and sterilise (Shanks 1992a: 69–75).

Around the world many ancient sites are in the care of the state and are open to the public. There is a very distinctive style to most. They are ruins, but consolidated. Loose stones are mortared in position. Walls are cleaned and repointed. Paths tended or created. Park benches may be provided to seat weary visitors. This is all justified in the terms of health (stopping the further decay of the monument) and safety or amenity (of the visiting public). However reasonable such a justification, it creates a distinctive experience of the visit to such a past monument. Masonry, earth and sky: such monuments are interchangeable, if it were not for their setting (Shanks 1992a: 73). And these ruins are, of course, not in ruin. These preserved monuments are **simulacra** of ruins (**simulacrum** – an exact copy of an original that has never existed).

Conservation is a potential sanitisation and sterilisation of the past. These conventional and legitimate archaeological approaches sometimes also neutralise their object. The life-cycle of things is occluded. Life and death are missing. They are actively avoided. In cleaning up the ruined building ready for the public to visit it can be forgotten that objects haunt. We can fail to feel the ghosts.

Ageing and decay, basic aspects of the materiality of both people and things, are today often considered negatively. Worn out things are thought to be of no use to anyone and, when cleaned up, only of interest to a museum or collector. To be old and retired is not always to be valued and respected.

Instead of this negative attitude, and with David Lowenthal, we make a plea for pathology.

Consider plant pathology. Most gardeners strive to eradicate slime, mould, rust and fungi. Yet these are natural, even essential adjuncts of plants they infest. Many attack weeds. Others create compost. Some, like entomophthora, kill off flies. But these ecological virtues still leave them unloved by flower-fanciers. When bacterial fasciation infects forsythia, clusters of distorted leaves tip plank-like shoots. Rather than cutting them off for burning, why not keep them? They do not spread; and their oddity adds varietal interest to any garden. Slime moulds congeal into a mass of powdery grey or sulphur and crimson spores, and enliven lawns. The intricacy of bird's nest fungus is a striking adjunct of stem decay.

(Lowenthal 1991b: 2–3)

Here infection, fungal and bacterial action, which also accompany decay, are seen as complements to the life and health of a garden. Lowenthal argues for the architectural value of age and decay, a sensitivity to the qualities of the materials of building. In archaeology the argument is that decay is an essential adjunct to a living past.

Conservation may stem processes of ageing and decay. Death may be delayed. But immortality cannot be achieved. This is not to hold that we should allow the past to rot away, but to have a living past we should cherish decay and ruin. This is about the way that we attend to the life of an artefact.

Both people and artefacts have life-cycles. Decay and fragmentation are a token of our symmetry with the physical world. Sensitivity to wear and decay is a mark of humility before the otherness and independence of material things. The signs of wear upon something that I have just acquired show that it existed before me; it was not created just for me, but has a particular history of its own. Historicity, the sense of the linear, directional flow of history and its events, depends on historiography, writing the plot of history. Writing distances us from cyclical routines of the everyday and the repetitions of life-cycle, and into which we can be immersed. So the marks upon an old pot are often also a form of writing, attesting to the history the pot has witnessed, its own historicity.

The decay of an artefact is a token of the human condition. The fragment, the mutilated and incomplete thing from the past, brings a sense of life struggling with time: death and decay await us all, people and objects alike. In common we have our materiality.

When a building collapses, the order of its construction and interior spaces disperses. We meet the commixture of materials and things in archaeological excavation whose object is, among other things, to reorder, to abolish the disorder of collapse and dilapidation, to find significance and signification in the apparent chaos. Archaeologists clear up and tidy the remains of the past. This too is the work of memory. But we might remember too that the litter and discard which accompany decay are interesting in their heterogeneity: juxtapositions of fibula and quernstone, gold ring and ox scapula in sifting through the cultural rubbish tip. The strange and oftentimes surreal juxtapositions of things with which archaeologists deal may be dismissed as distraction, or reduced to manifestation of cultural practices we know well; but a sensitivity to the strangeness of litter can reveal preconceptions about our cultural classifications, for example surrounding dirt (Hodder 1982b: 62f.; see also Douglas 1966). Such an everyday and mundane occurrence like litter can be surprising.

There is, after Nietzsche, a well-worked argument that discovery and innovation arise from metaphor, the juxtaposition of what was previously considered separate (discussed by Knorr-Cetina 1981: Chapter 3). Litter creates.

So too, the fragment of the past evokes. We can work on the archaeological fragment to

A.4   M.4   B.4   E.4

reveal what is missing; the shattered remnant invites us to reconstruct, to suppose that which is no longer there. The fragment refers us to the rediscovery of what was lost.

More generally it can be argued that the disfunction which accompanies wear need not, indeed should not be seen as a problem (see the discussion of Heidegger on disturbance and breakdown by Dreyfus 1991: 70–82). Disfunction refers us to the being of something; it draws attention to the artefact or social actor which is otherwise overlooked and ignored. We do not notice the working of a washing machine until it goes wrong, 'goes on strike', and then it is treated as a problem. But to accept disfunction as a revelation of being involves a project of *maintenance* – of getting on with something on a day-to-day basis. To treat disfunction as a problem calls for a project of *intervention* – not just getting on with things, but acting upon them. Furniture designer David Pye (1978) detailed an approach to design which accepts that nothing is ever purely functional in that useful devices always do useless things; design is always partly failure. Washing machines do and always will break down. Cars are comfortable ways to transport ourselves, but they generate noise and heat, they guzzle fossil fuels, pollute the earth, and they always break down eventually.

When disfunction and decay are not conceded there is a desire for dead things, things which do not change, essential qualities of things (abstract and unchanging), things which do not go wrong. This desire is encompassed by the concept of commodity.

The commodity form is a principle of abstract and universal exchange. Money, as a medium of universal exchange, allows the exchange of anything for anything else. The particularity of what is exchanged does not matter. Any transaction is the same as any other, and can thus be termed homogeneous or abstract. Because the commodity form takes no account of different things, no account of the particular and historical life of things, it is the principle of death represented by pure repetition.

The commodity form may find expression in the mass-produced object – the output of controlled, predictable, repeated and standardised production. Every commodity is seen as the same as any other. A particular washing machine is representative of its class of artefact and is held to wash clothes. This is compromised when it goes wrong; breakdown is a problem. We are detached from its life-cycle which runs through the relations of its production, distribution and processes of ageing. The washing machine goes wrong; throw it away and get another – repeat the purchase.

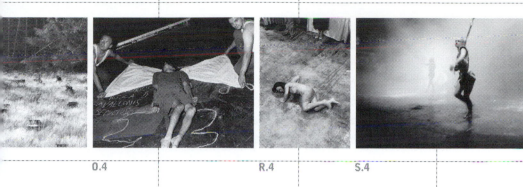

0.4   R.4   S.4

The death represented by the commodity becomes clearer if we contrast the mass-produced artefact with the product of craft, a piece of studio ceramic for example (Figure 8). The latter is a denial of pure repetition. Its life resides in its resistance to its making, its unpredictability.

Walter Benjamin (1970a, 1970b) related the rise of the commodity form to changing conceptions of aura. Aura refers to the sense of associations and evocations that cluster around an object, correspondences and interrelations engendered by an object. Aura is a sense of distance, no matter how close an object may be: it somehow seems more than what it is. 'To perceive the aura of an object is to invest it with the ability to look at us in return' (Benjamin 1970b: 190); it is the transposition of qualities of the animate to the conventionally inanimate world.

When we speak of something having sentimental value we are referring to aura; the article means something to us because it evokes memories of a common history; both the article and we have shared a life. Benjamin discusses the aura of works of art. Tourists cluster around the *Mona Lisa* in the Louvre because of the singularity of the painting achieved through its associations and evocations.

Consider rock brought back from the moon by astronauts in the late 1960s and early 1970s. The piece of rock displayed in a museum is not just any piece of rock. It is from up there, the moon. It is not of this earth. The rock is both present to the viewer now, but also beyond (admittedly also on the other side of the glass in the museum). Moon rock has an aura. It may be objected that this is something read into the rock, something which is not an attribute of the rock. If it were discovered that it was not in fact from the moon its aura would dissipate immediately and it would become just a mundane piece of rock. So what is the difference between moon rock and mundanity? It is life history. One has an everyday history; the other is part of a project which took people up in rockets and spacecraft for great distances and at great effort, and then back again. It ties in American political manoeuvres in the 1960s, and those ghostly figures on TV stepping down on to the moon surface. Aura is the mode whereby these associations and events are gathered around an artefact. Aura refers to the life of things.

Such particular relations with things can be lost with the rise of mass-production and the commodity form which deny any living relationship with the material world, treating it as the stuff of manipulation and controlled repeated production.

Aura and the commodity form are not, however, exclusive. In collage and montage the commodity can be treated as a heterogeneous fragment. Evocation, association, displacement, meaning, life can be found in the gaps between things, in difference and dissonance (Berger *et al*. 1972; Shanks 1992a: 104–5,188–90). This is made conspicuously clear in subcultural style – for example, the mobilisations of things and their associations in punk of the late 1970s (Hebdige 1979; see also Clifford 1988). Safety pins became unfamiliar – reused as body piercing. It is something many of us do everyday in juxtaposing in our homes and offices things brought from all sorts of aspects of our lives; together they generate meaning and association. They may bring homes and offices alive. This too is the life and fascination of litter and rubbish.

In the common process of life, life-cycle and history there are these many parallels and associations between people and things. Why then, and how, are things held to be different to people? We will attempt to counter the usual arguments.

Simplicity and complexity. Objects are often thought to be simpler than people. But many interactions between people are very simple; people often merge into the background and may be, in particular circumstances, treated far more simply than many machines. It is quite possible to have a complex relationship with a computer. Or indeed a work of art which can gather around itself many associations and connotations. Cognitive scientist Don Norman (1988) argues that most of the complexity of everyday knowledge lies not in people's heads but in the objects with which people surround themselves. There would seem to be a continuity from simple to complex irrespective of whether we are dealing with people or things.

Lack of consciousness. Objects, it can be argued, do not possess consciousness as do people. I am not necessarily for imputing consciousness to things, but it might be asked how could you tell? Think of the issues raised by Ridley Scott's film *Blade Runner*. If you create an artefact (a cyborg) which performs as a human and also give it personal memories, how is it different to a person? The now classic Turing test (Turing 1950) sets out to answer the question of the nature of artificial intelligence, and holds that if a questioner cannot tell from the answers to a series of questions whether those answers come from a machine or not, then it may be accepted that the answers come from an intelligent being. This is irrespective of the form or materiality of the entity answering. Whatever the validity of the Turing test, the field of artificial intelligence raises serious questions about the boundaries and interactions between human and object or machine worlds. Many objects do display extremely complex and independent behaviour. The mathematics of chaos deals with object worlds which are based on regularised principles but which nevertheless display unpredictable and independent, 'lifelike' behaviour. And what of animals? They may not have a consciousness as we understand it in ourselves, but this does not mean that we are absolved morally from treating them as equals. Why not also apply this to things?

But does this not involve a naïve anthropomorphism? Immoral because human suffering should not be debased by comparison with an object world which lacks feeling and consciousness (but see above). This criticism can be answered with other questions. Who mixes the worlds of objects and things? Doctors do. They connect people, chemicals, artefacts, bacteria. In what ways are they immoral? There are no simple ethical answers here (Latour 1989: 125).

Surely objects are passive, inert, inanimate? But consider a computer diskette. It looks like an inert and passive square of plastic and magnetic medium. Diskettes are inserted into computers. As a square you might think there are six different ways you could do this. But you can't. The diskette will not let you. It will allow only one mode of insertion. The diskette is active. So too are these bookshelves in my room, though they are apparently passive. They hold up my books and allow them to remain in order. Objects and artefacts can do work. Simply think of what a person would have to do to replace an artefact and then it can be seen how active the object world is.

Language: only humans talk, and when artefacts are said to speak it is through a human inter-mediary. But there has been an enormous amount of work associated with structuralism and post-structuralism which shows convincingly that a linguistic analogy can be applied to the material world: it is often structured like a text and communicates (see, among others, Hodder 1989 and Tilley 1990b for archaeology). But again this may be ascribed to an intermediary – 'society' making its classifications. There again some have argued for the death of the author (after Barthes 1986 and Foucault 1986b), that issues of linguistic and textual communication are not simply about an expressive agent or subject expressing. The easy integrity of the person and the self have been questioned in an historical and philosophical decentring of the subject. A monstrous elision of people and things is a continuation of the contemporary project of inscribing text on bodies and things, constituting agents in discourses (from Lévi-Strauss through Foucault and beyond; the focus on agency and the social theory of those such as Giddens).

Consider also representative democracy. Who is speaking when a Member of Parliament speaks in the House of Commons in London, a Congressman in the House of Representatives in Washington? Is it the member or their constituency? It is impossible to tell apart those who speak directly or indirectly, unless we start to argue about the nature of representation (political and other). There is no simple answer to the issue of language, agent and object. Consider again the constitution of science discussed in the previous chapter. In a scientific experiment the object world responds to questions put and trials made upon it – the natural world 'speaks'. Is this to be denied? Solipsism is the result if it is denied. No, it cannot simply be argued that people speak and objects do not. The issues are far more subtle.

The world of objects is that of objectivity; not anything can be done with the object world: it has its own logic and rules (laws of nature) which impose limits on human manipulation. In this argument we are getting to the nub of the matter. Objects are considered to belong to another order. People and things are inscribed into a series of dualities, from which they cannot, and indeed must not, be extricated (so it is conventionally held).

Objects are written into an order separate from the social:

human world	object world
society	environment
history	nature
the social	the technical
humanities	natural sciences
mind	body

The former may be held to supplement the material world; the latter to do with materials, science, technics, the environment, objectivity and the inanimate.

There are perceived dangers in not upholding the dualisms. The alternative to keeping things and people apart is represented by the spectre of the cyborg. It is an epistemological threat too. If the object world is collapsed into the social world (via notions such as the symmetry of people and things in their common life-cycles) it might appear that objective standards of truth are lost and relativism results; if objects and their materiality are historical, objectivity (the quality an object possesses) would be contingent. This is feared because the object world is seen as providing constraints and limits on what can be said and done through its quality of objectivity which is held to be beyond the historical particularities of the social. Society is seen as weakness, objectivity as strength. With no constraints there would seem to be idealism and all its dangers. Ethics and politics gets mixed up with circuit boards and robotics.

It is because of these dualisms that most archaeology and heritage cannot cope with the evocations of decay and morbidity; they threaten abstract and timeless objectivity, the solid rock upon which fact and truth are supposed to be built. Life-cycle is instead ascribed to the technical and the natural; decay is a problem and to do with preservative chemicals. Archaeology cannot have objects which are somehow on a par with people otherwise the dualisms threaten to dissolve. The past has to be killed off. This is the guilt at the heart of archaeology: in excavation archaeologists destroy that which they think they cherish.

We are arguing that the archaeological experience of ruin and decay reveals something vital about social reality, but something which is usually disavowed. Decay and ruin reveal the symmetry of people and things. They dissolve the absolute distinction between people and the object world. This is why we can so cherish the ruined and fragmented past.

What follows if it is accepted in this way that artefacts and people are similar, both having a material and historical nature which is expressed in the concept of life-cycle? People and the realm of the social become material, and the object world, nature, acquires a history (of different relations with people). So there is nothing purely social or technical, human or non-human. There has not been a 'pure' human social relation for perhaps over two million years, since artefacts came to regularly accompany hominids. If a pure social relationship is sought, reference should be made to primate society (Strum and Latour 1987; Byrne and Whiten 1988). So where are we now? We are inextricably mixed up with non-humans. Our histories are united. This is also to argue that society is not *sui generis*, but has to be materially constructed. It means that humans have always been part machines (Mumford 1966 to Law 1991). And if you do not like being part machine what are you going to do? Become a baboon? (cf. Deleuze and Guattari 1988.)

If objects and people are to be held in symmetry, what then is an artefact?

Consider again the perfume jar in Figure 5. What is it? It is a pot – a ceramic vessel of a particular kind. Does this answer mean that materially its object quality is that of the ceramic, while the rest – its social meanings, aesthetic qualities, all that we discussed above – are supplemental? If this separation of pot from 'context' is upheld, invoked are those dualisms, introduced above, of the social and technical, object and person. To identify this artefact as a 'pot' does not explain the particular life and historicity of this artefact – its movement through production, exchange, consumption, deposition, decay and discovery, reconsumption in the nineteenth-century museum and twentieth-century text. Are all of these contingent to its nature, its objectivity? If so, how did it come into being, then and here and now? How is it here now, as a picture in this book? Is this irrelevant to its reality? The very category of ceramic ('it is a pot') is a changing and historical one. For example, and in the context of this section on the temporality of an object, the attribution of this artefact to an objective category such as pot does not explain the origin (the genealogy) of the category 'pot'. The simple answer does not allow for difference: the ceramic substratum of 'pot' is here an essential quality, abstract and general. Although it is quite legitimate to unite things through qualities of sameness it is vital to consider also difference and variability, both within the category, and applied to the uniting category itself.

We have shown in a small way how the perfume jar ties people and things together in its life-cycle (raw material – design – production – distribution – consumption – discard – discovery, etc.). What did it unite? This particular artefact brings together clay and potter, painter and new brushes (for miniature work), a new interest in figurative work, the interests of patron perhaps and trader, heterogeneous elements in its figured designs (animals, warriors, monsters, violence, flowers, special artefacts), perfume (it is a perfume jar), oil (perfumed), the body (illustrated and anointed), travel away from Korinth (its place of making), ships, sanctuary of divinity, colonist, corpse and cemetery (pots such as this were given to divinities and the dead) (Johansen 1923; Payne 1931, 1933 and many works after; the pot is fully discussed in Shanks 1992b, 1995c and 1999). The perfume jar helped constitute the nineteenth-century art museum (albeit in a small way). This pot has been mobilised many times in defining the discipline of classical archaeology (see the biblio-graphical listings of Amyx 1988: 23 and Benson 1989: 44). And this life-cycle can be extended to include ourselves and readers – the pot unites us here even now, mobilised as it has been by us in this project of ours.

In its life-cycle the pot brings together all this, including aspirations, futures, distances, feelings, hopes as well as objects, people and social relationships. This is a network of heterogeneous actors. And in this network or assemblage, the pot gathers through people's interests and projects.

In this cultural assemblage we are dealing with what Theodor Adorno would have called the 'non-identity' of an object. Let us explain. Identity may be asserted with a statement such as 'this is a pot'. And/or the dimensions of association and affiliation may be followed through a life-cycle as we move from this to this through this and that connection, in an assemblage. Following these connections may involve holding back on deciding what the artefact is – its 'identity' is suspended. Regarding classification and identity, the self-contained identity of an artefact may be defined according to attributes – 'this is a pot with these attributes'. The discovery of identity may equally be made by following an agglomerative and synthetic articulation that is the artefact's life-cycle – following the artefact as it assembles heterogeneous actors (people, things, feelings, interests . . .).

We are here proposing a conception of the artefact as a multiplicity, an historical and hetero-geneous assemblage. Abstract identity (ceramic/pot) is bracketed as we follow the artefact in its life.

An artefact, as is accepted, is a multitude of data points, an infinity of possible attributes and measurements. Which ones are made and held to constitute its identity depends conventionally upon method and the questions being asked by the archaeologist. But we also hold that the arte-fact is *itself* a multiplicity. Its identity is multiple. It is not just one thing. The artefact does not only possess a multitude of data attributes, but is also itself multiplicity. We come to an object in rela-tionships with it, through using, perceiving it, referring to it, talking of it, feeling it *as* something.

This *as* is vital. It is a relationship of analogy – *as if* it were something. And it is always ironically something else – our references to the object are always metaphorical. That artefact in Figure 5 is not the word/label/category 'pot', though we can legitimately treat it as if it were, given certain interests and goals – projects. And these projects, interests and goals are culturally and socially constructed and meaningful. There are an infinity of possible relationships with an object and these literally make it what it is for us. The relationships are not abstract or given, but social and historical. So the materiality of an object has a history. This pot found by an archaeologist is not what it was.

We are back to time and ruin. Skara Brae in the Orkneys is an archaeological site, a prehistoric settlement in the sand dunes. An ancient place. It is the reality of the past, at least what is left of it. What does this statement mean? We are arguing that a site such as this does not belong to a singular date back then, and that its objective being has a history. Things have a history which is often tied to that of people. This means that Gordon Childe, who excavated Skara Brae with a team of archaeologists, is part of the (multiple) existence of Skara Brae. Just as Skara Brae is part of the biography of Gordon Childe, so too Gordon Childe is part of the life-cycle or biography of Skara Brae. Gordon Childe 'happened' to Skara Brae. We find ourselves in our relations with things, just as they come to be in their historical and cultural relations with us.

How could Skara Brae be conceived before the storm which blew away the sand and revealed the site to archaeologists and led to the excavation directed by Gordon Childe? Are we to apply his work retrospectively and suppose that Skara Brae was there all along, even without Childe, his workers, the British archaeological establishment, the funding agencies, the hard realities of archaeological work? Are we to project the present into the past, arguing that we know it here now and it must have been this way in the past? Isn't that what ideological archaeologies do? Nazi archaeologists find their political realities in the past, projecting back from the present and claiming that Aryan supremacy can be traced in the archaeological record.

Of course you may believe that Skara Brae was there all along, projecting back. But really it is of no necessary concern. And how would you prove it? Is there a time machine which would allow an archaeological team to excavate Skara Brae in the fourteenth century to check that it was there then? Is it not better to accept the gaps and lacunae in these life histories? To accept that the object world comes to be in our relationships with it? Gordon Childe and everything he brought with him is part of the historical reality of Skara Brae.

What is in this pot Figure 5? Well, probably not an aryballos; a perfume jar! So rather than saying that this illustrated object is a pot, we might also acknowledge that this object *becomes* a pot (and many other things), and these are due to our productive relationship with it. Of course, this does not mean that we can say it is an axehead, but we can make of it many things, depending on interest and purpose. We might explain its painted designs in terms of a history of animal art, or we might relate the form of the figures to ideological conceptions of the body, or we might imagine and investigate the haptics of miniature jars and perfumery. In all cases this may mean making no reference to the object being a ceramic form. We simply work on its materiality in a craft that includes archaeology.

We can never capture raw materiality. Why should we? The object always withholds some-thing. We put a thin section of the ceramic beneath a polarising microscope and it becomes another world of colours and patterns which technical skills can interpret as mineral inclusions and effects of temperatures. And even specifying chemical and physical composition is understanding 'as' something else. Metaphor and analogy are essential, as particle physics with its strangely named entities and forces conspicuously shows. The vital role of metaphor and analogy, for example in innovation, is widely accepted in the philosophy of science (Black 1962; Hesse 1970).

All this is to open space. That pot can take us in many directions – we are invited to follow the artefact and the people it unites through their projects and interests. To attend to the artefact. This is a sensitivity to its historicity, its life and the way it gathers many sorts of things, people, feelings, aspirations. The assemblages respect no absolute distinctions between cultural categories such as things and people, values and materials, strategies and resources, architectures and dispositions. And in this archaeological cyborg world we will have to talk a great deal of 'might' and 'if', of slippage and fluidity, of mess and what is missing, of gaps and bridges between different worlds, of time breaking up, moments lost and regained. We will need our dramaturgical imagination.

Heterogeneity figured in the presentation of experiences of war in the archaic Greek world, *Tetsuo* and *Full Metal Jacket*. Our digression into material culture and the archaeological has led to a further exploration of notions of assemblage, gatherings around artefacts and our working upon worlds of multiplicity. We have associated concepts of artefact, cyborgs and assemblage with performance and dramaturgy. We now shift direction again, to consider the articulation of past and present in site-specific theatre. Assemblage here is of specific dramaturgical elements which obey no hierarchy of text, performer, stage, props and viewing audience. Fragments are energised in an explicit and located cultural politics of performance. Another immediate link is the event and conduct of war.

Gododdin: the past in the present

It begins with a fragment of poetry.

> *Gwyr a aeth Gatraeth gan wawr . . .*
>
> *Men went to Catraeth with the dawn,*
> *Their fears disturbed their peace,*
> *A hundred thousand fought three hundred*
> *Bloodily they stained spears,*
> *His was the bravest station in battle,*
> *Before the retinue of Mynyddog Mwynfawr.*
> (From *Y Gododdin*, Jarman 1988)

Y Gododdin is one of the earliest surviving examples of Welsh poetry, transcribed in the twelfth century but commemorating an event in the sixth: an elegy for slain heroes and a eulogy of their excellence and bravery as fighting men.

The land of the Gododdin (the Votadini of the Romans) lay around, and to the south of, Edinburgh in Scotland. Sometime towards the end of the sixth-century AD, a small warrior-band mounted one last, suicidal attack from that region against the Anglo-Saxons who were already consolidating their occupation of much of present-day England, in the period of upheaval, contest and reorientation that followed the collapse of the Roman world. Fuelled by heavy drinking, three hundred met one hundred thousand in battle near Catterick in North Yorkshire. Inevitably they were slaughtered almost to a man. One of the few survivors was the poet Aneirin himself. His hundred stanzas celebrate the heroic disaster: the Gododdin and their exploits are remembered in this one epic.

> Y Gododdin wears the aspect of a genuine relic of a long forgotten strife, a massive boulder left high on its rocky perch by an icy stream which has long since melted away.
>
> (Brith Gof: Gododdin programme notes)

The language of the court of the Gododdin chieftain Mynyddog Mwynfawr was a form of proto-Welsh known as Brythonic spoken at that time down the western seaboard of Britain: a shared ancestry meant that the Gododdin could call upon brethren from Wales to join their cause. Y Gododdin records the assembly of warriors, a year of riotous preparation and training and the final, fateful conflict. But there is no linear narrative here. Instead the sequence of events is revealed in a fragmentary manner, as the exploits of individual heroes and groups of fighters are lauded and extolled. Whilst tonally familiar, much of this remains elusive and obscure to the modern Welsh ear.

Performance as political theatre

The decision to make a performance based on Y Gododdin came at the conclusion of a long series of productions, collaborations and training schemes organised by Brith Gof and based upon the theatrical animation of Francisco Goya's eighty etchings The Disasters of War and their captions (see Goya 1967). Thirteen major pieces of work, staged from Norway to Hong Kong, were inspired by the same graphic source. Gododdin was to be the penultimate manifestation. But the impetus to create the performance came with the darkest days of 'Thatcherism', a time when Margaret Thatcher herself proclaimed society dead. We had long harboured a desire to work with Test Dept, a group of industrial percussionists – 'a skinhead gamelan' – with several Scots members, whose own spectacular performances and collaborations – with such unlikely partners as the South Wales Miners Choir – had marked them as amongst the few authentic voices of artistic dissent and opposition. But together we resisted the temptation to create a didactic and hectoring piece of agit-prop theatre. Neither did we want to make some 'period' dramatisation of Y Gododdin with the music as a kind of congruent backing for the events of the epic. Of course, the metaphorical implications of the poem were self-evident. But in deciding to create a large-scale work, at the limits of our ability to achieve it both technically and physically, we aimed to echo the folly of the Gododdin, the small struggling with the impossibly greater. We wanted to constitute political theatre as sophistication and complexity, elaborating dramatic material and detail in all available media simultaneously, to work with the friction between the sensibilities and procedures of theatre and rock music and with anachronism.

> Defeat is never to be cherished, but the glorious rendering of their account against an infinitely stronger enemy lessens the smugness of victory and lends dignity to the vanquished. Culture then and now becomes a tool for survival. History brought alive through the power of a performance, no matter how times have changed. Today the wealthy invade for personal and political gain. Yet after thirteen hundred years there is nothing marginal about the issues at stake. The right to self determination, the growth and celebration of native language, looking back further than thirty years of 'pop culture', making huge visions concrete and breathing life back into characters who, like so many, were destroyed when a race first began to flex their colonial muscles.
>
> (Brith Gof: *Gododdin*, Test Dept in programme notes)

Gododdin was conceived, constructed and initially presented – for three nights late in December 1998 – in the engine-shop of the enormous, disused Rover car factory in Cardiff, itself a potent symbol of economic decline and industrial decay. The production included fragments of the poem sung and spoken in Brythonic and English within the musical spectrum; a highly amplified instrumental soundtrack played live and on tape; dynamic physical action which made no attempt to tell the story of what is, after all, an elegy and a scenography which 'brought the outside inside', an arrangement of hundreds of tons of sand, dozens of trees and wrecked cars, and thousands of gallons of water, the latter of which gradually flooded the performing area during the performance. Dramatic material was generated and manipulated in each of the constituent media, as libretto, as musical composition, as choreography, as architecture.

The dramatic elements were written, composed and developed in relative isolation in order to reach their fullest, unmediated potential and only then combined at a date late in the rehearsal process. To function successfully this required two working principles: the establishment of an agreed dramatic structure, in the case of *Gododdin* a sequence of named, thematic sections – with consensual agreement about the nature, purpose and emotional tenor of each – and the institution of a time-base with fixed durations for each section. The schematic sequence included entry, prologue, heroics, berserking, arming, journey, battle, lament, epilogue.

Clifford McLucas's scenography resisted all temptation to provide an anecdotal or naturalistic setting for the literal exposition of the text. Instead his rigorously formal arrangement of scenic elements – trees, cars, sand – distributed on the architectural principles of line and circle throughout the hundred metres by forty metres space engaged the entire room (McLucas and Pearson 1996: 211–34). The design centred upon the old factory clock suspended somewhat off-centre towards the middle. Immediately below this a mountain of sand-covered oil-drums was constructed. Around the mountain a circle of sand thirty metres in diameter and three inches deep was laid out, kerbed with concrete blocks, its surface raked like a Japanese garden. Around the circle were four groups of two cars, all distressed with thin white paint and with working headlights. Across one diagonal of the room stretched two rows of pine trees tied to the roof trusses and creating an avenue for the entry of performers and spectators alike. A row of yellow and black banners each five feet square hung down one long side of the room. Two rows of facing cars demarcated an additional area for use during the 'battle' section.

The sand circle provided the main arena for the physical action, the spectators standing around its circumference. Twenty minutes into the performance, the circle began to flood with water from hoses from above, turning the sand over a period of time into a circular lake retained by the concrete kerb. At one side of the circle was a large stage for the musicians; opposite it were the lighting and sound control desks. The light sources included the car headlights, follow-spots and strip-lights removed from the building and rehung in a circle around the sand.

The design was thus a juxtaposition of that which was of the place – cars, neon, metal – and that which was brought to the place – trees, sand, water. As a total designed environment it was from time to time indifferent to, and in conflict with, not only its host site but also with the activities pursued within it. The spectators were free to move throughout the space; during the battle section the performers burst out of the circle.

The soundtrack was constituted as a musical composition. First, a tape – which was to play throughout the performance – was recorded, providing a continuous undertow of rhythmic pulses and patterns, signalling timings for sections and cueing changes. Again the analogy of the practices of a sound-recording studio is useful: against this basic track, all the live instrumental and vocal elements were placed, elaborated, articulated and layered. For each section of dramatic development a fragment of text from *Y Gododdin* was chosen; other elements were developed through improvisation and trial-and-error. Test Dept's drumming provided the dynamic impetus to the performance, each section having a different rhythmic and tonal quality. Their drums, of wood and metal, included both orchestral instruments and 'found objects', from timpani to huge aluminium thunder sheets, from home-made marimbas to large metal tanks struck by swinging logs. Instrumental textures were then added on trumpet, cornetto, cello, bagpipes and animal horns and these were occasionally modified by electronic effects. All instruments were highly amplified. The use of contact microphones meant that on-stage samplers could be triggered by the actions of the physical performers themselves. For instance, by striking their own shields the warriors could create the sounds of battle, such as the screaming of terrified horses. This gave the sound engineers key responsibility for creating the complex sonic effects of the performance and for ensuring its dramatic coherence. All of the textual elements were sung and spoken as an amplified libretto. Finally only twenty-five stanzas were chosen, as much for musical qualities as for their meaning. Lis Hughes Jones sang in Welsh, her voice singular and haunting against the relentless percussion. Conventionally the use of amplification means that voices issue from the same locations. However, through the judicious placement of amplification speaker units, a sonic architecture was built within which particular voices could be placed, moved and panned, with text moving over, through and around the spectators.

The soundtrack now bore the principal responsibility for providing the dramatic shape and continuum of the performance: each section had a distinct musical atmosphere. Significantly, the physical performers had to accept that they could never compete with the volume of the music, their acoustic voices lost and despairing, their actions puny and pitiful. And that they could never hope to animate the entire scenography: they were figures in a landscape. They became one element in a locale where there were other things to see – active environment, musicians, other spectators – and to hear. The physical action then, freed from its role of being solely responsible for the exposition of the narrative, became schematic and non-illustrative. It was conceived as a series of group movements; as the manipulation of a limited repertoire of objects – oil drums, long wooden poles, banners – and semi-fixed scenographic elements such as cars and rope nets; and as a series of tasks, as a set of rule-based engagements and confrontations with the constructed environment. But there was no enemy. If there was an opponent it was the scenario, the tasks to be completed, with exhaustion as the ultimate failure. Or the scenography as the performers fought with the increasingly difficult environmental conditions, mirroring the frenetic energy of the hapless struggle of the Gododdin themselves. This became the more poignant as there were only six physical performers – two women, four men – lost in the cold, wet enormity of the theatrical concept. All were dressed in kilts, ubiquitous Dr Marten boots, jackets and shawls which could be transformed into banners: wrecking vehicles, using car bonnets as shields.

> Theatre in free space, reacting to (and conditioned by) the surrounding architecture
> . . . performers working at the very edge of their ability and stamina.
>
> (Brith Gof: *Gododdin* programme notes)

The articulation of the physical action was mediated by the environmental conditions, composed as much as a series of strategies and tactics for coping with difficulty as a complex choreography. It was as much rock concert or architectural installation as theatrical performance, as much political event as artistic endeavour. As such it prefigured the rave, that rush to the communal, to being part of the mass, to that subsuming of one's identity rather than dressing up to be seen as a member of a stylistic sub-culture, in reaction to the prevailing notion that the only safe place is a home. Here it's unclear who are the performers, who the spectators, as in a conventional rock concert. Following this model, performance may once again have to think of the 'we' rather than 'us' and 'them': the crowd may once more become exciting, dangerous and unstable. And this theme began to assert itself in subsequent Brith Gof productions.

In *Camlann* (1993), an examination of happenings in former-Yugoslavia through the myths surrounding the death of Arthur, with Arthur equating to Tito, the spectators were divided into Welsh-speakers and English-speakers, each group following different performers in different areas of the warehouse and only gradually coming together (Pavis 1996: 174–6). Each language was constantly heard over, through and in conflict with the other. In the open performance area of *Arturius Rex* (1994), there were no formal divisions between performers and spectators. Welsh and English were spoken at the same time, the spectator free to find and follow the voice of his choice.

Prydain: The Impossibility of Britishness (1996) was part-building site, part-performance, part-concert – a hybrid of action, music, architecture and audience participation – for five performers, ten technicians, two music groups – with a live soundtrack by Slovene composer Robert Merdzo and the 'techno/jungle' sounds of Welsh band Reu-vival. There were fifty spectator/participants and one hundred and fifty spectators. And some fragments of text by William Blake and Iolo Morganwg spoken, shouted and scrawled on walls, floors, furniture and inscribed on the naked bodies of the performers. Both Welsh and English were again present but – to match the theme of revolution – half-heard, over-heard, heard in fragments. Here the spectator had to negotiate her presence, moment by moment, deciding whether to participate. 'Who do I listen to?' 'What language is being spoken here?' Standing, moving, running with, running away. To decide where to stand, to work out what her *stance* was.

The main artistic conceit was that the whole show arrived on the back of lorries and was built during the performance, in an ad-hoc way, performance as field. Stage-managers, directors, performers worked to devise the theatrical effects as they occurred. So the performance was always in motion, being built and falling to pieces in and around the participants. It utilised small generators, megaphones, battery amplifiers, industrial lighting and a repertoire of utilitarian materials: scaffolding, plastic sheeting. A theatre in the making, a work of invention with nothing to watch and everything to do. Within this maelstrom of activity, the fifty participants were invited, urged, to take part, to be choreo-graphed. And this necessitated choices, commitments, courage ... the primal scene. Of this work there are few photographs. But then what could you photograph here, would you want to photograph here, from what standpoint and why?

Gododdin was subsequently restaged in a sand quarry in Italy, in a disused crane factory in Germany, in an empty ice-rink in Friesland and in Tramway in Glasgow. On tour, all of the production elements were regarded as kit of parts, a repertoire of

0.5   S.5   B.5   M.5

scenographic elements and performance sequences, to be reworked, reconceived, relocated for each separate architecture, according to the specifics of the location and the material means of the producer. All of the information necessary for a local construction team to create a given performance was enclosed in a strategic workbook: lists of materials, technical procedures, constructional timetables, line drawings of objects, diagrams, plans, sections . . .

In Polverigi, Italy, the open-air location allowed the use of motorised drum platforms during the battle section, high-pressure water hoses to repel the warriors, fire and naked flames, including a blazing log-slide which descended from the lip of the quarry to strike a large cement hopper. The topography of the site, where mounds of soil had been left to support electricity pylons which traversed the hillside, provided cliffs for scaling and an open arena within which to locate the various sequences, the spectators shifting from locale to locale. Two days before the premiere, heavy storms created a substantial lake in one area. Rather than altering the choreography to accommodate this, the battle ensued on, in and through it. The lament occurred in an area of thick mud, in the rain provided by upturned water hoses. All services such as electricity had to be brought to the site enabling the juxtaposition of fire and strip-lighting, the lighting tubes arranged vertically against one side of the quarry.

In Hamburg, Germany, a tower-crane placed at the centre of the circle allowed a wooden boat to be hoisted into the arena during the lament, circling and floating eerily a few centimetres above the water. In the restricted space of a site which usually functioned as a garden, the branches and foliage of trees and bushes were bound up tightly in muslin to protect the plants and to improve sight-lines. Metal mesh allowed the performers to climb high above the spectators, their bodies again beaten by water jets. Whilst the popular reaction to the performance was enthusiastic, some critics assumed that the presence of drums, boots, fire and naked torsos indicated fascist affiliations. It was with such ambiguity and reappropriation of iconography that groups such as Test Dept and Laibach from Slovenia toyed in the late 1980s.

In the empty ice-rink in Leeuwarden in the Netherlands it was decided to flood the whole space. This was, after all, a building designed to deal with water. Thus, as the performance progressed, the spectators became isolated in groups on islands created from

A.5   E.5   R.5

eight thousand sand-bags, a scene reminiscent of the flat Friesian landscape where communities stand on man-made mounds or *terps*. Here Gododdin was presented to another linguistic minority and as one newspaper commented 'Everyone was there'. Four local artists created a wooden war-wagon in the shape of a swan with a nodding head: huge milk containers were used as drums, such is the nature of scrap-metal in Friesland, necessitating the use of large, extremely soft drumsticks and mallets which created a deep, muffled ring.

In Glasgow, Scotland, the tracks in the floor of the old tram depot enabled the use of mobile spotlights mounted on boogies but the restriction of size meant that a stage for the musicians had to be cantilevered out, halfway up one wall. A ramp made of corrugated iron, for the warriors to attempt to ascend, was lowered only late in the performance. It was here that *Gododdin* revealed itself not only as a political act but as the earliest Scottish epic too: as the run of performances progressed the physical performers found themselves accompanied by kilted spectators eager to participate.

Performance: against theatre

Since the classical Greek period, theatre has been regarded as an institution in which a society reaffirms and articulates its common identity, turning its history into a story for the audience to include in its common memory. This representation is achieved spatially, and arrangement of performance and spectators is the result of and medium for concrete social practices. This is a place where a community is supplied with a socially acceptable and valid representation of its world, a spatial machinery of identity. The evolution of theatrical space has witnessed its gradual division into two distinct places built around the principle of separating the 'see' from the 'being seen', stage and auditorium, limiting perception to the stage alone and the increasing formalisation of this fundamental structure. The basic paradigmatic design for theatre is thus a box-shaped stage and a raked auditorium, the separation stressed by light on stage and darkness in auditorium, reinforced with the coming of electricity (See Roms 1993). The existence of the stage has allowed the elaboration of private places and restricted places, off-stage, places of preparation and storage and the development of scenic effects and machinery hidden from audience. In the nineteenth century, theatrical space becomes increasingly fixed and theatre serves as a verbal depiction of inner worlds and psychological spaces. So modern auditoria are **sociofugal**, throwing spectators apart, limiting their eye contact, discouraging social interaction with implications for the practice, function and meaning of theatre. Space becomes a static object whose structure is regarded as unchanging, representation as fixed, imagination as given, criticisms controllable. The role of the spectator in signification is denied.

Recurrent challenges to this model and development of aesthetic and political alternatives have taken two basic forms, both of which confront the concept of space as static and imagine a new role for the spectator. Within the auditorium, directors such as Robert Wilson have deconstructed the stage picture, suggesting for instance that we are glimpsing only one part of a much larger picture which continues beyond the frame of the proscenium (see Fairbrother 1991). In Brith Gof's *Patagonia* the whole auditorium was regarded as a **found** site within which another architecture, an acoustic architecture, was created. So the sophisticated 'miking' and amplification of 'on-stage' voices allowed the distribution, movement and stratification of voices throughout the auditorium, removing from the performers the need to project their voices, employing instead intimate modes and tones of address, with visual and aural expression sliding out of synchronicity (see Pearson 1996a).

Others have left the auditorium altogether. *Gododdin* is a political imperative. With few endemic dramatic forms, with no mainstream tradition defining what theatre should and ought to look like, with no National Theatre prescribing an orthodoxy of theatrical convention, with no great wealth of playwriting, no extensive circuit of auditoria, then theatre in Wales still has options. It need not aspire to the normative practices of its majority neighbour: the exposition of dramatic literature in English playhouses. It can fold together action, text, music, scenography, place and public into performance forms and manifestations with no parallel in England. It has the chance to address different subject-matters, using different means, in spaces other than the hushed and darkened halls of theatre spaces, to create a counter-discourse. Yet in its forms, preoccupations, themes, function and placement, Welsh theatre may be distinct, but it need not be authentic. As much as the country itself, it is a work of imagination and invention (see Williams 1985). For the fractured, problematic nature of Welsh society and the endless tension between conservatism and innovation may lead to the creation of performance **hybrids**, as unafraid to **abrogate**, **appropriate** and **mimic** (see Bhabha 1994) alien techniques and foreign aesthetics as they are to revisit and deconstruct traditional cultural motifs. Here dramaturgical assemblage unites with a very particular cultural project – located.

The lack of theatrical tradition doesn't mean that we commence empty-handed. Wales does have a sophisticated repertoire of musical, poetic and oratorical forms and techniques, enshrined in the cultural competitions of the *eisteddfod*, in the choral singing and preaching practices of the chapel and in the bombast of a fiery political culture: Welsh practitioners are used to performing, but on platforms and in contexts other than the auditorium. And these are highly instructive for new approaches to performance not only in informing the expressive techniques of performers, but also in suggesting alternative types of material – poetry, song, speech – and their sequencing. Welsh performance may include performers who sing as often as they speak, particularly in moments of deep emotion, without the work ever becoming a musical or opera, and who speak with the voice of the preacher, the politician and the auctioneer. It can employ the verbal and vocal traditions of poetic recitation, of wordless religious ecstasy and four-part harmony. It can substitute rhetoric and soliloquy for dialogue, declamation for discursive reason. And as Wales has only a limited range of auditoria, performance has naturally sought other locations, places in which Welsh audiences might feel more at ease than in the serried rows of the auditorium. Welsh performance can substitute real tasks or patterns of work for stage illusion and gesture, tasks which utilise the processes and rhythms of work, play and worship: recontextualised, mutated, re-energised. It can concern itself with the actions of nameless characters who look as much like rugby players as actors, who behave as much cultural activists as fictional characters. Often, Welsh performers are already politicised, beyond the subject-matter of the performance, in the degree of their engagement. Identities may actually be at stake here. Performance may exist for the performer over and above motivation, character, blocking . . .

It can draw themes and subjects from the common currency of myth and religion; from a rich literary tradition; from a political history of bureaucratic and state intervention; from the effects of industrial and economic decay, of emigration and immigration and from a love of language and landscape. Whilst applying the most recent of technologies, it can address the oldest of anxieties. It returns recurrently not only to the Bible, to ancient lyrics and to mythical stories but also to specific instances of injustice, repression and resistance. For, in a traditional society, history may be experienced, or characterised, as a series of crucial, **inciting incidents** around which opinion accumulates and which resonate in the present: history conflates. Thus the flooding of the Welsh village of Tryweryn to make a reservoir for the English city of Liverpool in the early 1960s is still a potent metaphor for heavy-handed colonialism. Theatre in a minority culture can thus assume a certain level of knowledge and approbation in its audience, which is finite in number and already 'in on something'. With the existence of such a collective consciousness, knowledge or memory, theatrical interpretation can be audacious, detailed and diverse. And it can anticipate more acute levels of criticism! This does not mean that the tacit affirmation, by a Welsh audience, of entrenched stances such as passive resistance to bureaucracy, civil disobedience and anti-Englishness, or of such familiar notions as *hiraeth* – the love of native land – should go unconsidered. Welsh performance can also resemble the political meeting or the *noson lawen*, a rural entertainment of songs and sketches. It can employ the conventions of the chapel service and the barn dance as its performance structures. It need not even be *in parenthesis*, signified as distinct mode of expression: performance can be as much an actual memorial service as a fictional story. This is the particular social and political context within which *Gododdin* was created.

Site-specific work and the material past

Theatre auditoria are sites of continuous occupation: the material traces of previous performances may still exist. There are traditions of usage and the memory of previous performances will certainly provide perceptual orientations for the spectators. But to understand the processes by which different performers are simultaneously manifesting different imaginary landscapes onto a fixed topography we may need to look at notions such as Jameson's '**cognitive mapping**' (Jameson 1991: 409).

The continuous use and reuse of locations bestows meaning upon them, affecting the way in which they are experienced. This is only partly to do with the configuration of the space, and partly to do with what one brings to the place: an attunement, an awareness of the place's historicity. The place is 'read' and thereby interpreted in the same way as the performance. Indeed, the reading of the place is a part of the setting of performance, as much for the performer as for the watcher. By a mirror-play, each site gathers its surroundings, in association and connotation. Places are reworked by playing upon and transforming past associations and meanings.

(Thomas 1994: 143)

Gododdin was created at the time when the term '**site-specific**' was first applied to performance. At site, no such traditions of theatrical usage exist. However, the traces of other usages are apparent occasioning a creative friction between the past and the present and drawing attention to the temporality of place. And within such places, free from conventions of dramatic exposition, performance may be constituted as a locale of cultural intervention, as a temporary autonomous zone, as both **heterotopia** and **utopia**.

Site may be directly suggestive of performance subject-matter, theme or form. Its usage, or former usage, may directly inform dramatic structure, the hand-in-glove congruence of performance about war-wounded in a hospital or constituted as a religious service in a chapel or as a political meeting in a council chamber. Performance, in turn, may reveal, make manifest, celebrate, confront or criticise site or location, and its history, function, architecture, micro-climate . . . Conversely, site may facilitate the creation of a purposeful paradox, through the employment of orders of material seemingly unusual, inappropriate or perverse at this site, site serving to recontextualise the material, relocating it and suggesting environment, equipment and working processes which might mediate and illuminate it.

At site, architecture and everyday usage may suggest a dispersal of activity and modes of performance. There may be an existing institutional arrangement of watchers and watched which can be annexed: the formal organisation of pulpit and congregation in a chapel or beds and visitors in a hospital. However, site-specific performance may allow the construction of a new architecture, imposing another arrangement, floor-plan, map or orientation which confounds everyday hierarchies of place and patterns of movements.

We might envisage performance which refuses the panoptic view, which is aware of what it brings to site, which makes no attempt to re-enact the million, million occurrences which have happened there, which is aware of its nature as a contemporary act, as the latest occupation of a place where previous occupations are still apparent and cognitively active, the friction of what is *of* the place and what is brought *to* the place. Composed as a number of different, overlaid and interpenetrating orders of material, fictions or conceptual frameworks – some temporal, some spatial, some thematic, some textual – performance in heritage contexts can conflate the documentary and the fictive within a given location or architecture, covering the full range of Tschumi's programmatic proposals without laying claim to historical accuracy or authenticity. No single story need be told here. Indeed the frameworks may be so different in nature that their juxtaposition recurrently creates new and unexpected meaning. The work can be ambiguous and provocative, exciting and engaging whilst revealing and complementing the auras of the place. Here is a fusion of the creative and the analytical, the past and the present, and the animation of individuals within a variety of dramatic structures which can evoke a richness and density of meanings, trapped neither in one period nor in the mannerisms of costume drama.

They are enigmatic, inasmuch as any one viewer may pay more or less attention to any one event in such a multi-focus field of material. For the viewer, they are inherently non-hierarchical - any of the work's components may, at any one time, provide the 'centre' or 'datum' around which other materials are working, but the responsibility for fulfilling this role is not carried by any one prime component (as, for instance, does the script in a piece of orthodox, narrative theatre).

(McLucas in McLucas and Pearson 1996)

Visiting the past: stories of heritage and authenticity

Gododdin re-enacted past in present and in a future-oriented project of performance against theatre. This chapter began with a section on sovereignty which juxtaposed diverse elements to generate interpenetrating and multifocus frictions. We have dealt with notions of artefact and site, and, throughout this chapter, with a fusion of the creative and the analytical. We move to another set of locales where past and present percolate – museums, heritage sites and interpretive centres.

By the village of Saint Fagan's near Cardiff is Amgueddfa Werin Cymru, the National Folk Museum of Wales. The wooded valley is setting for cottages, farmhouses, rural industrial buildings, a methodist chapel. The buildings have been brought from all over Wales and rebuilt here. Guidebooks give information about the different buildings: timber construction or the arrangement of accommodation for animals and people together in a long house. Uniformed museum officials are at hand to answer questions. But wandering around the exhibited structures is less about information than it is an evocation of pre-modern, pre-industrialised times. Fragmented – a collage of spare puritan methodism, dark smoky interiors, warm glow of blacksmith's fire, rural labour. No particular dates, simply pre-modern. You may buy traditional stone-ground flour and bread, taste organic farm cheeses. Schoolchildren visit, dress up, sit on old school benches and listen to teacher forbid them to speak in Welsh.

At one edge of the museum is a more recent addition. A 'Celtic' farm has been constructed – round houses in a small palisaded enclosure. The draughty walls and puddles on the earth floors do not make for congenial interiors. But a primary focus in the other buildings at Saint Fagan's is the homely interior. Period detail; contemporary consumers are sensitive to style and design. The bedspreads and furniture in Llainfadyn cottage; country kitchen of the Abernodwydd farmhouse from Powys. Period style. Perhaps we would all wish for such a country cottage.

The round farmhouses are called 'Celtic': here are connotations of those who are indigenous, belonging before Roman invaders. This is the Welsh National *Folk* Museum. The Museum's theme is the folk, a term which raises images of folk costume, ideas of national identity, belonging and attachment to the countryside, land, the soil. It may be somewhat quaint too: folk-tales and fairies; cauls and love-spoons. Hitler's *Volk* was more than a little different.

The institution and discourse of the museum supply an authenticity – this is all accredited by an academic and authorised body. Money and resources have been invested by the state. The transported buildings were carefully chosen because of their value to history, to *Welsh* history, to the history of the Welsh *people*, the lowly folk rather than great public figures. The museum curates, takes care of the material history in its keeping. There is no trace of ruin (the litter of some rusting farm machinery, yet to be attended to, is hidden behind bushes). The past is here pristine.

Complaint may be made that this is a very particular authentic Welshness which is being presented. What of the major nineteenth- and twentieth-century experiences of the South Wales valleys – coal mining and steel production? There is a row of industrial workers' cottages, but again the vehicle to understanding is domestic interior. Saint Fagan's is reminiscent of John Ford's film *How Green Was My Valley* (1941) – Welsh miners' singing community, wandering down the hill from the colliery pit head, mams at doors with roast dinners waiting. Staged romanticism.

The comparison with Hollywood, and indeed the costume dramas produced by British TV companies and marketed worldwide (numerous novels by Jane Austen, Dickens, Trollope), is not an arbitrary one. Outdoor museums such as Amgueddfa Werin Cymru invite comparison with heritage centres and theme parks. The lack of heavy and detailed interpretive presence offering information and historical, chronological and social context could bring the criticism that visits verge on the historically incoherent, being more to do with spectacle and entertainment than the 'real' past.

Authenticity and the romantic fallacy of the 'real' past

But what is the real past now? What does an authentic past look like? Is this visit to St Fagan's an experience of an authentic past? The issue of authenticity is one at the heart of our project of theatre/archaeology.

Outside of Paris and east along the Marne is to be found Disneyland Europe, or Eurodisney as it was first called. There you can fly in a gondola through a window in a London terraced house, out with Peter Pan into the night sky and over to Never-never Land. On an underground boat trip swashbuckling model pirates sack a town of oldendays; a stuffed goat bleats as the runaway goldrush mining train careers out of control; ancient holographic ghosts feast in Norman Bates's house from Hitchcock's *Psycho*.

It is a strange experience, out of time and place, for where and when is this all supposed to be? Much of Disneyland Europe makes reference to time and temporalities – lost and better pasts, nostalgias, storyland historical romances, progress and technological futures. Heritage generally, taking it as legitimate to write of a unity 'heritage', references time and the past. The archaeological, that is, the material past, is being used more than ever. And a major complaint against heritage is that it involves an ignoral or distortion of the 'real' past; heritage contaminates. A typical response of an archaeologist may be to check the references to the past that are made in the cultural work of heritage, proposing instead a 'better', more real or authentic account, less contaminated by spectacle and the present, more in line with the discipline of archaeology.

Authenticity? The country cottages of the Welsh National Folk Museum are as authentic as they can be; they are the real thing. You might expect Disneyland to be cheap and shallow – it is not. The old disused mine is carefully staged with all sorts of 'genuine' artefacts and equipment brought from industrial workings in the United States; in this it fascinates and is not easily dismissed as superficial. In 'Toad Hall', which is presented as an English pub (without the beer), are served fish and chips. Cliché perhaps, but the designers have, in detail and ambience, excelled in producing a non-pub which is far more 'authentic' than many English pubs we know.

So what is the difference between Amgeuddfa Werin Cymru, other sites aiming at historical and archaeological respectability, and places such as Disneyland?

Archaeologists gather objects and nominate sites. Archaeologists interested in the past do not want fakes. They select those to be studied on the basis, ultimately, of age and authenticity, originality. But authenticity is not an intrinsic property or essential quality. What would be an essential quality of 'authenticity'? Truth to self? If so then the hope for a quality such as authenticity involves abstract definitions of self (object self) and truth, on the basis of which the inessential and contaminating may be excluded. This is all very philosophical and difficult. Alternatively, and more usually, the archaeologist prefers to guarantee authenticity through context and association – where the object comes from, the traces remaining of the object's 'present', the artefacts and features of a site remaining from a time past. Although the traces of the past are now part of our present, authenticity and the value of a genuine artefact to (archaeological) knowledge depend upon it being *removed* from the present. If you mix up old artefacts and spectacle, entertainment, interests of the present, then that old artefact is supposed to be of less use to proper archaeological concerns such as producing knowledge of the past.

It may be argued that a proper and respectable mixing of authenticity and entertainment is that for purposes of education. The designers of Jorvik Viking Centre in York, England were some of the first to learn a great deal from Disney's 'imagineers', and produced an entertaining trip in a time car to a reanimated Viking settlement and through to an archaeological excavation frozen in time (Wishart 1984). But, arguably, Jorvik is considered more respectable than Disney. Why? Because the spectacle sticks to the facts of the past and is educational? Or because the profits go back into archaeology?

We have made reference to value and use. What use is an entertaining experience to archaeology? What is value in this context? Value may be exchange value, what something means to someone else, the value of something for an other. Or it may be use value, the relevance of an object to a purpose or interest. Use value refers to the object as a tool. Tools are fitted to some purposes, and are useless for others. Use value is the relevance of an object to a purpose or interest. Archaeologists, in their professional work, exercise choice in selecting and gathering artefacts (and experiences) according to archaeological purpose or use. It is important to note that both forms of value include acts of *choice* on the part of agencies beyond the object itself. In this way authenticity and value are about *desire*.

To think of authenticity as essential and intrinsic obscures the relation of exchange which exists between past and present. It is to forget that the object's value is decided in moving from past to present through the work of desire. Archaeologists, or Disney imagineers, *want* what they find and use. What is found is not naturally 'authentic'; its 'original' context is not natural. For what is natural about the comminglings of the cultural garbage heap, of the abandoned home? Only perhaps the entropy, decay and rot. There is no archaeological 'record', just a ruined mess. What is found *becomes* authentic and valuable because it is set by choice in a new and separate environment with its own order, purpose and its own temporality – the time co-ordinates of the discipline archaeology which give the object its date and context. This is a moral setting, when authenticity is considered good, as opposed to deceitful fakery.

The systems of value according to which archaeologists gather and order their 'finds' are not natural then, but tactical and strategic. This is *not* to write arbitrary. But the archaeologist's choice is *no more or less meaningful* than the choices and juxtapositions of Disney imagineers. To recognise choices made makes archaeology and Disney comparable and commensurable. No longer are there archaeologists on one side virtuously holding on to the past while on the other Disney corporation adulterates for contemporary interests of profit and perhaps the American way of life. In this latter case there is no reasonable choice to make between the experiences of Disneyland and the archaeological profession, and we can only suppose that all those people who visit Eurodisney are stupid, conned or uninterested in the past. But with this view of authenticity as a mediation and relationship of past and present, we can see that both archaeology and Disney are mobilising heterogeneous assemblages of artefacts, reason, ingenuity, experiences, knowledges, interests, purposes.

Disney's choice of things is made according to criteria that are very different from those of archaeology. Heritage, more generally, is not about the attractive presentation of a past as it is understood by archaeology. The power of heritage, its seduction, is that it is about signification – things' meaning for what we are now. Heritage is a symbolic exchange like sacrifice, wherein a victim is given in exchange for a favour from an other – this for that. Heritage is a sacrifice of the past for the present. But this does not mean that the past is necessarily of no importance. In fact the opposite is true of sacrifice; it is vital that the victim is appropriate and correct for its purpose. It must be scrutinised thoroughly to achieve the power of sacrifice which is communion with an other. What is this other? It depends upon the heritage site, but it is, *ex hypothesi*, to do with things and qualities which are **desired**.

The symbolic exchange of heritage is about sacrifice and consumption (of the past) rather than accumulation and the hoarding of new knowledge. In this heritage logic the meaning of the past does not lie in the dusty cellars of a museum. The meaning is what the past can do for the present. Nor does consumption mean that the past is necessarily served up for a consumer society, suitably trimmed and cooked. Consumption (potentially) means that it is taken within the self.

The Welsh National Folk Museum offers an experience of a rural heritage authorised by its national status, its academic officials, its period details in a pastoral location far from the contemporary city and suburbia. Further west is another offering of Welsh heritage under a different authorising notion of authenticity. Set in an old squire's house, *Celtica* offers experiences. The visitor is guided through a sequence of sets, dioramas, stages which all mix time, narratives, character, viewpoint. There are evocations of megaliths, extracts from Celtic mythology, accounts of Druids, a Celtic village diorama, with an actor/interpreter in character (an Iron Age blacksmith when we visited), surreal and mystical settings (misty ancient oak groves) for projections and soundtrack.

The message is that the ancient Celts were a spiritual, warlike, fiery, passionate and highly creative race of people who dominated central and western Europe. Though marginalised in late antiquity, they are still with us now, we are told, found on the 'Celtic fringe' of Europe, still speaking their old languages, still embodying their ancient characteristics. They are the Scots, Irish, Welsh, Bretons, Catalans. Celtica is a story of genealogy and the true identity of the Welsh. Authenticity is here directly connected with continuity from past through to present; authenticity is here associated with the aboriginal.

Gwydion, a Druid's apprentice, is cast into the vortex and tells the future from the past, shown to the audience on video. 'Can you still see our craftsmen?' asks the Druid of Gwydion. And the flickering video clears to show modern industry. Rugby playing merges into the contemporary *eisteddfod* – descendants, it is claimed, of those ancient warlike and artistic qualities. So what has happened to this great Celtic people of old? The answer is confirmed again at the end as a Welsh choir sings Dafydd Iwan's song 'We are still here'.

Predictably perhaps, after the guided visit to megaliths, oak trees and mystical vortex, the visitor is directed to a more conventional learning experience, an historical timeline recording various events on the continuity from Celtic past to present. This, explicitly affirmed at the beginning of the exhibition, is all authorised by an academic team, again.

The eclipse of academic values of 'rational' knowledge by sentiment, sensation and melodrama may be termed 'Romanticism'. The mobilisations of the past in the service of nationalist and regional identities (with no necessary reference to the academic) add weight to the use of the term, given the traditional association of romantic ideologies and nationalism. The association between language, soil, society, culture, and a smoothed-over continuity of history is great ideological force. There are grounds here upon which criticism can validly be made. Sensation and melodrama often use cliché, stock characterisation and scenes for a predictable and easy response. The particularity, otherness and difference of the past may be ignored because upon these work is required. The past is not attended to. We may wish to criticise nationalist sentiment when past evidences are ignored. And all those notions, at the heart of the Celtica agenda, of a Celtic people and unity of culture are, for archaeologists and historians, deeply problematic. Again, however, we stress that these criticisms cannot claim that the past is hereby being contaminated by the present (it is always past/present). Criticism is of the *character of the relationship* between the past and the present.

Celtica is heavily dependent upon media of diorama and video projection accompanied by simple dramatic enactment – pretending to be a Druid or a blacksmith. But here we note a paradox or contradiction which confirms our point about the authenticity being dependent upon the character of mediation or relationship between past and present. The actor in the Celtic village, speaking modern Welsh, performed the past. His language, far from being contemporary, was proposed as archaic, signifying the ancient, the Celtic, the continuity. 'These words were then'. So although he was playing an ancient role, we also had to simultaneously suspend our belief, because the role of the actor was his physical presence, a nice modern Welsh boy, speaking Welsh. It was this modern identity that was the crucial point, making him an authentic intermediary. We will take forward this theme of dramatic re-enactment.

Rupture and the authentic imagination

Dramatic replication of the past is fraught with difficulties. Theatre is constituted as a sophisticated system of simulation, of illusion of place and person. Its nature is towards unauthenticity; our distance from the stage precludes the need for exact similitude. We accept the codes of repre- sentation. Sadly, re-enactment at heritage sites recurrently takes the conventions of stage practice – the rhetorical devices of acting – and the technical means of the auditorium – lighting, sound, fabricated decor – and applies them in contexts where they are singularly inappropriate and where the spectator is asked to accept their very unauthenticity as authentic, as a true window on the past. Here it is the intention that is at fault, a process which reduces the complexity of the past to the linearity of dramatic narrative, changing the 'it was this and this and this' of the visitor's imagination to 'it was this'.

There never was a *then* for this place: it *is now, was then* and *all points in between*. At least in the auditorium we the spectators collude in the deception of theatre. We suspend our disbelief, we acknowledge the fiction, the illusions and simulations of place and person. We are supposed not to do this at places like Celtica. Nevertheless many visitors spend much effort in trying to expose the fraud, revealing the performative nature of representation by, for instance, confronting the historical personages with contemporary objects. At least this is playful, indicating that the relationship can never be other than theatrical, that spectators will always view such interpretation with scepticism, resisting closure. But why bother in the first place then? Awkward questions about attempting to control interpretation arise.

Within such contexts actors are often presented with an impossible task. They are caught between **now** and **then**, between the need both to explain and to re-enact. Yet the actor/spectator interaction occurs in the public domain of the present not the past: it is inevitably tempered by the social norms of contemporary society and by the transactional conventions of modern theatre practice. Re-enactment then is often neutered, without extremes of emotion or action. The actors cannot become dangerous: we don't see them defecating, having sex, sleeping . . . And whilst it remains a fascinating project, we rarely see any attempt to reconstruct the gestural conventions, particularly the private ones, of a particular period, as opposed to the linguistic affectations (which are surely no more discernible than physical activity). These people, these actors, cannot do otherwise: they never have enough knowledge of 'how to go on', how to improvise 'as if in the past'. And whatever the degree of verisimilitude of costume drama, we always suspect that they are wearing modern underwear.

Training prepares actors for the strange half-turned – speaking out, speaking across – conventions of the proscenium stage. Once removed from this protected environment, the actor becomes three-dimensional, in an alien environment. As the stage picture, his normal workplace, is characterised by omission, by a series of design concepts which hold the elements together, there is little wonder that he may appear swamped in denser aggregations of site and objects. Inevitably, he must find ways to survive. The blacksmith fiddles with props in the mock-up Celtic village. He might include a certain knowingness or collusion, communicated to the spectator as an 'I know you know this is not real, so we're all in it together' attitude and undoubtedly of the present. Or the creation of *character*, a construct of biographical fiction, speculative motive and response, and personal technique. Both lead to a closure of dramatic potential and ultimately to a banalisation of the past. He's just a nice Welsh boy really; and this, as we have shown, is the point.

Consider now the *Big Pit*. Up another of the South Wales valleys is a site of industrial archaeology, the Big Pit at Blaenafon. On a bleak and scarred hillside, snow-flecked when we last visited in October, is one of the few remnants of the South Wales coalfield, in its heyday at the turn of the century the biggest in the world. The pit was closed in 1980, then opened again three years later as a visitor centre, though its future still remains uncertain. The colliery is not cleaned up, other than at the entrance and reception. Bits of machinery lie around. The pithead is worn, dirty and used. Ex-miners take visitors down the pit and walk them around the now disused workings. The miners speak about the history of coal mining, but the chronology is imprecise. They speak of the way it was; *was*, because work stopped. No romanticising of the past, very little nostalgia. Just talking about what they did and showing us where and how.

Here was a simple contact with another order of experience. Mediated by a vitality – the life of the ex-miner and his experiences expressed in anecdote and incidental detail, and by a site which had not been sanitised, but left. In the pit baths, again just left empty, a plain photo exhibition expanded with old pictures of miners and a few stories told mostly through contemporary journalism. They added to a physiognomy of Blaenafon.

The guide at Blaenafon Big Pit also told of his times and points out things of note. He just shows you around in circumstances which are as staged as Celtica. The character there just shows you around too. You know it's not 'real'. He is a character, and plays his part well. Visitors are there to use their imagination. In this perhaps Blaenafon and Celtica are not comparable. But there is another difference, in the type of experience afforded. Much of Celtica is as sterile as the magic oak in whose roots we are supposed to see the future; which is not to say that it does not attract. The story may well be perceived as a good and relevant one. It has been academically authorised and an accompanying conventional exhibition goes to great lengths to provide archaeological and historical authorisation. Empirically it is supposed to be correct. But it isn't. The underground machinery has mostly been removed from Blaenafon and the coal workings are empty. In this it is not anything like the way it was: Blaenafon has *changed*, and the visitor perceives this. But the empty underground stables echo, resonate, evoke. Blaenafon haunts. The ghosts at Celtica are the faces projected when you push the button on the mystic stone.

Again we want to stress that the haunting of the past is not to do with 'authenticity', meaning the simple material and empirical presence of the past. Many museum displays, traditional and contemporary, are as sterile, sanitised and dead as Celtica. The authenticity of Blaenafon is the character of the changes we perceive it has undergone. Thus we argue that rupture is essential to the *authentic imagination*.

Work such as *Gododdin* never claims authenticity. Yet, like the National Folk Museum, Celtica and Blaenafon, it is inherently archaeological. *Gododdin* worked with the traces of the past, in this instance a text and a legend, and makes something of it in the present.

And heritage sites differ from the locations chosen for Brith Gof's site-specific work in designation only. They may be equally susceptible to the oblique strategies and approaches of an experimental theatre which has gained the experience and expertise to deal with the most diverse of sites. It may be possible to create theatrical presentations which are not reliant upon the re-enactment and singularity of interpretation of conventional dramatic practice, which make no pretence at verisimilitude, which juxtapose alternative interpretations simultaneously, which reveal site continuously and which serve to evoke rather than to monopolise meaning, rupturing rather than consoling. Such interpenetrative hybrids may include anachronism, lack of congruence, fantasy, the overlaying of 'like' and 'unlike' in order to stimulate the imagination of the spectator, to provoke questioning and to embrace her in an interpretive and critical process. Their parts never fully coalesce and they contain irreconcilable discontinuities within their juxtapositions of material. They are purposefully unauthentic.

Monuments and morbid echoes: choreographing the prehistoric body

We have dealt with things, the performer, mediation of past and present, rupturing authenticities and enduring pasts, evocative and haunting. We move on now to consider more of architecture and site. Our subject is performative behaviours seen through European prehistory.

Site and place in prehistory

> *I am the family face;*
> *Flesh perishes, I live on,*
> *Projecting trait and trace*
> *Through time to times anon,*
> *And leaping from place to place*
> *Over oblivion.*
>
> *The years-hiered feature that can*
> *In curve and voice and eye*
> *Despise the human span*
> *Of durance – that is I;*
> *The eternal thing in man,*
> *That heeds no call to die.*
>
> ('Heredity', Hardy 1993: 103)

On a hillside in west Wales looking out towards the sea, stands the elegant structure of Pentre Ifan. Its simple sculptural form – three uprights and a capstone, in local stone – resembles a contemporary art-work, an intervention or **interruption** in the landscape (see Kastner and Wallis 1998: 72ff.). Yet it is over five thousand years old, an example of those built structures, with an insular flavour, which emerged with what has been described as the advent of the neolithic period. During a period of cultural change and innovation, soil, timber and stone were fashioned into a new range of architectures, cere-monial sites, avenues and circles which reached their developmental zenith with the final phases at Stonehenge and Avebury (Thomas 1993: 32). This may have involved the adoption of new beliefs. It certainly witnessed the advent of a set of new body practices manifest in space and in relation to the dead, as new attitudes to the human body, both as active agent and as corpse.

> My mother heard a gasp in the bed beside her and my father was dead. In his dream was there sudden black, the jolt of a fall, or just another page turning in the wind?
>
> (Brith Gof: *A Death in the Family*, 1991; text by Mike Pearson)

Prior to the neolithic, social life was lived out as a series of encounters, in the face-to-face co-presence of other participants, in highly localised arenas (see Giddens 1984: 75–92). These encounters occupy regions of space and time, the opening and closing of the bracket marked by mechanisms and techniques of entry, body positioning and turning away. They may have been informal for the 'figures in the landscape' – on path, in clearing, around fire – the human body experienced in relation to environmental features and to impermanent dwellings. Or more formally at oft-visited places, recurrently or seasonally visited, in a complex narrative weaving of time and space. So there are meetings with friends, kin, strangers . . . and these probably have to be formalised to prevent misunder-standing and violence. Initially we might have to signal our presence – by smoke signals, by use of the voice; shouting, yodelling, singing as Pygmies do in the Congo jungle . . . and then use a series of conventionalised and mutually understood postures and gestures to clarify our intentions. We may have to perform our identity. Inevitably this will include *proxemics* – placing the body in particular relation to those of others, and *haptics* – partic-ular kinds of touch, rubbing noses and such, as well as meaningful gestures. And then we begin to tell of what we have seen and done – to describe, to represent, experiences of other places, other times. To sing, to gesture, to enhance our telling. And perhaps this telling is about a shared history, recited to hold it, and us, in place. Inevitably we exaggerate, we dramatise our story to keep the listener interested. And we may too begin to imitate and impersonate others, humans and animals, mimicking their postures, movements and voices to make then present in the moment. Shouting across the valley, whooping in the hunt, calling out greeting, chatting around the camp-fire, wailing in front of the corpse . . .

Fred Machin did a good job, calm and deferential; the frayed cuffs on his suit at the crematorium burst any pretence. His mortuary was a breeze-block shed in the yard, a small wooden cross above the door to distinguish it from several others.

The dead were disposed of then in ways which we can barely discern. Perhaps they were just left on the ground for carrion or thrown into the nearest river, got rid of. Or slightly more formally, hung in a tree for the birds to eat or covered in a pile of animal bones or cast in the same midden as the food remains. Environment – topography, climate, flora and fauna – and body – living and dead – in a field of fluid, tactical and improvised engagements.

He looked serene, the blond hair that lingered at his temples neatly brushed. The rest, as is the way with the Pearsons, he lost in his early twenties, whilst sticking his head out of a Liberator bomber, over Ceylon, or so he said. And in the cream silk suit of the coffin, he looked like a cardinal. Whether through some alchemy of the embalmer's art or the sudden release of all fear, strain, tension, his face was completely without lines.

Monument and architecture

And then – earthworks, great stones moved and arranged, quarries opened up, chalkland scarred, uplands dug. It begins with the construction of **place**. These new architectures separate and demarcate: they mark out, mark off and set aside space. They are the trans-formations of space through objects: linear and circular configurations and constraints which affect and regulate the way space is experienced and interpreted (Thomas 1999: 35f.). They inscribe the newly cleared landscape. They are 'special places' where the human body is framed and observed in relation to new facades, backdrops and screens; where movement is controlled and channelled; where the voice is contained and amplified; where encounters, events and physical and vocal intercourse may be prescribed and choreographed and where actions and performances are staged (ibid.: 41f.; Bradley 1993: 48f.; Barrett 1994: 9f.). They are as much about the movement of people as they are about the stars. They are the locations of events: feasts, gatherings, burials. Within enclosures and at locales and settings, in places specially allocated and 'bracketed off' from other activities, in places of meeting and of regionalised practice, individuals are brought together in time and space. Here the space may act directly upon the body, causing irregular movements and orientations, channelling the eye, regulating patterns of visibility and hiddenness, controlling the spacing and timing of encounters. And here there can be the formal and strategic deployment of the body and the voice in extra-daily practices. At such places there is an articulation of interior and exterior, inclusive and exclusive, watchers and watched. And discourses are protected from evaluation through restricted access (Whittle 1988: 149–50).

She bent down and kissed him on the cheek. Only later would she stagger and wail – and here I can make no impersonation of my mother – 'He's not coming back to me'. She had known him since she was 6 years old. 'Touch 'im, touch 'im, you 'ave to touch 'im', hissed my grandmother, responding to some age-old imperative. Slowly, my hand slid to his. And then I realised it was all wrong. The nails were clean, manicured, no trace of soil. And the skin was smooth, waxy, like the skin of a potato.

John Barrett identifies places where performance is more or less likely – processions in avenues, presentations at stone settings or locales (Barrett 1994: 15ff.). Performance may have four axes of manifestation: space, time, pattern and detail. This model might cause us to seek those places in the past where architectural surface and closure might necessitate and prescribe certain altered behaviours and bodily orientations. But we should never forget that movement defines and articulates space just as much as walls or columns and that 'performed movement' is our elemental means for the realisation of space-creative impulses. Movement in space is at once a 'reading' and a 'writing'. Barrett supposes that the stone rows of southern Britain are the physical manifestations of the existence of processional activity: setting out from and arriving at henges, along avenues. He suggests that the architectural settings of Bronze Age monuments created formal opportunities 'to enter and leave each other's presence, to observe passively or to act, to lead processions or to follow' (ibid.: 29). Here he distinguishes between those included in the activity and those excluded and 'amongst those who were included were those who led and those who followed' (ibid.). Body practices of leaving, moving, entering; leading and following; observing and acting.

There were no flowers. Instead, a collection to buy a defibrillator for the Scunthorpe Ambulance Service, which was ironic, as during his second event they almost killed him with one. Without time even to grease the terminals, they slapped them straight on, leaving two huge burn marks on his chest. The funeral service at the crematorium was the usual public affair: family, friends, colleagues, those come to make their peace, those come seeking some sort of retribution. And the body is surrendered into the hands of others. And as it slides from view, a link is cut.

In regular and sporadic cycles of physical engagement, of encounter between body and environment, social and ritual generate people's understanding both of themselves and their surroundings. Acting as 'stations' in this network of movements, features which have been constructed by human beings will have a constraining effect on the interpretive process. That structuring then of a landscape through the building of monuments, is actually the 'making' of human subjects and their consciousness. 'For these constructed features have a constraining effect upon interpretation' (Thomas 1999: 36). They channel and direct movement, the encounter between body and environment, in choreographies which prescribe time and sequence and which ultimately map patterns of practice and of belief.

In fact, it's not easy to dispose of a body. Burial always leaves a trace. Even in the most acidic of soils, a black shadow remains or perhaps just a concentration of certain minerals, potassium for instance. Head of femur, teeth, usually resist burning.

Amongst the earliest sites are the causewayed enclosures, discontinuous ditches surrounding a central area and crossed by . . . causeways (Mercer 1990; Parker-Pearson 1993: 28f.; Thomas 1999: 38f.). These ditches demarcate; they don't defend. And they are filled with extraordinary debris. At all levels, there are the disarticulated remains of dozens of individuals (350 at one site): scattered single bones, and parts of skeletons – limbs, torsos and the pelvis/femur/lower vertebrae assemblage which is the last to fall apart, because of the strong muscle attachments. Also single skulls and bundles of bones. And enveloping them, the remains of feasts: animal bones from meat-rich parts of the body and quantities of unweathered drinking cups and bowls. The conjecture is that these were vast mortuary enclosures or open-air cemeteries, where bodies were left on the surface of the interior to rot, decompose and naturally deflesh – in a process called *excarnation* – and then handled, carried, used, deposited – in fragments – in subsequent rites. The access of the living to this reeking site was restricted to the narrow causeways. And there they ate and drank amongst the remains, in a conflation of choreography and improvisation and sensual contacts with organic objects which many performance artists will doubtless appreciate. Significantly, certain parts of the bodies are underrepresented.

What to do then? Throw it into a river like they do in the Ganges. Feed your victim a special breakfast porridge, garrotte him and throw him into the local bog. Where the leathery skin will turn up generations later in the unforeseen quest for peat. Bury it where no one will expect to look: in a cemetery for instance, as they did during the Dirty War in Argentina.

The henges have a circular ditch with an external bank and one or two entrances, a marking off of space, rather than a defensive structure (see Burl 1991). Inside there are concentric settings of timber uprights, perhaps buildings, perhaps circles of posts. Movement is channelled towards a facade which draws attention to the place of entry, across a platform and depositional area of hearths and meat-rich animal bones – principally pig - and into the concentric area where it must turn aside or approach the fire at the centre. Also within the henge are localised settings or stages – locales, architectural and depositional – to amplify and focus activity, to act as backdrop or screen, with in-front and behind. Places for events and for offerings.

But perhaps you don't want to get rid of it. Perhaps you want to keep it, hanging on the wall, embalmed. Death is easy to look at in the cool, clean, odourless catacombs of Palermo. But Death always laughs back. The priests in their vestments have faces pulled into grimaces, hands tightened into talons.

Simultaneously with the causewayed camps, new tomb types emerged, apparent today in the landscape as long mounds. These mounds cover a number of different structures, in two basic traditions. In the south and east, they are of timber and turf; further west are tombs with dry stone masonry and stone-built chambers, which were entered over centuries. And in the far west, there are the table-like structures – uprights and capstone – also in stone of the classic megalithic dolmens, as at Pentre Ifan. Both traditions involve communal burial rites: the tombs include the skeletons of many individuals ordered, sorted, reordered, mixed, reassembled over centuries of re-entry (Shanks and Tilley 1982; Thomas 1993: 37). Here the identity of the individual is subsumed within that of the community, albeit the community of ancestors. They become literally 'of the one body'. But we should never see them as monuments, as mausolea, merely as depositories of the dead. They were sites of long-term, though intermittent activity, functioning as shrines, as the locale for rite and ritual. And we should not isolate mortuary practice from social practice: these are places of the living and the dead, of lamentation as well as silence.

Bones and bodies

In all types, the bodies were defleshed elsewhere, the bones gnawed by rodents and invaded by terrestrial land snails, perhaps in temporary pits or on platforms as in native North

American practice (Parker-Pearson 1993: 46). And again all the parts are not here! There is a suggestion that some parts of each body are in the tombs, others in the enclosure ditches! What is certain is that the placing of bones in mounds was only one stage in a complex process and that the internal patterning may be the end-product of a long sequence of additions and removals from the burial deposit, whilst the mortuary structure was still accessible. Bones and parts of bodies were circulating, disarticulated, like religious relics. Perhaps the corpse was seen as unstable, dangerous, polluting, with corruption marginalised to the enclosures, whilst bones came to represent the ancestor as opposed to the individual.

Auschwitz is all you expect. 'Arbeit Macht Frei' above the gate. Rooms full of shoes, suitcases, hair, spectacle frames. The killing wall where death came swift and savage. But Auschwitz is a brick barracks, not the image in the mind. That is two miles away. And however often you've seen the photographs, nothing prepares you for the reality of Birkenau. There is the gate-house with the railway running beneath . . . there the wooden watch-towers . . . there the acres of broiler houses . . . there the platform where man played God – 'To the left . . . To the right' - as the band played on. And there are the crematoria where the disposal of bodies was turned into a science. And even if all of this were obliterated and every trace of human remains removed, you would still know that this was a place of death. It lingers in the atmosphere in this place where God looked away.

Physical access to the bones was controlled. At the earth sites, there is an embanked linear zone across which may be a bedded timber facade; an avenue of posts aligned to the mortuary area and an enclosure, chamber or platform (Thomas 1999: 131f.). So whilst the corpses were available for the selection and manipulation of bones, entry was limited and channelled directionally. The bodies were defleshed elsewhere, on occasion the flesh even being burned off in an investment of effort by others (ibid.: 136). The arrangements of skulls and long bones and variation in the number of ribs and vertebrae indicate conspicuous selection, the deposition being only the final phase in a circulation and the pattern a result of additions and removals (Shanks and Tilley 1982). Bones were even moved from one side of the mortuary to the other. There are piles of male and female, patterns of laying out and grouping, breaking down and reuniting. Eventually, earth was piled on the wooden structures – frames, mortuary houses, rows of posts – and on the pits and hearths.

They seem to have succeeded in the early Iron Age, no burials, no bodies. Perhaps nobody died. The Oglala Sioux believe that we all leave a trace: 'Aye, footprints I make, footprints I make.'

This involvement with the bodies of ancestors was much more protracted in the chambered tombs, such as West Kennet (Thomas and Whittle 1986). Here, over several hundred years, bones were being moved and removed: placed in, taken out, resorted, rearranged, the remains of previous generations mixed with those of the present (Thomas 1991b: 103f.). The tomb consists of five chambers, with a facade and forecourt area bearing the remains of hearths, pits, platforms and pig feasts. Defleshing occurred outside, perhaps on the forecourt itself. In the five chambers, individuals were separated according to age and gender. But the bones are sorted, skulls in one area, long bones in another. Skulls are often underrepresented (Shanks and Tilley 1982: 138-50).

Entry was possible, to allow an approach by the living to the dead. The architectural complexity stage-manages the encounter with the remains. But perhaps not for everyone. The spaces are restricted; few people can fit physically at one time. They require stooping, bending, squatting, in a poorly lit charnel house. This has led commentators to suggest that there are two groups present (Whittle 1988: 181–2). Only protagonists with specific knowledge of layout and contents could enter. Here perhaps the privileged feasted with the ancestors, as evidenced by the smashed drinking vessels, burnt soil and bones. They would then return to a larger audience outside, with new knowledge or even to display body fragments. So, details and contents remained private and public rituals occurred outside. Megalithic tombs represent a stage for the performance of rituals (Barrett 1991: 8). Rituals involve the manipulation of space and material objects; they represent a microcosm of the world which can be manipulated within a bounded analytic space – passage, chamber, forecourt – in a combination of display and secrecy.

Barrett (1994: 57f.) proposes that the facade distinguishes those who face it from those who face out from it, passive spectators and active protagonists or performers. The front space is a stage, the chambers a back-space. He imagines a turning away, an entry, a re-emerging. Inside a series of choices are presented: left/right; front/back. Bones are added or withdrawn for display, consulted, reordered, reinterpreted and placed in new spatial configurations, in a complex interplay of burial and rite, of the living and the dead, in a confined space. There is a physical constraint on the way in which the chambers are experienced. Entry is on a specific axis, traversing a courtyard through its pits and hearths, into a passage of limited height.

And this is highly suggestive (Shanks 1992a: 194-206). We might begin to envisage a series of **entrances** and **exits** signalling dramatic **thresholds**. And a pattern of **inciting incidents** and their **trajectories**. Changes of consequence. **Crises**. **Ruptures** or sudden shifts in orientation. **Nodes** or densities of activity. Breaks or pauses. **Irrevocable acts** such as the display of the dead. And **decay** as in the breaking of vessels. We might envisage the existence of the event for the participants as a chain of physical orientations and mutual re-engagements. As an **interrupted practice** of different modes of expression, of varying types and intensities, from display to disengagement. As a **discontinuous activity** including changes in style, mode, material. As a kind of **incoherent behaviour** switching from whisper to oratory within a performance continuum. We can envisage changes in *proxemic* and *haptic* engagement, in quality of light, surface-texture, tempera-ture, odour . . . **kinesic** restriction inside the tomb, the facade as framing backdrop outside, different tones of voice inside and outside. And we might suggest that the demeanour of the watched was different confined in the chamber than in front of the crowd.

And the ring passed from his finger to mine in two days.

E.6   A.6   B.6

Giving voice to the past

The haunting past is an issue of embodiment.

Significantly, these sites and structures enhance the voice: channelling its effects, amplifying it, echoing it; enabling its manipulation and elaboration; allowing its employment in new and unexpected articulations and modulations within and in relation to man-made architectures. For the first time perhaps and even leading to its formalisation. Here the voice constructs and is simultaneously constructed. New discourses, new ways of telling, appear. These are places of, and for, the voice.

Bernard Tschumi might give voice to the 'insiders':

> Space is real, for it seems to affect my senses long before my reason. The materiality of my body both coincides with and struggles with the materiality of the space. My body carries in itself spatial properties and spatial determination: up, down, right, left, symmetry, dissymmetry . . . here is where my body tries to rediscover its lost unity, its energies and impulses, its rhythms and flux . . . One can participate in and share the fundamentals of the labyrinth, but one's perception is only part of the labyrinth as it manifests itself. One can never see it in totality, nor can one express it . . . We cannot both experience and think that we experience.
>
> (Tschumi 1990: 20–21, 28, 27)

We can suppose that different tones of voice were employed from time to time both inside and outside and by both watchers and watched. But can we ever get close enough to hear the voices? Can we 'read off' what was happening here from the architectural remains? After all, we usually assume that places are more or less suited to the activities they contain. Surely, these places suggest hushed, reverential tones. Yet there are enough smashed cups inside to equally suggest a riotous carousal. What we need is a model which allows us to embrace a multitude of possibilities – what might have happened, what could have happened – of the million, million things that perhaps happened here during its long history. But within this precise set of material conditions. We will need to use the word 'if' a lot . . . 'If this happened, then this would have been the result'.

The relationship between event and space in Bernard Tschumi's work may be instructive as it suggests that linkages may be other than causal: it may be reciprocal but it may also be indifferent or in conflict. Thus we cannot infer from these structures that they were places of reverence. Of

S.6   O.6   R.6   M.6

course, they might be. But they might also be the scenes of violence; they might be the location for a celebratory party as much as a liturgy. And whilst one can whisper and chant in these spaces, one can also wail and shout. The relationship of voice and architecture can be **assymetrical**. It is not enough to say that these places were about lowered voices simply because their enclosure necessitates little vocal projection, though of course it does. We know, for instance, the effect of the sudden, piercing cry in the gentle murmuring of funeral prayers.

Further, we might suggest employments and engagements of the voice at and within these tombs which are akin to Tschumi's **programmes**. If then we propose a spectrum of vocal exposi-tions – whisper, speak, shout, sing – and a variety of articulations – loud/soft, with energy/without energy, solo/group or even transformational devices like Tschumi's and apply them with **indiffer-ence**, **reciprocity** and **conflict**, then we can begin to imagine the effects of the tombs on the voice, and vice versa, not only for those inside but for those outside. Not to say this is what happened but to say this is what the effect could have been had these vocal expositions occurred. And perhaps the best way to understand this might be to go there ourselves and try ourselves, to engage the site, using our contemporary voices as a kind of 'experimental archaeology of phenomena'.

Now this might not be saying much but we can elaborate our model somewhat by considering the work of both Goffman and Hall (Goffman 1971a; Hall 1966). Goffman's notion of '**region**' (1971: 107–40) may lead us to suspect that a formality of layout may prescribe and direct the nature of discourse. Within them, behaviour can be ordered, stylised, carrying a message. Both have a public and a private area, fore-stage and back-stage. The public is more staged, laid out, lit in a particular way; the private is ad hoc, improvised. The question we must ask ourselves is, at our structures: 'What is the "off-stage" and what the "on"?' And whether modes of formal discourse, heightened vocal address, occurred outside or in. If in, then the effect for those waiting might be muffled, resonating, emerging from deep within. And Hall's work on proxemic zoning may help us discern the relationships being honoured and transgressed here. Thus whilst we might suppose that the relationship of watchers and watched on the forecourt is in the public zone, occasioning vocal projection, oratory, public pronouncements, communal singing, entry into the tombs forces some bodies together, perhaps even transgressing daily codes of closeness and touch. And this may enhance particular modes of vocal address which again may be appropriate or inappropriate, in relation to the everyday modes of discourse, within the varying zones: singing in someone's ear.

The spatial enclosure may enable the use of quieter tones of voice. However, if those outside are intended to hear what is going on, then the repercussions inside might be deafening!

And so in combining Tschumi, Goffman and Hall we begin to create a dizzying map of vocal potentials. Yet our constant premise must be: 'If the voice was used in this way then the effects might have been these.' In this way we do not monopolise the past but make a creative engagement with a given set of material circumstances. As our ancestors surely also did.

Walking in the past

As noted previously, Barrett (1994: 9f.) suggests that a prime feature of emerging sacred landscapes may have been procession, setting out from and arriving at henges, along avenues. Examination of the performative nature of procession might illuminate body practices of leaving, moving, entering; leading and following; observing and acting.

Procession is a release of energy, a concerted effort on a particular occasion. And whilst it may be purely a means of reaching site B from site A, it may indicate 'meaning through movement'. For, it manifests 'walking together', communal endeavour and vitality; it may denote renewal and invigoration. It has to begin and end somewhere. We can thus suppose that it has at least three phases: departure, journey and arrival. Prior to this may be preparation and organisation. And subsequently, change and dispersal. In each of these phases, different activities, different emotions and different modes of intercourse are evident.

Organisation takes place adjacent to the processional route. It requires space or area which may be especially designated. Its first period may be informal, including dressing, 'warming up', greeting fellow participants. This is followed by a semi-formal period of assembly in which an amorphous group begins to order itself. This may be the communication of the rules of engagement or a 'getting into line', the creation of the processional form without motion. Or it may involve the creation of another configuration from which the procession will emerge. This may resemble a coil ready to unwind; or concentric rings of participants who will pass through some filtering aperture such as a porch. Departure is a setting out. It may involve a separation. And the revelation of participants and those left behind or abandoned. It may be accompanied by well-wishing, embraces, turning and waving, signs of regret and/or expectation. There may be explicit signals to begin, both aural, such as instrumental blasts or 'strike up the band', and visual, such as the hoisting of banners. For the participants the engagement may be instantaneous, experienced as a push from behind, or gradual, as the wave-like motion, which spreads from front to back, is experienced as 'following' or 'joining in'.

If there is to be a division of watchers and watched, then the moment of engagement is the moment at which distinction is drawn. It may be marked as the crossing of a threshold, an emergence from a private place of organisation into the public arena and the difference in formality and attitude this may engender for, or necessitate in, the participants. A narrow doorway may act as the filter through which an amorphous shape becomes a linear one. Even though they may make no direct appeal to the outside through the employment of spectacular techniques and improvisation in response to audience reaction there may be watchers and watched. If there are watchers and watched, then journey generates two basic and different experiences: moving and passing and standing and being passed. Participants will rarely have an impression of the totality of the procession, experiencing it rather as a transitive 'being part of', as leading and/or following in two basic states: move and stop. Move may vary from slow to fast and may be subject to stylistic diversification. Stop may simply be 'marking time'. It may also include rest, the opportunity for stylistic change and energetic re-engagement. Those being passed, the watchers, will have a complex and individual impression of a three-dimensional organism with length but no face.

Journey may occur along a prescribed route and it may have an immutable sequence. Arrival may be experienced with a sense of satisfaction, accomplishment or relief. There may be an intensification of emotion towards climax and jubilation in conclusion. It may be accompanied by greetings, congratulations and the reintegration of watchers and watched.

When a procession encounters a resistance, when it 'hits the buffers' or comes to rest, it must change its nature in order to prevent its participants piling into each other! On some signal, it may simply halt and then fragment or disperse. It may, however, take up or adopt another shape or form. This may be suggested, and indeed channelled, by entry into another architecture, such as a church, or by the physical arrangement of those waiting. Or it may reorder itself in relation to a particular focus, such as a grave or fire. The procession thus becomes a filling, an encircling or an ordered dispersal. And as it comes apart, it may reveal, within its body, different orders of participants whose hierarchical status is suddenly reinforced by their elevation to raised areas or placement at the centre of circles. This may signal a change in activity and a new distinction between 'who the watchers' and 'who the watched'.

Our archaeological neolithic shades into Bronze Age. The landscape of southern Britain was inscribed in even more substantive ways by the construction of a range of ceremonial structures from the enigmatic banked enclosures of the cursuses to the great trilithon structures of Stonehenge. All required vast amounts of labour, using rudimentary tools such as deer horn picks and shoulderblade shovels. The fact that this may have been by the 'many' for the 'few' suggests hierarchies, literally the 'incrowd' and the 'outcrowd'. But this loses sight of the communality of labour, the recurrent, perhaps seasonal gathering, to work, to sweat, to talk, to build social realities. We see these sites as finished monuments, designed, built, preserved. But perhaps they were never completed, more like building sites or locations of changing practice.

Eventually the tombs were filled and blocked. The last acts included the reconstitution of individuals from scattered parts, the construction of 'virtual' individuals, the separation of piles from several individuals, the grouping of skull, mandible and one or two long bones, and the uniting of crania with different jaws (Shanks and Tilley 1982; Thomas 1999: 151). The latest tomb types have a long passage and a single chamber, with a mass of intermixed bones. In Brittany, at Les Pierres Plattes and at a date slightly earlier than in Britain, the passage turns through a right angle. Suddenly, you are bending, crawling, in total darkness. In torchlight, the walls are revealed to be covered in carvings – of ribs and torsos (Thomas and Tilley 1993): a passage like an internal organ. Your body is in a body, with bodies. Perhaps this 'theatre of death' was experienced alone as an extraordinary encounter with one's ancestors, a rite of passage, all one's senses alert. Or as a graded, deeper and deeper, access. Or perhaps it involved a guided reading, a performed interpretation for a small group, huddled in front of the images. At Gavrinis, the whole tomb interior is covered in swirls, axes, ribs, a dizzying, disorientating other world, which unites the bodies of the living and the dead within this one theatre.

And in these places I can imagine that had I screamed in terror, chanted in reverence, talked to myself, sung in the darkness, whispered to my fellow initiates, as I am doing now, then it would have been just so.

3 THEATRE/ARCHAEOLOGY

It has so often been said that history does not exist, it is created by historians . . . and then of course, decorated perhaps, if you are fortunate, even illuminated by poets, writers, painters, composers.

(Greenaway 1993)

In a third phase, what we term 'theatre/archaeology', the two disciplines are no longer held discrete. They coexist within a **blurred genre** (Gregory 1993: 296; Tilley 1994: 1) or a science/ fiction, a mixture of narration and scientific practices, an integrated approach to recording, writing and illustrating the material past. Here archaeology and performance are jointly active in mobilising the past, in making creative use of its various fragments in forging cultural memory out of varied interests and remains, in developing cultural ecologies (relating different fields of social and personal experience in the context of varied and contradictory interests) and in their joint address to particular sites and themes, a significant resource in constructing and energising contemporary identities, personal, communal and regional. This necessitates a broader definition of possible objects of retrieval, new approaches to the characterisation of behaviour and action, different **ways of telling** and different types of recording and inscription, which can incorporate different orders of narrative. It suggests mutual experiments with modes of documentation which can integrate text and image, new approaches to museum practice and the creation of joint forms of presentation to address that which is, at root, ineffable.

In theatre/archaeology documents, ruins and traces are reconstituted as real-time event. In this chapter we attempt to show what this may involve. But we do not present theory, method and case study separately. Instead we have adopted a katachrestic format. There are three main interconnected sections set in several places or locales, real and typical, and dealing with various themes within the archaeological and performative. This is a combination of performed material, narratives and ruminations on the theory and practice of theatre/archaeology. At pivotal points we consider concepts of landscape, temporality, interpenetration, evocation as an oblique strategy of representation, site-specific theatre, story-telling, the guided visit, deep mapping, memory and identity – those practices which help constitute both city and country.

In this blurred genre there are convergences with other academic, artistic and cultural efforts. Here then is that symmetry, interpenetration, commingling of our practice and a particular focus of interest, a **heterotopia**, a ruined farm in West Wales, Esgair Fraith. A series of innovative approaches at site, off site and within the electronic media have interwoven the social history of the farms, the politics of afforestation, the architectural interpenetration of events and places, the romance of the ruin and the phenomenology of decay. The elaboration of this **poetics** of the past is thus a process of cultural production which takes the remains of the past and makes something out of them in the present, involving various communities, various social and political constituencies. And such **critical romanticism** – an attitude suspicious of any final account of things – acknowledges the importance of the material past to communities, pays attention to the local and particular and to contested interpretations. It might help engender a **sense of place**, providing insights into regional and cultural planning.

Within the composite approaches of theatre/archaeology we might regard performance as an experimental archaeology of the interpretive. And as information technology brings further challenges to the discrete nature of individual disciplines, archaeology and performance might be drawn into joint endeavours for which, as yet, we barely have names.

Landscape: walking

It begins with a sheet of whiteness, at once both page and landscape, a field for action. (And a niggling question: 'Whose sheet?')

> There is no seduction here. No half-hidden, half exposed. No objects of desire. No one to call you by name. No one to look you in the eye. No one to see you, from over there. No trees with the promise of shade. No verticals at all. Just an endless horizontal. The only possible cinematic 'shot' is the 'pan'. As easy to lose your mind as to lose your way.

> (Brith Gof: *Patagonia* 1992, text by Mike Pearson)

As a page, it awaits our mark. In George Orwell's novel *1984* (1990) Winston Smith's downfall in the totalitarian state begins when he finds a notebook in which he could write – criticism, biography, poetry – all potentially dangerous and subversive. Its whiteness then challenges us . . . to begin. And as we write, a text forms and is frozen. Inevitably with nothing to guide us, it travels horizontally from left to right (though not perhaps if we are Japanese or Iranian or . . .), top to bottom, obliging the reader to follow our tracks in the same way we made them. First nothing, then a few signs which orientate us, and those who follow us, a rudimentary map. So writing plots a journey. But it is discontinuous, riddled with blanks, pauses, spaces over which we jump because we know the direction. And just occasionally we pause or we leap here and there, to the footnotes, to the index.

> It's worrying, being out in the desert, no frames for what's going on. A solitary figure on the horizon, too soon to know whether coming . . . or going. But erect a vertical – a post for hitching, a doorway for standing, a wall for leaning – and desire begins. The desire for that position, that place.

> (Ibid.)

Our speeds and techniques of writing and reading vary according to the place, time, mood: we scribble notes, we scan-read, we compose our diary with care. And also according to the surface:

its quality, its texture. And sometimes our journey is slow and laborious: using a dictionary, trying to decipher the scrawl, stopping to reflect . . .

> He'd seen the dog-shit first. Birdie said it was a flag. The Owner wrote, 'It was a flag'. But he knew dog-shit, had scraped it off his fingers, on his knees, dead drunk, in Bute Street. Nature displays nothing black here. And it was so black. Dog eat dog. Dog eat dog-shit. Dog eat man-shit. Man eat dog. Quote: 'They licked their cracked lips, unable to take their eyes off the delicate cutlets spread on the snow.' And his hand . . . pulsed.

> (Pearson/Brookes: *Dead Men's Shoes* 1997)

Georges Perec (1997: 13) suggests that 'This is how space begins, with signs traced on a blank page', as invention: space as the relationship between this word and that. So as I begin to write, to decide what is of significance to me, I begin a journey across the page. In later days I will come back to this map of my trip and try to remember why I made that mark, what it means, to reorientate myself in that field of ideas that is this chapter. Of course, the first question is how to begin: 'What pen shall I use? What shall I write and what not? What will be my strategy of notation . . . think/write, write/write . . . and how will it change?'

> And then there were paw marks, dozens of paw marks. And it dawned that they were second, that the Norskies, the dog-eaters, had beaten them. 'Many thoughts come to us and much discussion we have had', the Owner wrote.

> (Ibid.)

As a landscape, its whiteness is dazzling, matched only perhaps by the wastes of the Antarctic Plateau. Step onto it, and we can see a long way. Many miles before they reached the South Pole, Captain Scott and his team realised they would be second there.

> They'd found the tent easily enough, a little black job with a single bamboo pole. They wandered around a bit. Eight hundred miles to wander around, aimlessly. Bill sketched, as usual. Birdie took some photos eleven in all working the shutter with a piece of string. At first, they all changed places. Then he just sat down and let them move, around him. But what had they expected? A candy-striped barber's pole sticking out of the ice? Something, anything, different. And where was it exactly, this point from where everywhere else is north? 'Proceeding south' their telegram had said but the Norskies hadn't found it. And all they'd found was the Norskies.

> (Ibid.)

In his visionary work *Flatland* of 1884, Edwin A. Abbott (1998) imagines a two-dimensional world – a vast sheet of paper – where the inhabitants are triangles, pentagons, hexagons and irregular figures. They move around freely on the surface but since all geographical shapes appear as straight lines when viewed edge on – and the edge is the only possible view in Flatland – then the inhabitants must feel around each other when they meet, to work out how many corners they've got, for proper recognition.

But we stand tall and this world is three-dimensional. Our senses are working overtime. Even in this barren waste, we are aware of at least two phenomena: surface and climate. Beneath our feet the land may be rough or smooth, hot or cold, hard or soft. And the temperature, the climatic conditions – wind, rain, blizzard – may vary similarly. As yet this is a world mainly of horizontals for no verticals catch our eye, though at the horizon itself there may be a distinction between the land which stretches away from us and the vault of sky which covers us. And of course this vault is liable to spectacular variations, from towering clouds to the visual displays of the Aurora Borealis.

> Cold is when the snot freezes in your nostrils, is when the matter in your blisters turns to ice, is when your crystalline breath snaps like a fire-cracker and falls as icicles in your beard, is when you can cut off your thumb . . . and pass it round. Cold is when the nerves die and your teeth crumble, is when your body 'chatters' in paroxysms of vibration, is when your lips are so raw that even smiling is painful, is when the sweat freezes on your body and you jump up and down in a shower of splinters. And the daily hygiene ceremony? Cold is when you can shit in your pants . . . and shake out the frozen lumps.
>
> (Pearson/Brookes: *Dead Men's Shoes* 1997)

And perhaps too we suspect that there is depth to this plane, that we are not suspended in mid-air, but that there is something under us, layers, strata. The law of **super-position**, the basic principle of geology and archaeology, states simply that, layer upon layer, the deeper you go, the older it gets – to dig down is to dig into the past.

We look, we listen, we touch . . . we begin to inhabit and measure this world through our sensory experience of it. 'And in so far as my hand knows hardness and softness, and my gaze knows the moon's light, it is as a certain way of linking up with the phenomenon and communicating with it' (Merleau-Ponty 1962: 317).

> To be human is both to create this distance between the self and that which is beyond and to attempt to bridge this distance through a variety of means – through perception (seeing, hearing, touching), bodily actions and movements, and intentionality, emotion and awareness residing in systems of belief and decision-making, remembrance and evaluation.
>
> (Tilley 1993: 12)

A.7   B.7   S.7

THEATRE/ARCHAEOLOGY

The human body then is the fundamental mediation point between thought and the world (ibid.: 13; Barrett 1994: 14) and it is at the beginning of our understanding of space(s).

So as we stand and look out, we can begin to orient ourselves: to make distinctions between left/right, top/bottom, within reach/beyond reach, within sight/beyond sight, here-and-there polarities. We begin to make perceptual judgements about distance and direction, near or far, this way or that way. We begin to understand this place through its capacity to enable or restrict our bodily actions and movements. Of course, our emotional response and awareness springs from our previous experiences and from our beliefs and ethical stances. If this were a nuclear test site, we might not want to be standing here; if a sign had told us to 'keep off' we might not feel able to anyway!

> Cold is when your breath solders your balaclava to your face and your head is encased in a block of ice, to look up or down impossible without inclining the body. Is when your clothes turn to armour, hard as boards, sticking out in folds and angles, and dressing is a three-man process of bending and thumping to achieve body shape. Is when your sleeping bag becomes an icy coffin, prised open with care lest it shatters like glass. Real cold is when you adopt the pulling position immediately on rising so that your clothes can freeze, in the most useful position, as you stand.
>
> (Pearson/Brookes: *Dead Men's Shoes* 1997)

We begin to walk. We feel the ground beneath our feet, the wind in our face. And as we do, we leave traces. We are **involved** in the landscape (Kastner and Wallis 1998: 114ff.). We leave the prints of our body, the touch of flesh on metal and stone. We constantly wear things out, with our hands, our feet, our backs, our lips. And we leave the traces of singular actions: the unintentional, the random, the intimate, unplanned touch of history's passing: we break twigs, move pebbles, crush ants ... all the signs that trackers learn to read. We leave footprints, as Neil Armstrong did on the Moon. It was when Robinson Crusoe found Man Friday's footprint that he realised he was not alone and colonialism was born: there was another being present, to subjugate (Phillips 1997).

And we discard things – we throw things away, we lose things – material which, in years to come, others will regard as artefacts, as the remains of past actions. In Antarctica, where nothing

E.7   0.7   M.7   R.7

rots, you can still find the remains – cans, harnesses, clothes – of Scott's expedition, Shackleton's expedition, Amundsen's expedition . . .

> They found the old 'Discovery' hut, the 'Royal Terror Theatre', full of ice. Shackleton, the bastard, had left the window open. But it was all still there, as if everyone had just stepped out. A sixpenny copy of 'The Story of Bessie Costrell', read and left open, the Contemporary Review, Girl's Own Paper and, encased in a block of ice, Stanley Weyman's 'My Lady Rotha' which was thawed out and read by everyone, the excitement increased by the fact that half the book was missing. Mind, he preferred Alexander Dumas or Dum-ass as he called him, something with 'a bit more plot', 'The Three Musketeers'. On the table, bread rolls with the impression of bites given them in 1909, sauces, pickles and a half-empty tin of gingerbread as crisp as the day it was opened. In the tent, five hymn-books, Bovril, Rowntree's cocoa and three-year-old cheese and biscuits, which they ate. In the drifts, the hoof marks of ponies long-dead. And the wrappings from Frank Cooper's rhubarb, Tate's granulated sugar, Heinz baked beans, Lyle's golden syrup, Colman's cornflower . . . It was eerie, ghost-like as if the people would walk back in at any moment.
>
> (Pearson/Brookes: *Dead Men's Shoes* 1997)

What of our sheet of paper? Perhaps because we have only one sheet, we have begun to try and fill all the space, writing smaller, writing down the margins and ultimately writing over our own writing. We begin to create a **palimpsest** – writing over writing over writing – in a kind of stratigraphy of text.

Perhaps we became frustrated and threw it away, a love letter that wouldn't compose itself. But as we retrieve it, we realise something unusual. Points which were once separated in time and space are now adjacent, in a new non-linear relationship. And perhaps this is how history really is: as our memories constantly fold into each other, when we meet people we haven't seen for years or visit childhood haunts. We try to straighten it out. But of course we can't. It has developed a kind of topography of creases, folds, bumps, rips, all of which will now influence how we might move across it.

> They all kept their diaries, writing for another audience, in another time, another place. What they didn't realise was that they were writing a tragedy.
>
> (Pearson/Brookes: *Dead Men's Shoes* 1997)

But these are not the only marks we might make. The artist Yves Klein dragged and rolled painted bodies across paper (see Goldberg 1988: 144–8) and Jackson Pollack dripped paint onto his in tracks which mimicked the trajectories of his actions (see Lewis 1999).

And our landscape? Twin forces are here too at work, changing its nature: environmental erosion, the steady run off from rain, the catastrophe of flash floods and the endlessly protracted processes of geology, gradually bending, tilting, folding, fracturing . . . So the land becomes seamed and detailed, with hills and valleys. High points appear which obstruct our walk but which also reveal new vistas and horizons for the first time. And gradually it becomes covered in

THEATRE/ARCHAEOLOGY

vegetation: from grassland to jungle. Occasionally fires rage across the land, but as yet we have made no fundamental attempt to change it. And for many millennia of human history we lived on the land in this way.

Acting out the land

Walter Benjamin once said, "When someone goes on a trip he has something to tell about." He'd always told stories. On the march he built their teetering structures, castles in the air, line after line, twist upon twist, topping them off with just the right punch-line. They filled the time, kept his mind off food...and grievance. They held him in the present. Every event he could romanticise, mythologise –'the compulsive raconteur' – forever talking, joking never bloody shutting up. To defuse the tensions of the Owner's moodiness, irritability, depression. And now, they collapsed. And he ...withdrew, went quiet. He said . . . nothing. He'd . . . lost the thread. He . . . couldn't even remember how to speak English.

(Pearson/Brookes: Dead Men's Shoes 1997)

Late in 1911, Captain Robert Falcon Scott attempted to walk to the South Pole accompanied by four others, three officers and a seaman. The fate of the officers is well enough known: they kept their diaries to the end. It was they who wrote the script. The final three died in their small tent just eleven miles from a depot of food and fuel. But the Welshman, the sailor Edgar Evans, remains enigmatic, always marginal, slightly out of focus, a preternatural story-teller, silent and silenced. The polar journey is the theme of *Dead Men's Shoes* (Pearson/Brookes 1997).

The solo narrative was performed against a forty-foot long white screen upon which seven computer-controlled projectors showed dozens of images of Scott's expeditions: original photographs – including those eleven taken from the camera found on Bower's body – the two most of us know but also the one in which they all moved from shivering; the one in which the shutter went off accidentally, casting the shadow of Bowers's bulky body across the group – blown-up, trimmed, enhanced, modified, changed; creating a parallel narrative – complementary, contradictory; casting doubts on the veracity of the Scott myth. And more poignantly than the text can ever hope to be because we know these men are dead, we know how it will end, we have the evidence: the bodies. All except two. Oates . . . who 'went outside'. And Evans . . . who lies somewhere out on the Beardmore Glacier.

At the Scott Polar Research Institute in Cambridge are the albums of photographs of the earlier 1902 *Discovery* expedition, the first occasion upon which Evans accompanied Scott to the Antarctic. In the middle of one volume are two extraordinary pictures, one of a group of men in *drag* , the other in *black-face* . . .

On 25 June 1902 the shore-hut, renamed 'The Royal Terror Theatre', opened its doors. There was stage, footlights, and a backdrop showing the ship and the volcano, Mount Terror. Chairs for the officers, benches for the men. Part One of the programme was 'various singers'. But Part Two was 'Ticket to Leave', a screaming comedy in one act. He got 'dragged up' – in full make-up – and he gave 'em the works. The house was in uproar, no need of a plot. And a waste of time learning the lines with such a loud-mouthed prompter. And the notices from The Owner? 'Rarely been so gorgeously entertained. Great histrionic talent'. By 6 August, it was minus 40 Fahrenheit outside – 70 degrees of frost – just right for the first appearance of 'Massa Johnson and the Dishcloth Nigger Minstrel Troupe'. He made suits of vivid colours and grotesque forms from calico, shirt fronts and enormous collars from paper and wigs from rope dipped in red ink. 'Bones' and 'Skins' had movable top-knots worked by pulling strings . . . just like Birdie's camera. They presented jokes and conundrums in authentic 'nigger' language and sang 'Oh, dem Golden Slippers, oh dem golden slippers' and 'Way down upon de Swansea Ribber'.

(Ibid.)

Yet we tend not to roam endlessly: we stick to a patch; we become familiar with it; we grow attached to it; we begin to feel 'at home' there. Our human activities become inscribed within a landscape such that every cliff, large tree, stream becomes a familiar place. The landscape then becomes embedded with memory. 'Daily passages through the landscape become biographical encounters for individuals, recalling traces of past activities and previous events and reading of signs – a split log here, a marker stone there' (Tilley 1994: 27). We begin to give names to signifi-cant places – descriptive names, names which commemorate certain events. And certain places we visit recurrently, along paths that become well-worn. Our familiarity begins to informs an art, a right way of moving around in the landscape. So we might see landscape as 'a series of named locales, a set of relational places linked by paths, movements and narratives' (ibid.: 34).

Walking then is a spatial acting out, a kind of narrative, and the paths and places direct our choreography. This regular moving from one point to another is a kind of mapping, a kind of narra-tive understanding. Paths link familiar places and bring the possibility for repeated actions. Different paths enact different stories of action. Walking is like a story, a series of events, for which the land acts as a mnemonic. And we are aware that our ancestors have also walked these paths no more so than in Australia where features in the landscape – often invisible to the uninitiated eye – mark the sites of ancestral acts (Tilley 1994: 37f.). To travel across such a land-scape is to remember it into being, it is sedimented with human significances. And the pathways are song-lines, long narrative excursions which remember places in song. To travel the land is to sing the world into being again (Thomas 1999: 35). And Aborigine maps – geometric patterns of lines and dots – represent not only places but creatures and events in the story of the locale.

Folded in the land

It is the matrix of particular folds and creases, the vernacular detail, which attaches us to a place. In Wales there are a number of spatial notions which describe the Welsh **sense of place**. These notions operate as a series of cognitive maps. *Y filltir sqwar* (the square mile), the intimate land-scape of one's childhood, that patch of ground we know in a detail we will never know anywhere again. Site of discovery and putting names to things, people and places. Working with difference and similitude. Favourite places, places to avoid. Neighbours and their stories. Textures, smells. Also of play, imagination, experiment. Finding the best location for doing things. Creating worlds under our own control, fantasy landscapes. A place of exaggeration and irrelevance. Of making rules and breaking rules, of learning to distinguish between 'do' and 'don't do'. A place of improvised responses, rules of thumb – where, as Ned Thomas said (1991: 86), 'the child first learns everything which is of real importance, history and geography'. And of which D.J. Williams noted (1987: 12): 'when the many things I remember actually happened, I haven't much of an idea. But I can locate most of them with a degree of certainty – where such and such a thing happened and where I was standing when I heard what I heard.'

- ❖ *Y fro* (neighbourhood, home district, heimat), where, as Thomas again observes (1991: 85), 'everyone in the community is joined to everyone else by a mesh of stories and incidents if not by family relationships'.
- ❖ *Cynefin* (habitat), that area where we feel we belong, the immediate environment, the surroundings which impress themselves upon us in the formative years between 5 and 15.

Bedwyr Lewis Jones suggests (1985: 122) that land and language are two strands that tie the Welsh-speaker to his cynefin. There are other links, such as remembrance of things past . . . Cynefin is more than landscape and scenery. It is a piece of earth where a community has lived, – a community with whom we identify. In this bond, language has its essential place, and here again the local factor is to the fore. The language of each *bro* has a distinctive hue . . . a storehouse of the transmitted legacies of experiences and imaginative constructions of those particular parts.

In these notions, landscape is not separate from the lives lived there. But they are cognitive devices – not precise territorial zones, rigorously defined, delineated and patrolled – and they vary (in importance) place to place, individual to individual. This is slippery ground, places without firm boundaries, places which perhaps only the poet can map. Such notions have long informed and animated the Welsh poetic imagination: the performance of poetry and narrative are simultaneously acts of memory and creation. As poet Waldo Williams writes 'This was my window, these harvestings and sheep shearings' ('Preseli' trans. Waldo Williams cited in Nicholas 1975: 8). T. H. Parry-Williams (1974: 58–9) examines the ways in which the natural environment moulds human personality and the relationship between family and locality, body and land in his native Snowdon mountains: 'This is not a mere madman's fantasy-thinking. There are bits of me scattered all over that land.'

The notions circumscribe that area where we feel we belong, what Raymond Williams called 'an attachment to place, the landscape, in which we first lived and learned to see' (Williams 1973: 84), the immediate neighbourhood, the window through which we view the world, a personal construct of land, language, history. The site of familiarity and identification. Where scenery is not separate from the lives lived there. Where the minutiae of morphology and tradition are preserved in idiom, dialect, proverb, lore. Where history is experienced as contemporaneous and the past still operates on the present. A ground level experience, landscape not as scenery but as a social construct, a **palimpsest**, marked and named by the actions of ancestors. 'All present experience contains ineradicable traces of the past which remain part of the constitution of the present' (Ashcroft, Griffiths and Tiffin 1998: 174). To represent such places adequately we might need a **deep map**: such depth is cultural and historical. For as Ned Thomas again suggests (1991: 72):

> even the landscape takes on a different quality if you are one of those who remembers. The scenery is then never separate from the history of the place, from the feeling for the lives that have been lived there . . . always the outlines of the scenery are deep in the Welsh consciousness as if scored in thick paint on canvas.

And as Waldo Williams suggests, we are *'Keeping house in a cloud of witnesses'* ('Pa beth yw dyn?'/'What is Man?' in Williams 1991: 64):

> Me? I nearly went back, once. Wilf died and the family house lay empty. But there was nothing there for me: "There's nuthin' 'ere for ya', duck". So we sold it quickly, cheaply, to avoid the pain of watching it decay. 'Limestone cottage. Needs modernising. Suitable project'. Project: more like a bloody attack! They hacked off the rendering outside, chipped off the plasterwork inside, pulled down the false ceilings. All the patinas of occupancy, they destroyed. Everything Wilf had dreamed of, had fantasised about, they found: oak beams, inglenook fireplace, priest's hole, paving made from old grave-stones. 1670 they reckoned, give or take. And then they dug up the floor . . . and the end fell off . . . finished up with a pile of oolite. Me Mam wasn't sorry!
>
> Our family house has fallen down. But it has yet to disappear. For we make the house . . . and the house makes us. We are of one body . . . Of course, we are in the house: it is marked by our presence . . . and by our passing. With each new layer of wall-paper, each new lick of paint, each new change of surface, colour, texture, the family writes its story: each repair or decoration another paragraph in our history, a crucial moment of discussion, argument, decision and communal action . . . And every house bears the scars of our actions: scuffs on the skirting-board, spilled coffee on the carpet . . .
>
> It's in these traces – the result of accident and habit, event and ritual – that the family's biography is revealed. And now all this is lying on the village tip. Our family house has fallen down . . .
>
> But the house is also in us. The house in which we were raised is physically inscribed in us. 'The feel of the tiniest latch has remained in our hands' (Bachelard 1964: 15). Enter that house again and 'the most delicate gestures – the earliest gestures – suddenly come alive, are still faultless' (ibid.). We remember where and how to turn, to sit, to bend, to lean, to reach . . . when to stoop to avoid banging the head. Here is that network of contacts which our body remembers. For hands: knobs, handles, switches, taps, window latches, locks, banister. For bottom: toilet, chairs; ears, eyes, mouth, feet, heels, knees . . . 'We are a diagram of the functions of inhabiting that particular house, and all other houses are but variations on that theme' (ibid.).
>
> In a tin shack in Queensland, in a jerrybuilt castle in Ceredigion, in a buffalo-hide tent

in Canada, in a terrace in Cardiff, that house is there with us . . . in a way of sitting, a way of slicing, a way of sleeping, in ways we barely discern. We may emigrate, integrate, colonise, go feral, go native, lose ourselves in a wilderness of tundra or jungle, in a barren desert of hatred, in the wastes of the city, in the vastness of a foreign language. But we can never leave them. We can never wipe the slate clean. For occasionally as we reach for an unfamiliar knob, we unlock the familiar cupboard of memory, of all those other times . . . The 'book' from which we learn our vision of the world is read with the body. And our family house has fallen down . . . (see Bourdieu 1977: 89ff.)

(Pearson/Brookes: *The Man Who Ate His Boots* . . . 1998)

Walking, looking, marking out

'A working country is hardly ever a landscape. The very idea of landscape implies separation and observation' (Williams 1973: 120). How easily the notion of 'land-scape' becomes a purely pictorial construct, a framing of artificial viewpoints and perspectives, the appreciation and consumption of artistic artifice. In Welsh, there are two words for landscape: *tirlun* and *tirwedd*. *Tirlun*, which includes the words *tir* (ground) and *llun* (picture), implies a pictorial construct, something to be apprehended by looking, something available for the appreciation and consumption of the visitor, a commodity: viewpoint, perspective, vista, frame. *Tirwedd* has more geographical connotations. But both can be represented by maps, those colourful virtual documents where rivers are blue, roads yellow, forests green. And both concepts work with surface, with morphology.

Thomas Johnes must have hired some of the local silver miners from Cwmystwyth to do the job. You walk past the remains of the iron suspension bridge, along the edge of the deep river gorge. The path turns a corner and the note of the river changes – something ahead, as yet unseen. But instead of turning off, away, up and over the back of the rocks, a neat tunnel opens into the hillside. It is designed as a light trap, with a 90-degree turn halfway along. It funnels the noise of the torrent as you half stumble along to find the light at the end. Turn to the left and the tunnel exit, squared off neatly by the miners, frames the view, right into the midst of the waterfall.

Landscape has connotations of a pictorial perspective, from a fixed point of view, a piece of scenery, a visual phenomenon. And the contemplation of landscape has been a cultivated pursuit which involved a lot of screwing up the eyes, moving to and fro to get the view right. This is an active reconstruction of the land in the imagination into a composition. The best perspectives – where the scene is perceived to be arranged in lateral bands away from the viewer. And names were given to particular effects.

Edmund Burke (1998) suggested that the **sublime**, a mood prompted in the viewer by some overwhelming or awe-inspiring natural feature, should create an unsettling fear or astonishment. Sublime objects, such as the ocean, are vast and painful, objects of terror. On the other hand, the picturesque which emerged in the 1790s was based on variety, intricacy and partial concealments that excite active curiosity. It accepted real environmental change rather than an idealised view of nature, preferring foreground side-screens with middle and background of differing shades. Ruins and humble cottages and farm animals were regarded as more picturesque than monuments and mansions. And it inspired 'picturesque tourism', particularly in Wales.

It is perhaps not surprising that concepts of the picturesque were worked out on the Hafod estate near Aberystwyth in the late eighteenth century, and the wilderness made wilder, made more natural, by the strategic planting of trees and the building of waterfalls and gardens. Thomas Johnes worked to organise his property according to the principles of the picturesque aesthetic. The elements of roughness and wildness were essential. Johnes built paths which introduced the visitor to a sequence of contrasting scenes as perfect pictures, even if this meant building water-falls. There were dynamic contrasts between sheltered paths in the riverside meadows and dark, gloomy depths of the overgrown torrents. 'All that is here done, has been to remove obstructions, reduce the materials and conceal the art; and we are no where presented with attempts to force these untamed streams or indeed to invent anything' (Cumberland 1996: 6).

Simultaneously, other changes were occurring. The enclosures of the late eighteenth century were fundamental in completing the landscape of lowland Britain which we still see today. For centuries, much of the English landscape was of large, open fields surrounding relatively isolated villages and extensive sheep-walks. The characteristic sense of space was circular, around the village. Agricultural improvement swept all this away; above all it introduced linearity. It was about measuring and rationality. The large fields were ironed out, broken up and reallocated, hedges planted, roads straightened, ditches dug, the details of topography erased, the minute and intricate divisions of landscape abolished: all was utility and functionality. And the **sense of place** was threatened.

One of the casualties of this change was the poet John Clare, whose own village Helpston was enclosed in 1809; his own attachment to a particular lived experience of landscape was severed. It is the form of Clare's poetry itself which makes a stand against such imposed linearity in its description of place. So the landscape is presented a multiplicity of simultaneous experiences, with a tendency towards disorder. He attempts in his work to express a manifold, or continuum, of related impressions. In 'Emmonsails Heath in Winter' (Clare 1967: 74), John Barrell (1972) identifies his use of hypotaxis to describe this experience, through the use of words such as 'while', 'beside'. Even in the following section which tends towards parataxis, he is *in* the landscape: he sees the woodcock, feels the bog beneath his feet and hears the fieldfare simultaneously.

Up flies the bouncing woodcock from the bridge
Where a black quagmire quakes beneath the tread
The fieldfare chatter in the whistling thorn

[Ibid]

Reading into the place

The attempts to enclose Ceredigion in West Wales were particularly fraught, for they challenged a set of relationships with a locale which were bound in a set of traditional and customary rights: the right to cut peat and turf for fuel, the right to pasture sheep and cattle, the right to squat and to build upon the common. People resisted, long and violently, loath to believe that any action by the gentry would benefit common people. Somehow the Commissioners finished their work but then sold part of the land to a young Lincolnshire man called Augustus Brackenbury to defray their costs. When Brackenbury tried to prevent customary access to his land the trouble really began.

On Sunday 23 August 1998, Mike Pearson walked for five miles across Mynydd Bach, near the village of Trefenter, south of Aberystwyth: following footpaths, sheep trails, farm tracks and wind-farm access roads; winding along a line, as the crow flies, from Llyn Eiddwen to Pwllclai. He was wearing leather boots, leather gaiters, embroidered waistcoat, frock-coat, top hat, lilac gloves . . . radio microphone, battery unit, earpiece and receiver, and carrying a halogen lamp. Victorian gentleman meets hi-tech in the creative frictions of anachronism. He was accompanied by collaborator Mike Brookes, who carried a backpack radio transmitter and a torch. But they were not entirely alone: out on the mountain sat a BBC engineer in his relay car; in the Radio Ceredigion studio in Aberystwyth were other collaborators, all chattering excitedly, non-stop, in our headsets. Company members managed the traffic out on a tiny one-track road. And across the mountain were scattered groups of people, huddled in groups, sitting in their cars, doing something which they probably haven't done since the 1950s, listening communally to the radio. They were all engaged in, and with, *The First Five Miles . . . /Rhyfel y Sais Bach*, a performance work for radio broadcast and live performer. And all probably equally 'in the dark'.

The conceptual bases of the project were simple enough. At 9 p.m. a local radio station, Radio Ceredigion, began broadcasting a specially created bilingual drama/documentary on the abortive attempts of Augustus Brackenbury to enclose 850 acres of peat-bog and mountainside near Trefenter in the 1820s, sold to him by the Commissioners to defray their costs, and the concerted efforts of local people to prevent him. In what was to become known as 'The War of the Little Englishman', we see worked out all those fears and uncertainties which the enclosures, which the change in the nature of place, which the erasure of familiar topographies, brought to Britain. And the first use of those techniques of resistance – nocturnal meetings, threatening letters, maiming sheep, parading effigies, use of disguise (including men dressing as women) – which were later employed in the Rebecca Riots, against toll-gates, in Wales (see Rudé 1981; Molloy 1983) and the Captain Swing riots, against the mechanisation of agriculture, in England (Rudé 1981).

Simultaneously, we began walking.

Whilst I was permitted to remain within the range of the light from the fire I saw that several of the persons assembled had covered their faces with handkerchiefs and disguised themselves. I believe that other of the men were dressed in women's clothes and that the two who detained me were armed with guns. I did not know any of the persons so assembled neither did I those who detained me. Nor can I describe their features for they held me in such a position that I was rendered incapable from restraint and fear to mark their features or dress.

(Pearson/Brookes: *The First Five Miles* . . . 1998)

From time to time, my voice, as that of Brackenbury, was mixed live into the programme, travelling from my microphone to the backpack transmitter to the BBC vehicle to a satellite and thence to Aberystwyth. Or so we initially, naively thought. In fact, from the satellite it travelled to

Goonhilly Down in Cornwall (images of Raymond Baxter enthusing 'Yes, yes I can see a man's face' from Goonhilly, during the first transatlantic link, come to mind) and then by land-line to Wales. Well, perhaps . . . There is a chance that, to reach Aberystwyth, it was automatically switched to the next nearest tracking station, which is in Norway. Trefenter – Norway – Aberystwyth. And in all this, it was essential that I never heard my own voice, for it was being broadcast almost a second after I spoke. It was elsewhere, disembodied, travelling, boundless . . .

The broadcast itself was in stereo, with the Welsh texts panned towards the left and the English towards the right. Through this – and by attributing the two languages to voices of different gender, tone and mode – we attempted a form of bilingualism which is not about direct translation. It is rather about the coexistence of two languages, simultaneously saying different things and in different ways in such a way that the individual ear can favour one or the other. For the English ear then, the Welsh perhaps becomes a *melissma*, a sonic environment equating to that milieu within which the historical events occurred. For the Welsh ear, the English text – particularly that of the original documents and legal depositions – has all the authority, pomposity and presupposition of the colonial experiment as it was worked out, internally, in Wales. And hence it becomes a kind of static or white noise – background noise, relentless, ever present, but never saying much.

The soundtrack – a music for violin, guitar, and drums – was at once provisional, improvised and on the verge of falling to pieces. Most of the texts were spoken by actors. We had hoped to include the voices of local people who had family stories about Brackenbury. We did record Beti Ty'n Draenen (House in the Thorns) singing a ballad about 'Y Sais Bach', in her kitchen, eating fairy cakes, then discussing what it is like to learn Welsh, to be without an accent, to be close but never quite close enough. But only during the broadcast, and immediately after, did the conversations begin, did opinions clash, did details of memory begin to emerge: anecdotal, fragmentary, speculative . . . all those things which we might never regard as authentic history but which go to make up the **deep map** of the locale.

Our greatest disappointment was that the police helicopter couldn't fly. It was to have tracked my walk with a circular pool of light, pointing at Pearson but at the same time moving on, never turning the landscape into a pictorial backdrop for the performance, never appropriating it, never illuminating it, never pretending that this story of colonialism is of the place. A point rather than a perspective, the landscape as a place to be *in* rather than to be *against*. But the weather was foul – strong winds, low cloud – and the pilot decided it was too dangerous to fly. Of course, we should have expected this. This is, after all, where they built the wind-farm.

I dressed at 'Tan y Castell', 'Below the Castle', down on the bog. In the next field one can see the moat which Brackenbury dug to protect his second house, a provocative fortress-like tower with slit windows. To little avail. The mob demolished and burned it as quickly as they had done the first. Every time he tried to build – fences, houses – huge mobs appeared, often accosting him, and for years. Down the road is ('Cofadail' 'Monument') his third house, where they finally left him in peace.

In our walking we eventually reached Brackenbury's mountain estate. Scattered across the plateau are the remains of maybe a dozen farms. By the 1890s, there was a community of

144

perhaps ninety people living here, prospering in that agricultural boom during which so many houses in West Wales were built, and so many traditional long-houses demolished as old-fashioned. By the depression of the 1930s, there were none. Dai Morris bought all the tenancies piecemeal but he never moved people back onto the land. He had made his money as a builder in the South Wales valleys and he knew where profit lay. Every farm he stripped: slate roofs, timber work, anything that moved. Used to go up with a hand-cart. Like Brackenbury he just wanted the shooting and the fishing. In years to come their cleanliness will present an archaeological conundrum!

But the land was exhausted. What looks like natural grass today, it has taken Dai Williams thirty years to grow. When he first came here it was nothing but moss, the result of overcropping and bad husbandry and of squatting the land. He professed to know little of history but it was he who showed me the banks and ditches built by Brackenbury, the sunken roads, the stone gateposts with holes bored right through them for the iron bolts; he who showed us two *tai-unnos*.

In the eighteenth century, squatters believed in the existence of a traditional law which stated if they could build a house overnight and get a roof on and a fire going by dawn, then they where entitled to the land. And they could lay claim to that within the compass of an axe, thrown from the door in all directions. They cropped it to exhaustion. One can identify the *tai-unnos* because they have three necessities nearby: a small quarry, running water and a peat bog. The geology helped, alternating layers of building stone and shale. Chip out the shale and you can break off stone of different thicknesses for everything, from flag-stones to gable-ends. Here we were on the Telychian deposits of the Llandovery series of the Silurian. (Interesting that the three earliest periods of geological history have Welsh names: Cambrian, Ordovician, Silurian . . . four, if you count the Pre-Cambrian – the 'Before Welsh' – before outline, before topography, before people, before language. The geologists were here too.) Most have the remains of a rectangular banked garden, the hedges now grown out into full trees; several have potato graves, pits for storing the precious crop. The current map shows a few open squares, the symbols for deserted building. That of 1906 shows Blaen-Camddwr, Garn-fach, Pant-yr-ala, Esgair-ddu, Lluest las, Blaen Wyre-isaf, Blaen Wyre-uchaf . . . The names go, with the people. As John Aubrey had it: *mors etiam saxis nominibusque venit*: death comes even to stones and names.

And in each is a ruined hearth, *yr aelwyd*, point of revolve, the focus of family life. Each to his or her own seat or place, holding together, creating, a world picture by talking, gossip, stories, incidents, anecdotes, genealogies, memories, opinions, biographies, thoughts for the day. The approvals and disapprovals of family lore and communal tradition, told *soto voce* in whispers; opinions expressed openly to an unforgiving world; incidents worked and reworked, endlessly. The site of eulogy and elegy. Also of daydreams, shadows, personal reflection (Peate 1972). 'For our house is our corner of the world. It is our first universe, a real cosmos in every sense of the word' (Bachelard 1964: 4). And around each – *y filltir sqwar* and *y fro*, a world of infinite detail without foreground and background, where anything is potentially significant, where anything can take the eye.

Long after the broadcast of *The First Five Miles* . . . had finished, Pearson and Brookes were still walking.

Site-specific performance – work which is specific to this place and no other place – addresses such depth. But of course, it might equally be in conflict with, or indifferent to, site. For these places are no essentialist Eden. Here too was incest, suicide, sexual abuse, misogyny, ruthless materialism and religious hypocrisy. And all that which comes from elsewhere, via trade, immigration, the media . . .

And we have doubts about the **appropriation** of place (Ashcroft, Griffiths and Tiffin 1998: 19). Perhaps then it is only in landscapes such as Mynydd Bach, places of contest, where claims and counter-claims have long been made, where issues of land and language constantly rub against each other, where we can, and indeed must, create work which has none of the dogmatism of the theatrical performance, of architectonics and that distanced aesthetic – framed up, laid out for our pictorial inspection and approval. So that the very **inauthenticity** of the performance allows room for manoeuvre, allows stances, of ownership, identity and interpretation, to be confirmed, challenged, confounded at the same time.

The First Five Miles . . . was constituted in the non-place of the airwaves, blowing in the wind, the visual screen turned down, the theatrical experience including environmental apprehension without it ever becoming a backdrop, personal interpretation including immediate phenomenological involvement with the place, discontinuities of attention, simultaneity of sensual experience. We attempted to reconstitute the notion of audience as a spatially and temporally discrete entity. Such work makes no claims to authenticity, to speak 'on behalf of'. And as immigrants, immigrants into a cultural minority, perhaps the best that can ever be done is to articulate the immigrant position, which is always at once critical and desirous of integration, through work which is fractured and provisional. For the immigrant can never be of this place, never have the knowledge, the words for people and places which come from having been raised in this place. There will always be tension between what you know, what you can find out and what you can never know.

And that tension we might now best represent technologically. In *The First Five Miles* . . . the fascinations are twofold. First, where was it being generated, in one place, or many places? Second, how was it being apprehended? How did the audience decide to constitute themselves: deciding to sit snugly at home or to be out on the mountain? Favouring English or Welsh? The work is a reading 'onto' and 'into' rather than a reading 'from'. And it complements, rather than subsumes, local knowledge and traditions of interpretation. Stirring up memories, thoughts of past times . . .

And it poses a series of questions: How can we read a landscape? How do memories attach to places? What is the relationship between landscape, experience and identity? How do we make sense of the multiplicity of meanings that resonate from landscapes and memories? What constitutes a sense of place? What is the relationship between personal and public memory? How does place act as a mnemonic for memory? How do we use the past to help create a sense of identity? How are notions of place operational upon us? Are they still relevant in an era of mobility and notions of shifting identity?

And how can we tell about them?

Cityscape: walking

Desire maps

> Their story begins on ground level, with footsteps.
>
> (De Certeau 1988: 97)

In his book *A Seventh Man* (see Berger 1975), John Berger describes the experience of the migrant worker, elaborating the great pilgrimage of the twentieth century, the journey from the village to the city. Most of us now live in cities, it is the urban, the congregation of strangers, which defines our contemporary experience. We can never know more than a fraction of our fellow inhabitants and we can never know the whole geography in any kind of detail. We are destined to be one amongst a great many, 'so many lives, jostling, colliding, disrupting, adjusting, recognising, settling, moving again to new spaces' (Williams 1973: 164).

On 4 November 1999 Mike Pearson walked for eight hours in the city of Copenhagen with archaeologist Jonna Hansson in a project entitled *Footloose*. It was organised by the Interactive Urban Landscapes initiative. The strategy was to constitute 'walking in the city' as a kind of anthropological and archaeological enquiry. Having identified shoes as a potential area of non-contentious enquiry, they aimed to work from the particular – in examining those moments, places and encounters where foot and city meet – to the general – in proposing such an approach as the creation of a **desire map**; to begin by knowing what they want to look at, and proceeding without fixed itineraries, without maps; to work at ground level, eyes down, close to the surface; to reveal the city through purposeful activity, taking full responsibility for their own actions and intrusions.

❖ *Pursuing*: manifestations and traces of a particular theme or topic which constitute an object of desire: shoes.

❖ *Rambling*: guided by disciplinary interest and expertise (as archaeologists we look at the vernacular, in detail), by the directions and instructions of informants ('Where is the nearest shoe repairer?' 'Take the first left and it's on the right . . .') and by the need to avoid certain, potentially dangerous or confrontational encounters.

❖ *Seeking*: the sites where shoes have left their traces, either as accumulative marks (prints, scuffs) or as erosion (depressions on worn steps, chipped paint on door frames).

❖ *Identifying*: ephemeral or transitory marks (wet footprints, impressions in builder's sand) and those of varying degrees of permanence: erosion of paint on zebra crossings, worn linoleum, pavement subsidence. And those places where 'wear' has ceased, where the building is locked and grass now grows around the threshold.

❖ *Finding*: artefacts (discarded shoes, boot scrapers, doormats).

❖ *Encountering*: those intimately involved with shoes (sellers, repairers), those who wear special footwear (policemen, meat packers, builders) and those who daily rely on their shoes, who work on their feet (shop assistants, hairdressers).

❖ *Enquiring*: of shoe menders: about the nature of wear, the relationship of individuals to their shoes and the fickle vagaries of fashion; of thrift-shop assistants: about lack of interest in buying second-hand shoes as opposed to clothes; of fashion retailers: about the identity of those who buy shoes as a style statement.

❖ *Discovering*: 'underground' shoe cultures – S&M footwear (with spikes inside); fetish fashion.

❖ *Observing*: moments of fleeting contact (a cyclist resting his foot on the pavement); places especially for shoes (foot rails in bars, bicycle pedals) and the sites where the density of marks or depth of erosion indicate traditions of social usage (the habit of kicking open doors).

❖ *Speculating*: that the city even smells different at shoe level.

❖ *Resembling*: those archetypal figures of the modern city: De Certeau's *walker* (1988: 91–110), Benjamin's *flâneur* (1999: 417–55; Buck-Morss 1991: 304–7) and Deleuze's *nomad* (Deleuze and Guattari 1988).

The walker

We may all *want* to go up the Eiffel Tower, to see the city from above, to be god-like, to gain optical knowledge, to achieve a total(ising) view. But in fact our elementary experience of the city is as 'walkers', 'whose bodies follow the thicks and thins of an urban "text" they write without being able to read it fully' (De Certeau 1988: 93). It is our intertwined paths which link places together; pedestrian movements form 'real systems whose existence in fact makes up a city' (ibid.: 97).

Such walking could be inscribed as routes on maps, but that would miss the practice of our meandering, stopping and starting, window-shopping, passing-by. There is always a tension then between the possibilities of the constructed order – 'I am only allowed to go there and not there' – and our own improvisation. De Certeau distinguishes tricks in the arts of doing (1988: xviii), the ways in which we subvert constraints. So whilst layout and street plan might prefigure our activity, we are always seeking the short-cut. This he regards as delinquency because it endorses the privileging of the route over the inventory. So 'walking affirms, suspects, tries out, transgresses, respects the trajectories it speaks' (ibid.: 99). Step by step we decide how we will do it, how we will read the text of the city: we gain our understanding through movement.

> The 'moving about' that the city multiples and concentrates makes the city itself an immense social experience of lacking a place – an experience that is, to be sure, broken up into countless tiny deportations (displacements and walks) compensated for by the relationships and intersections of these exoduses that intertwine and create an urban fabric, and placed under the sign of what ought to be, ultimately, the place but is only a name, the City.
>
> (De Certeau 1988: 103)

So the urban space is a frequented place, an intersection of moving bodies. It is the pedestrians who transform the street into a space. Yet this walking is often orientated. We are drawn back to significant places, familiar places, memorable places, weaving them together in improvised narratives. We both read and write. Through memory and imagination, we can claim a measure of control.

The *flâneur*

De Certeau suggests that walking is an act of appropriation which includes three aspects: walking, looking and being looked at. And this contains echoes of our second figure: the *flâneur*. In origin the *flâneur* was a detached and self-contained poetic figure, distanced from the crowd by his superior aesthetic sensibilities. He aimlessly wandered the city streets to gain inspiration, at once part of, and isolated from, the urban crowd, whom he studied; at once a bohemian and producer of written commodities, 'at home in the ebb and flow, the bustle, the fleeting and the infinite' (Baudelaire, cited in Edensor 1998: 217). The poet-*flâneur* had the freedom to loiter, to witness and interpret passing scenes and incidents (Edensor 1998: 217). And the premodern street was a place of diverse activities, unpredictable juxtapositions, fleeting occurrences, multifarious sights and sounds. With the advent of the modern city, the concept of the *flâneur* has come to stand as a metaphor for the contemporary urban dweller, moving through the flux of the city, as a mode of being in the world, in relation to the dazzling consumer spectacles: in a modern shopping centre we are all *flâneur*: gazing, grazing, consuming . . .

The nomad

The nomad shifts across the smooth space of the urban desert using points and locations to define paths rather than places to be, making the most of circumstance (Cresswell 1997: 364). The enemy of the nomad is the state, which wants to take the space and enclose it and to create fixed and well-directed paths for movement. And the nomad, cut free of roots, bonds and identities, is the enemy of the state, resisting its discipline.

The rambler

Jane Rendell (1998) identifies a fourth figure, the *rambler*, who rethinks the city as a series of paces of flows of movement, in pursuit of pleasure: moving between sites of leisure, pleasure, consumption, exchange and display. And such rambling is a gendered activity. She suggests (1998: 84):

> Urban design organises bodies socially and spatially, in terms of positioning, displaying and obscuring. Architecture controls and limits physical movement and sight-lines; it can stage and frame those who inhabit its spaces, by creating contrasting scales, screening and lighting. (Friedman 1992). Such devices are culturally determined, they prioritise certain activities and persons, and obscure others according to class, race and gender. Urban space is a medium in which functional visual requirements and imagery are constituted and represented as part of a patriarchal and capitalist ideology. The places of leisure

in the nineteenth century city represent and control the status of men and women as spectators and as objects of sight in public arenas.

Perhaps then walking is promiscuous, 'a mode of movement which celebrates the public spaces, streets and excitement of urban life from a male perspective' (ibid.) – looking at any woman with a consuming gaze, as an available object.

Urban time-spaces

Walking: affirming, suspecting, trying out, transgressing, respecting the trajectories it 'speaks'. The French anthropologist Marc Augé (1995: 56–74) uses three simple spatial forms to map anthropological space: line, the intersection of lines, and the point of intersection. In the city, they correspond respectively to paths which lead from one place to another; to crossroads and open spaces where people pass, meet and gather and which are sometimes large in order to satisfy the needs of economic exchange (as with markets); and thirdly to monumental centres, places of institutional complexity – the town hall, seat of government, palace, cathedral, etc. Routes, cross-roads and centres – though they may be found elsewhere, they are all found in the city. The notions of itinerary, intersection, centre and monument begin to describe the urban space. Thus individual itineraries in the city are constantly drawn towards centres where they intersect and mingle. Augé suggests that there is then the possibility for polyphony, the interlacing of destinies, actions, thoughts and reminiscences.

Cities are multitemporal. The remains of the past are all around us: architecture survives. Here a Georgian townhouse exists next to a modern designer home. Some buildings are thought worthy of preservation and restoration. And some fragments of buildings become integrated into others as if they are half-digested, stratifications of past occupations, repairs and constructions, the superimposition of different time-scales. Other buildings are repaired, their function changes: a chapel becomes a disco. Their identity is unstable. Survival, juxtaposition, discontinuity. There is no linearity here.

In cities, history accumulates. Many exist on their rubbish, their debris endlessly accreting beneath the feet. Not only does waste gather but buildings are constantly knocked down and others erected on their site. In some parts of London, the Roman city is twenty feet below the surface. The history of the city is revealed as a horizontal layering and a vertical accumulation of surfaces. In places, erosion reveals underlying strata (tarmac over tarmac over cobblestones); in others, processes of reconstruction and refurbishment cut down to reveal a classic archaeological 'section' of superimposed layers. Here the contemporary overlays the past (yellow lines painted over a variety of surfaces); there past and present meet in discontinuities of material fabric (tarmac abutting cobblestones); there present cuts through to lie next to past (pipe trench).

In *Footloose* were performed a series of encounters, always occasioned by discussion of shoes, with others (from various ethnic backgrounds, ages and professions). Except for the project they might expect never to meet and indeed may even have avoided each other. It leads to a fuller appreciation of the multivocality of the locale and inevitably, through the stories and experiences of others, to a sense of history, with the city inseparably spatio-temporal.

THEATRE/ARCHAEOLOGY

Talking at length to a shoe repairer. Asking him about whether he could see how people walked from the wear on their shoes. 'Of course', he said, 'though most walk, feet slightly splayed, on the outsides of the heels.' Asking him about what happens to shoes that people don't collect. 'I keep them', he said, 'in plastic bags in the cellar beneath our feet.' Asking him about the fickle vagaries of fashion. 'Well', he said, 'first they're pointy, then they're square, then they're pointy, then they're square.' And his thesis borne out by the display of medieval shoes in the Danish National Museum.

In the city we all create an itinerary of locations. The vernacular detail of the locale which we can now recurrently identify and which we can use to locate and orientate ourselves in an unfamiliar landscape without recourse to maps, diagrams, guides or needing to view the city as if from above. Such an interaction may then constitute a **desire map**: as 'strangers in a strange land' we pursue cultural phenomena – here shoes – which we knew from elsewhere and as we allow their manifestations to bring us into social encounters.

And, despite the walking, there is a suspicion that all around Copenhagen, approximately one metre from the ground, on walls, entrances, doors, window frames, there is a line, a datum, scored by the passage of millions of pairs of handlebars . . .

Landscape: standing still

A field of tensions

This notion of landscape, this cultural locale, as we have called it, of archaeology, is ridden with tensions. It is the implied separation and observation noted by Raymond Williams above, distant horizons and distanced vantage-points. It is that uneasiness we feel about the figures in many classic picturesque landscape paintings. The peasants dancing in the limpid evening light of a Claude, the locals 'going about their business'; the figures in the foreground as Turner captures the sublimity of a ruin against a sky (cf. Daniels 1993: 112). Or indeed for us it is the uneasiness invoked by the delicate constructions of land artist Andy Goldsworthy. Ephemeral ice sculptures, leaves woven together with thorns, photographed in morning light, beautifully reproduced in an art book (consider Kastner and Wallis 1998: 68-9). It is about an absence perhaps, this tension, in spite of the skills of artist, in spite of the aesthetic paradigm to which we all react. Nature turned to beauty in an aesthetic gesture of an artist like Goldsworthy, relationships turned into things to be painted, photographed, written about. We find ourselves asking, just what is going on there? John Berger famously connected the Gainsborough painting of Mr and Mrs Andrews, standing before their estate, to sentiments of property ownership (Berger 1972: 106-8), contrasting the commod-ification of their relationship with land to an implied authenticity of working relationships; though, and this is again the tension, he also failed to account for the attractions of such images (Fuller 1980).

Part of it is about such relations between foreground and background. It is also the relation-ship between here, the here of the viewer, and there, the there of the image or the worlds from which it borrows: for example, the Tuscan countryside of so many eighteenth-century pastoral idylls. In the idealised vision of many landscapes and landscape art there is a contrast between the way we are, and the way we might be, or the worlds we might inhabit, in harmony with nature perhaps, in a cottage in the countryside, a cabin in the woods, or in a carefully designed environment. Hence from the eighteenth and nineteenth centuries landscape as representation has been linked to various projects of achieving a correspondence between a pictorial ideal and the countryside itself. This manifested itself as landscape gardening and estate management, all the way through the garden cities of Britain, the lairds' villages of Scotland built to house the commoners and to supply picturesque backdrop to the management of aristocratic estates, suburbia to city planning and landscape architecture today. Of course it includes a tension, linked to industrialisation and processes of urbanisation, between city and countryside. Actuality of place and potentiality of improvement and design is also a temporal relationship between the quotidian and the timeless, the latter often associated with the beauties of place. Particularly now we are sensitive to those relationships between the general or the global, and the local. Here we feel uneasy about the myriad local landscapes made similar in their aesthetic treatment, in their assimilation to similar processes of understanding and representation.

In contemporary archaeology the tension is very apparent. Techniques of environmental analysis, tracing remains and evidences of geomorphology, plant and animal communities, climatic change, with powerful topographic mapping, and Geographic Information Systems to manage the data, enable increasingly detailed reconstructions of ancient environments. Spatial science reached a height over thirty years ago (Harvey 1969), as described in Chapter 1, and remains a formidable set of resources for controlling geometric space, as the 'backdrop' or medium of history and culture. But these advances have left far distanced the humanism of the landscape history of Hoskins, for example. Working in that paradigm of Aubrey and Stukeley he combined accurate observation with a facility for synthesis and narrative (in the classic *Making of the English Landscape,* 1955). We can think of no effective translation of these developments into even a descriptive mode of representation. The potential naturalism (as defined above) of these techniques has not been realised.

Meanwhile humanistic geography has developed a greater concern with the sociocultural and political processes which shape landscape, and with a focus on the ideological. Denis Cosgrove and Stephen Daniels edited a seminal collection of essays on landscape as a way of seeing (1988), drawing in concepts of iconography and textuality, with landscape regarded as a field of signifiers, the interpretation of which reveals cultural attitudes and processes. The earlier work of David Lowenthal and Hugh Prince (1964; also Lowenthal 1985 and 1991a) investigating the impact of national taste and social class on landscape creation, is to be noted here, taken up later by Daniels (1993).

The broader context is the investment of geographical interest in, indeed the redefinition of cultural geography as the time-space structures of human society and culture (Cloke, Philo and Sadler 1991; Johnston, Gregory and Smith 1994; Cloke, Crang and Goodwin 1999). Two key concepts here are **locale** – the settings in which social relations are constituted, and sense of **place** – a local structure of feeling. As we mentioned above, here are intellectual roots in the focus on the cultural landscape, human relationships with the environment, represented by Carl Sauer and the Berkeley School, and many after. Hägerstrand and the Lund School represent a time geography, investigating patterns of coming and going (references given above). Much recent work has paid attention to non-material and ideological aspects of culture in relationship with place, locale and landscape. Tapping more roots in social theory than biology and history, the effect of linguistic theory is significant, with the meanings of place contested, related to the discourses of particular human groups divided along axes of class, ethnicity, culture and gender. We consider important here that line of critique which goes to the heart of any geographical project – the question of the division of nature and culture. Anthropologists have been doubting the distinction and easiness of the relationship (Strang 1997) and considering the cross-cultural relevance of concepts like landscape.

Tied to these developments in cognate disciplines, archaeologists too have been considering the cultural constitution of space. John Fritz (1978) examined the symbolic landscape of prehistoric Chaco Canyon in the American south west in the 1970s, under a project of cognitive archaeology – the archaeology of mind. By the 1990s an archaeology often describing itself as phenomeno-logical has come to celebrate cultural experience and **lifeworld** – the totality of a person's direct involvement with the places and environments experienced in everyday life. Studies have appeared, for example, of prehistoric landscapes (Tilley 1994; Bender 1998; Edmonds 1999), with archaeologists again walking the land, this time asserting the primacy of the constitutive imagina-tion. For example, in Tilley's subjectivist critique of spatial science, meanings are given to external phenomena through intuitive experience and relationships with them, and captured in prose and photograph (1994). Visuality and movement are the two principal modes of engagement with the ruined monuments of ancient landscapes in Britain and northern Europe. 'Here people walked and understood the world in this way', is the recurrent motif. And past and present are brought together through walking and looking under a sensitisation to the way it may have been felt and thought in the past. This is achieved through the use of ethnographic analogies and particularly of cosmology, rather than through environmental reconstruction.

Hence Tilley begins his *Phenomenology of Landscape* (1994) with ethnographic cases of land as penetrated by cosmology, and is able to assert that 'writing about an economic base in relation to resource utilisation or landscape use seems quite irrelevant' (1994: 67). There is a problem though in thus giving primacy to a subjectivist aesthetic – walking the land with an eye to the experience can easily lapse into a 'past-as-wished-for'. In spite of its humanistic and critical commitment to an ethnographic sensitivity, the validity of Tilley's phenomenology is based upon the sophistication and subtlety of his projection back into the past from present landscapes. This conspicuously includes reliance, in all his illustrations of archaeological landscapes, upon that distinctive distanced aesthetic which we have been so concerned to denaturalise; the photographs and plans hold no surprises. And it is a pastoral aesthetic in this rejection of any involvement or engagement other than empathy informed by reading. For Tilley it sometimes seems we are to walk the ancient countryside in order to escape the constraints of social science.

We are reminded of that old distinction between Descartes's language of objectivity versus Vico's language of involvement. Here are polarisations between absolute position or point and relative or meaningful place, between the notion of a map as a geometric model of all possible routes, and the practical space of journeys. Our aim is not to separate and treat these as polar opposites, but to realise the relationships between them and understand where they come from. It is not as if we want, or can, make the tensions we have described disappear, somehow. For us landscape is a field of process and relationship, a contradictory nexus, itself to be explored.

We are left indeed with a technical issue of writing and representing, with our project of documentation, the partial and oblique strategies required in opening up a site and documenting a heterotopia. Barbara Bender has referred to Berger's call for another way of telling (1998: Chapter 6; Berger and Mohr 1982) and we concur. But an historical consciousness of the tensions simply in walking the land prompt us to rethink this task. We need an involved aesthetic yes, but we also need to consider political economy, the changing material conditions of living in the land; we need maps and geometries, as well as evocation. These tensions in landscape present us with a field of (political) potential linked to somatic memory and experience. For what is at stake is twofold – modes of visiting and the character of ruin. We stress again the concept of the archaeological and the need for a theory of ruin. By this we mean an ecology of interpenetration between past and present, with the visit treated as a performative event which witnesses absence.

A ruin buried in a forest

On a hillside outside Lampeter in West Wales, they are felling the pine plantation. And as the forty-year-old cash-crop is harvested, the ruins of perhaps twenty farmsteads re-emerge in the landscape. They were never quite totally lost. One could always spot the luminous green of their deciduous trees, beech and sycamore – the remains of gardens and grown-out hedges planted when the farms were created – against the monochrome canopy. Esgair Fraith ('Speckled Ridge') is one such substantial farmstead built as part of the enclosure of the parish in the 1830s. Sited on what was a piece of rough grass and wetland and often mistakenly described as a hamlet, its walls, paths and buildings seem too numerous for an upland agricultural concern. Indeed from the outset, they may have been more. For the first owner was a local weaver, an outworker in the important Cardiganshire wool industry. He was 46 when he moved to Esgair Fraith with his family who seem to have followed him into his trade. He may have been supplementing his income by farming. But it seems likely that these buildings were always partly industrial, with weaving and cloth storage sheds near the house, dams in the river and the remains of a horse-whim, perhaps for fulling. By the late 1880s the family was much reduced and subsequently only one daughter was living there with her own illegitimate daughter, masquerading as her aunt. And so the first trajectory of energy runs its course. The next occupants, the Davies, took Esgair Fraith solely as a farming enterprise around 1890. A dated stone of 1904 in the garden marks their energetic engagement. Mrs Davies died in 1926 and the old man lived there alone until 1941, when the farm was abandoned. The roof was off by 1949. Local memory has Mr Davies doing smithing, tinkering and shoe-mending, and in one roofless shed there are still traces of his work, baths and pans, leather and nails. The history of Esgair Fraith is thus the narrative of two families, of two sets of biographies.

A thick blanket of moss and lichen now coats the ruined walls. Its reappearance presents archaeology with a quandary . . . and with an opportunity.

For these are not merely domestic relics. They are examples of the way in which over the past sixty years places in Wales have been removed from maps: through the flooding of valleys to create reservoirs, through the sequestration of military ranges, through afforestation and through open-cast mining. Each episode of loss involved the removal of population and the destruction of communities. And each in turn inspired political response, campaigns of civil disobedience, the foundation of organisations of opposition: Plaid Cymru, the Welsh Language Society, the Free Wales Army, Meibion Glyndwr. For they function as **inciting incidents**, those irrevocable acts around which opinion clusters, reaction concentrates and through which a small nation marks its particular history.

This is never simply a matter of the loss of land and soil. It is always a matter of homeland and native soil. And more than that. What is lost here is not land but the lived experience of land – all that turns site into place and occupancy into identity – a continuity of experience which finds expression in a particular language and which is preserved in a particular oral and literary tradition. As the playwright, academic and activist Saunders Lewis said at his trial for arson in Caernarfon in 1936, 'The development of the bombing range in Lleyn into the inevitable arsenal it will become will destroy this essential home of Welsh culture, idiom and literature' (1983: 118). For him, land and culture are intimately intertwined. For him, place, language and identity are inextricably bound. Not surprising then that the poetic response should be as virulent as the political one. Of the afforestation around his ancestral home near Lampeter, Gwenallt, the poet who best captured the tensions between rural and industrial Wales, writes, in Welsh,

> And by this time there's nothing there but trees
> Impertinent roots suck dry the old soil:
> Trees were neighbourhood was,
> And a forest that once was farmland.
> Where was verse-writing and scripture
> is the South's bastardised English.
>
> ('Rhydcymerau', Jones 1986: 285–6)

Not only then do places disappear, they are also silenced. What is lost here, literally and symbolically, are those locales where Welsh discourse, where Welshness itself, is generated. We say symbolically because the Welsh sense of place is enshrined in that series of cognitive maps surrounding home and neighbourhood where particular discourses, discrete ways of telling, are engendered.

These 'sites of disappearance' continue to animate the political and poetic imagination in Wales: these ruins, traces, memories persist as places where meanings and identities, local, regional and national are indeed 'represented, contested and inverted'. They too resemble **heterotopias**. Their loss has been worked and reworked to illustrate Welsh cultural and linguistic decline. Even in their absence they become akin to Pierre Nora's **lieux de memoire** (Nora 1989), those sites where cultural memory is constructed and presented.

And then suddenly with the felling of timber, the years of recurrent drought, the demilitarisation of Europe, and with some irony, they return. Their return challenges us to revisit them, to re-address them, to re-enfold them, to remap.

M.8   S.8

The quandary. How is archaeology to deal with these ruins, rising amongst the felled trees? We could excavate their dereliction, record their house-plans, document broken pots, hoping to reveal how these places once were. Such archaeology is rooted in a desire for plenitude, the fullness of times lost, reversal of the mouldering decay which accompanies burial and time passing. Under this impulse and as we have described above (page 43), archaeological reconstructions often aim at photographic verisimilitude: a moment arrested before the viewer, or a simulacrum to be photographed. Their desire is naturalism, an adherence to the appearance of things, a replication of external features, the way things once were.

But to what end? Places like Esgair Fraith are neither so exceptional nor so old that their inscription is of particular importance. They are fairly recent phenomena, not more than one or two hundred years old, the result of both squatting on the commons and legal enclosure, particularly in the mid-nineteenth century, in response to population rise and the need to supplement the fluctuating fortunes of semi-industrial workers such as weavers and miners by homesteading. And as this break-up was one of the great changes in the Welsh landscape since the Bronze Age perhaps we shouldn't be too sentimental about its own subsequent demise.

Equally and instead we might accept the loss, whilst attending to Adorno and Horkheimer's admonition (1979 [1941]:148): 'what is needed is not the preservation of the past, but the redemption of past hopes.' Decay and morbidity are the condition of archaeological enquiry. It is not just that things happened in the past, but that they may be touched, somehow, and now. This quest for sensuous knowing and corporeal knowledge is often what draws people, archaeologists and others, to the material past. The tangibility of remains of times gone offers access to what was thought lost, drawing on the energies of loss and restitution.

The opportunity. These places are saturated with meaning: whilst little of physical worth is at risk here, everything of cultural value is at stake. They offer a series of challenges to those archaeologies which call themselves **interpretive** and **Romantic**, effectively to document and represent a locale that itself resembles a **heterotopia** and **palimpsest**. They require a 'rescue archaeology' not of physical remains but of cultural identity. For any approach to them must take into account the endless narratives, the political aspirations and disappointments, which have accumulated around them. It is not enough to confine them to the past, to say, 'this is how they were then'.

In the invitation to return and revisit, these places posit fundamental questions about methodology: What is to be recorded, how and why? How is the past to be written and on whose behalf?

B.8   R.8   A.8   E.8   O.8

What are the politics of interpretation and representation? How might contested interpretations of the past be embraced and presented? They may therefore be susceptible to those practices which are aware of their plurality of motive, which pay attention to the local and particular and which are suspicious of any final account of things; to practices sensual and phenomenological, which are bound to be subjective, emotional and provocative, which are as unafraid of poetry as they are of politics. 'Through poems, perhaps more than through recollections, we touch the ultimate poetic depth of the space of the house' (Bachelard 1964: 6).

Intimate to this concept of the archaeological are personal identities (always socially and culturally mediated) and their location in the material of our bodies, things owned, found, lost, lived amongst. This will necessitate new and extended approaches to site including creative and technical innovation in the recording, writing and illustrating of the material past – an experimental archaeology rooted in creative reinterpretation of social fabric.

Such is the resonance of these sites that any re-encounter will be inevitably political: reawakening memories, stirring emotions, mobilising causes. For it recovers that which we thought was lost: the disputes over ownership, over the proprietorship of interpretation. And it is here that archaeology has a chance. It could hide behind its scientific objectivity but, as we maintain, it could equally reveal itself as a process of cultural production which takes the remains of the past to make something out of them in the present. By the creative use of the various fragments *of* the past archaeology can become a significant resource in nurturing cultural memory, in helping to develop rich and plural cultural ecologies based on alternative notions of heritage and ultimately in constructing and energising contemporary identities.

But what does this mean in practice?

Let us first remember that realistic representation is not only or necessarily naturalistic. Realism is a project, not a set of formal conventions. As James Clifford (1988: 100) puts it, 'realistic portraits, to the extent that they are "convincing" or "rich" are extended metaphors, patterns of associations that point to coherent (theoretical, aesthetic, or moral) additional meanings.' Realism involves allegory. The construction of narrative is but one aspect or possibility here. In looking at things found we make stories, relating our looking to our experiences, to connections we see and imagine.

How are we to make sense of these places? Meaning comes from making connections and exploring contexts. This is something constructed or brought to a place by the maker and the viewer – what, after all, is a 'natural' context? It may involve considerable deviation – temporal, spatial and conceptual – away from naturalism. To understand Esgair Fraith, we may need to tell a story of quite another time and place.

Visitation

For Forest Enterprise, a state agency and the owner of the hillside, these places are regarded as a leisure resource: it is eager to provide public access. Since they are to be revisited, we might base the framework of a research project around the notion of the visit and its close relative the guided tour.

How might archaeology illuminate such visitation? First perhaps, by doing nothing. By leaving it as it is, providing access, saying nothing, letting the remains speak for themselves, letting the visitor address them in her own way. For these tumbled walls are equivocal, romantic, serving as a backdrop or scenography for any narrative or fantasy which might be projected onto them, any knowledges and aspirations, any interpretation which might be brought to them. A visitor's experience of the same place may invoke reactions and associations entirely different from that of the inhabitants: it is possible to be in a place without realising its significance for the groups of people who have historically inhabited it. For some, the response will be aesthetic and individual, the romance of the ruin. For others the very ruination is evocative of the cultural decline which it symbolises, with the deciduous growth representing a kind of dogged resistance. A pile of old stones to walk your dog over or the defeated hopes of a nation? Take your pick. Imagination here is the implement of excavation. Whichever, the senses of the visitor are accosted by the smells of decay, the textures of moss and dead leaves, the image of collapsed walls, fallen lintels, the gloom of forest shade. Here, the very processes of the archaeological are apparent: mouldering, rotting, disintegrating, decomposing, putrefying, falling to pieces. And that sense of the passage of time – and of our own mortality perhaps – which the manicured sites of heritage culture are so keen to disguise. And the visitor is aware that each surviving doorway was once entered, each window was once looked through. On this bleak hillside, where it will inevitably rain during your visit, humanity survived.

Second, archaeology might provide some sort of orientation, something to inform the reading: directions, a map. In that these direct movement *around* the site, then they could demand an energetic engagement *with* the site; they may come to resemble choreographic scores or diagrams. Such a choreography of the visitor could be *of* the site, following paths, crossing thresholds, entering rooms. Equally, it could delineate unusual trajectories of movement – straight lines, circles, arcs, traversing the site – revealing unexpected viewpoints, demanding altered stances and body engagements, all serving to defamiliarise the visitor, inviting her to look afresh at detail and at prospect and to sense the place. And it might suggest not only where to look but also how to look, in close-up, in long shot, with wide-angle. As, of course, people have always done there. But still the visitor has little to go on. She begins to ask questions: What is this place? What happened here? Who lived here? She wants to put a past onto the phenomenological experience of being present: she needs quite simply a **deep map**. So if we map, it is not as some banal planning or recording of the ruined structures. Any guidebook will have to be adequate to the task of elaborating the complexity of narratives which have accumulated and which are in contest here. We will need to be able to read between the lines. This will demand what we have termed '**incorporations**': juxtapositions and interpenetrations of the historical and the contemporary, the political and the poetic, the factual and the fictional, the discursive and the sensual. These are proactive documents: their parts do not necessarily cohere. They will require work but they leave space for the imagination of the reader. The interpretive instinct of the visitor is not denied: meaning is not monopolised. As such, they may function as an alternative kind of site-report.

Third, we might accompany visitors to site. And here the archaeological and the performative might make common cause, for the document, the equivocal, multivocal working of ruin and trace, could be constituted as real-time event. Performance itself can be a rearticulation of site: language can return a reading onto and into it. Performance occasions reinterpenetration (Phillips 1995: 51–2).

The solo narrative, some equivalent of the explorer's account, the traveller's tale of strange sights and smells, might be an effective means of rearticulation. It can exhibit a high order of intertextuality, of dialogue between texts: anecdotes, analects, autobiography, the description of people, places and pathologies, poetry, forensic data, quotations, lies, memories, jokes. Indeed, it must vacillate between the intimately familiar and the infinitely strange, if the visitor's attention is to be held. The teller is inevitably at the centre of events. The interpreter is foregrounded and interpretation becomes a performative practice. Here in the **grain** of the voice (Barthes 1977: 179f.) is where the story comes to life; and so too in all those techniques of the performer's art: physical re-enactments, impersonation, improvised asides, gestures, eye movements. 'After all, storytelling, in its sensory aspect, is by no means a job for the voice alone' (Benjamin 1992: 107). Here we might find employed all those modes and techniques, those social discourses, which inhabit and animate the cognitive maps of a Welsh sense of place: chatting, lecturing, reciting, orating, seducing in modulations and intensifications of speed, tone, volume, rhythm, emphasis.

What such work so often elicits is other stories, and stories about stories. It catalyses personal reflection and the desire on the part of the listener to reveal her own experiences. It works with memory: raking up old ones, stimulating new ones. These places continue not only to commemorate but also to animate. We work them so that their silencing is not forgetting and their disappearance is not amnesia. Memory preserved, over generations.

Site-specific performance

More complex site-specific work at such sites might use different varieties of narrative, factual and fictive, historical and contemporary, creative and analytical, in parallel and in sequence. It can overlay the documentary, the observational and the creative within a given location or architecture without laying any claim to accuracy or historical verisimilitude.

They arrived at dusk, taking nearly half an hour in the coaches to follow the forest tracks to the site, several miles from road and amenities. From the old quarry they picked their way over a rise, past the generators, towards the lighting rigs, into the conifers and the planked seating, set raked into the trees. Before them as picturesque a ruin as could be, but transected by two rigidly geometric cubes of steel tubing, two stories high, floored and lit, transparent architectures to accompany the stone walls and gable ends, some tables and chairs, a bed, a TV, buckets of fluid, and a dead sheep, stinking under a white cover. Thus it was in October 1995 at Esgair Fraith that Cliff McLucas directed a Brith Gof production – *Tri Bywyd* ('Three Lives') – a site-specific performance (McLucas 2000).

Instead of simply re-enacting the place and its history, it was decided to build two new architectures at, and indeed through the site, and through each other! These scaffolding structures were inspired by the architectural designs of Bernard Tschumi (1994c) and based on a cube structure divided into twenty-four separate 'rooms' of eight feet in each dimension – formality in the forest; wood and steel; straight and curved – and truly 'ghost-like' in their presence. Each frame represented a specific set of rooms – 7 James Street in Cardiff and Llethemeuadd in Pencader, Llandysul – as accurately as possible, in orientation and layout. All furniture – beds, chairs, tables – were constructed from scaffolding tube to echo the fabric of the frames.

In these three coexisting architectures were located three separate stories. They were about three lives, and three deaths. And about the domestic, set into historical and conceptual landscapes of rural life, urban anomie, charged tensions of community and enquiring authority, appropriation and resistance. Taking 1860, approximately the date of the building of Esgair Fraith, as the datum, one story was of period but not site, a second of site but not period and a third of neither site nor period. The narratives unfolded simultaneously in parallel, in a convergence of congruence and incongruence – katachresis and hypotaxis, one always seen through or in juxtaposition to the others, whilst never acknowledging each others' existence.

The first story was that of Sarah Jacob, the fasting girl of Llandysul, a nearby village, who in February 1866 contracted scarlet fever and was bedridden for two weeks. She recovered but in February 1867 complained of stomach pains and was put to bed. After a fortnight she developed strong muscular fits. She became emaciated and all her hair fell out. On October 1 1867 she ceased to take any food at all and lived for the next two years, one month and one week with no visible sustenance whatever. Lying in bed, saint-like and dressed as a bride, she became a major tourist attraction, not least with the coming of railways. Guides even met visitors from London's Paddington station alighting at Pencader, in the next valley; trains formed a recurrent motif in the performance soundtrack. She was perhaps receiving food from her sister, passed from mouth to mouth, under the arm. In May 1869, the editor of the medical journal *The Lancet* questioned the authenticity of her case and implicated her family and the local community. There were vitriolic arguments in the press – a clash of Welsh mysticism, Methodism and the rational discourse of English science. Four nurses from Guys Hospital, London arrived and placed Sarah Jacob under surveillance: within ten days she had starved to death. She was 11 years old.

The second narrative was that of Lynette White of Cardiff, murdered in the early hours of Valentine's Day 1988. She had worked as a prostitute in the run-down docklands, scene of the city's economic heyday in the nineteenth century. She had been stabbed fifty-one times and her head was all but severed from her body. With a mish-mash of contradictory testimony, confession, witness reports and forensic evidence the police arrested and saw through to conviction four local men, immigrants, not so well educated. The case of the 'Cardiff four' was a gross miscarriage of justice picked up by the media (Williams 1995); the men were later freed. And Lynette White, her own story, of which we have so little, and which is so symbolic of the death of old Cardiff, needs to be remembered, not lost in the journalism, in police record.

> At first, it was as if everyone was trying out stories to see if they would stick, to other stories – editing, trimming, rewriting. But then it moved on and James Street became a stage-set upon which everyone was free to choreograph and direct the behaviours, actions and motives of the protagonists. To create the scenario. To write the dialogue. To give oneself a starring role. To use scenes and characters from other times, other places. Eye-witnesses did it. Defendants did it. Police did it. I do it too.
>
> [Brith Gof: *From Memory* (*Body of Evidence*) 1995; text by Mike Pearson]

The ruins of Esgair Fraith itself hosted a specially composed fiction portraying a matter of contemporary rural concern, but one which is rarely discussed – suicide. The small farms of West Wales are less able than ever to survive economically in a context of rationalisation and commodification of rural life. Young people look elsewhere for viable futures; communities face a need for difficult and radical change. The sheep in the north of Wales are still quarantined after the Chernobyl nuclear accident (light rain on a fateful day). Those that are deemed healthy reach but a few pounds per carcass at market, yet in one of the supermarket chainstores in the same town a lamb fillet sells for more. Cattle raising has been devastated after mad cow disease makes it more profitable to build an incinerator to burn suspect cattle than to keep them on the farm. Caught with hope gone and bleak futures, often never married and with few family left, older farmers, like the one who lived over the way from one of us in Tawelfan ('Peaceful Place'), shoot themselves. This narrative was performed by an old local couple. Cliff McLucas wanted Dai to slaughter a sheep. It wasn't that he couldn't, only it wasn't allowed – it can only happen now in a licensed abattoir. Particularly poignant was their slow recitation of the names of the farms they knew and are now lost across the hillside. 'But over and beyond our memories, the house we were born in is physically inscribed in us. It is a group of organic habits' (Bachelard 1964: 14).

The dramatic structure was of thirty-nine sections of two minutes' duration, punctuated by three re-enactments of death, one at the beginning, one in the middle and one at the end, giving three intertwining trajectories of dramatic development and decline. Each story had nine sections of textual material including first-person testimony, descriptions of location, character portraits, autopsy details, account of death. Poetry, data, documents, lies . . . There were also three monologues by the perpetrator, a male figure moving from one story to the next and playing respectively murderer, doctor and land-agent. The choreography of the non-verbal sections was constituted from the reconstruction, deconstruction, reassembly and repetition of physical details from the events of the narrative. An accompanying sound tape relayed the historical and archaeological details of Esgair Fraith and provided a soundscape for the voices of the performers, all of which were amplified. The lighting included neon strips and large light-bulbs suspended within the architecture, gantry-mounted spots and floodlights, flares carried by the perpetrator, all at once unexpected, incongruous and anachronistic in the forest.

Tri Bywyd, site-specific representation as evocation, suggests approaches which can embrace

the multitemporality of place and juxtapose different orders of material and alternative interpretations simultaneously, whilst revealing site continuously. Performance is certainly a medium within
which meanings and identities are constantly represented, contested and inverted, the best
medium perhaps within which to represent another heterotopia.

Deep mapping

Places which once were lost, now are found. And they are complex places. They challenge archaeology to experiment with its means of writing and representing the past not only to inscribe and
embody the fine grain of lives lived there but also the myriad causes – of ownership, authority and
interpretation – clustering around their appearance and disappearance. Reintegrations of place and
language become essential to the energising of cultural distinctiveness. Archaeology becomes
part of an integrated, social and political practice active in the creation of personal, communal, local
and national identities, a practice unafraid to be sensual, interpretive, romantic.

Unfortunately, these are places which come and go: access can be denied. And we want to
speak of them at other times, in other places. Equally evocative performance can still be created
off site. Indeed, away from the romance of the ruin, the heady odours of decay and unencumbered
by the pleating of topography, narratives may be free to stand their ground, naked, revealed. A
multimedia performed lecture entitled *Deep Maps* was developed and presented by us at several
venues on different occasions. It too aimed to evoke rather than to describe Esgair Fraith. The
spoken text, for two voices, included three short pieces interspersed with three performance
fragments. It was accompanied by three types of projection: video (an oblique peregrination
around Esgair Fraith), slide (images congruent with the performance text) and computer-generated
(words and images in counterpoint to the themes of the spoken lectures). The lectures took as
their themes 1798 and Wordsworth's visit to Tintern Abbey, 1835 and Edgar Allan Poe's story
'Berenice', and 1942 and David Davies's presence at Esgar Fraith. The performances were based
upon memories of a grandmother and superstitions concerning death, the various occupants of
Esgair Fraith and the autobiography of the Welsh rural story writer D. J. Williams (see Williams
1987).

What follows is an amended and edited version of this performed lecture, designed now to
work with the rest of this chapter and the rest of the book. We take up the subject of the
landscapes of west Wales where we left them above . . . with Edgar Evans in the Antarctic,
Lincolnshireman Augustus Brackenbury at Trefenter, and in the streets of Copenhagen!

Esgair Fraith: a sedimentary map

1789 the Wye Valley

We begin again elsewhere.

In the Welsh Marches along the river Wye is Tintern Abbey, a ruin now in the care of the
National Trust. William Gilpin used the Wye Valley in his definitions of the picturesque (1782,
1792). Girtin painted it in 1793, Turner in 1794. Tintern Abbey is an archetypal beauty spot,

a jewel of English heritage. William and Dorothy Wordsworth visited the Wye in 1793 and again in 1798.

The second visit became the reason for a poem whose subject is the interplay of memory and imagination. William Wordsworth had visited five years earlier; he examines his memories, his experience of place and what memory and time have done with them. The poem is *Lines composed a few miles above Tintern Abbey during a tour. July 13, 1798* (Wordsworth 1973). The date is the eve of Bastille Day. The title makes it clear that the poem is not about the abbey, but the Wordsworths were on a tour such as those commended by Gilpin. The poem may not be about the ruin, but it does reflect on the meaning of place, natural objects and sensation. I suggest that a great deal of archaeological interest can be gained from a reading of this careful exploration of relations between self and what was, between self and that which is other. Under a 'dark sycamore' (10), Wordsworth compares his memories with what he now sees.

> And now, with gleams of half-extinguished thought,
> With many recognitions dim and faint,
> And somewhat of a sad perplexity,
> The picture of the mind revives again
>
> (58–61)

He writes of the mind's picture, but the poem is not simply concerned with pictures represented by words:

> Once again
> Do I behold these steep and lofty cliffs,
> That on a wild secluded scene impress
> Thoughts of more deep seclusion; and connect
> The landscape with the quiet of the sky.
>
> (4–8)

Here are fusions and translations which go beyond the pictorial: the cliffs impress *thoughts of more deep seclusion*, and the thoughts connect the landscape not to the sky, but to its *quietness*.

> I cannot paint
> What then I was. The sounding cataract
> Haunted me like a passion: the tall rock,
> the mountain, and the deep and gloomy wood,
> Their colours and their forms, were then to me
> An appetite; a feeling and a love,
> That had no need of a remoter charm,
> By thought supplied, nor any interest
> Unborrowed from the eye.
>
> (75–84)

The colours and forms of waterfall, rock, mountain and wood are the elements of a painting of the picturesque postcard. But here the waterfall haunts like a passion, and the forms and shapes of things are experienced not simply in themselves but as an appetite, a desire for nourishment. This is all beyond mere thought. Here feelings and things intermingle in evocations and associations of experience.

Such evocation and association involve the work of imagination upon experiences and relations with natural, objective things. The 'natural' world of objects is

> the mighty world
> Of eye, and ear, – both what they half create,
> And what perceive; well pleased to recognise
> In nature and the language of the sense
> The anchor of my purest thoughts, the nurse,
> The guide, the guardian of my heart, and soul
> Of all my moral being.
>
> (106–11)

Here is a creative union of person or self and object or nature. We half create as well as perceive nature because senses are not wholly passive but highly selective. Choice of what is perceived amounts to a kind of creation and it is guided by memory, searching for continuities in the linking of earlier and later experiences of things. But this creativity is also the natural and empirical anchor of 'purest thoughts'.

This is a unity then with the object world. Rooted in creativity and the imagination, it is more than a simple sharing of materiality or corporeality or objectivity. It is a principle of reciprocity between self and object world. So Wordsworth hears humanity in nature:

> To look on nature, not as in the hour
> Of thoughtless youth; but hearing oftentimes
> The still, sad music of humanity,
>
> (89–91)

And the unity is a disturbing one:

> a sense sublime
> Of something far more deeply interfused,
> Whose dwelling is the light of setting suns,
> And the round ocean and the living air,
> And the blue sky, and in the mind of man:
> A motion and a spirit, that impels
> All thinking things, all objects of all thought,
> And rolls through all things.
>
> (95–102)

Things are not fixed but shifting and flowing in a creative communion between self and otherness.

What has happened to his memories of standing by the river Wye? He has felt the forms of scene, the 'soft inland murmur' (4), 'plots of cottage ground' (11), 'hedge-rows, little lines of sportive wood run wild' (15–16). Forms felt and restored, renewed in 'purer mind' (29). These are not accurate images, simply pleasurable snapshot memories of the picturesque. They involve feelings of 'unremembered pleasure' (31). These are feelings and moods which cannot be put into words. And they bring to him an

> ... aspect more sublime; that blessed mood
> In which the burthen of the mystery,
> In which the heavy and the weary weight
> Of all this unintelligible world,
> Is lightened
>
> (37–41)

The strangeness, otherness and unintelligibility of the object world become sensible:

> We see into the life of things
>
> (49)

We may consider Wordsworth's examination of these experiences as mystical and irrational. Unlike Wordsworth we may be content with picturesque sensation and spectacle, postcard tourism. We might ascribe them to a field separate from the archaeological. But is it not an impoverishment to hold that the only contribution an archaeologist may make to the understanding of a visit to a site such as Tintern Abbey is to supply a measured plan of foundations? Who are we to look to, if not to archaeologists, for guidance about the action of time upon material culture, about the place of the past in the present, what may be done with it and how it may be perceived?

Tintern Abbey holds that simple picturing or representation are inadequate models of memory or experience. There is more to reality, objects and experiences than what can be captured by reason's dissection of the empirical. This is revealed in Wordsworth's consideration of the temporal gap between his two visits to this place. Memory selects and elaborates, working on associations and evocations. This work has been part of the changes he has undergone since the first visit. So the experiential loss of the past, its ruin, is converted by the imagination and by reason or thought, contemplation, into poetic gain:

> That time is past,
> And all its aching joys are now no more,
> And all its dizzy raptures. Not for this
> Faint I, nor mourn nor murmur; other gifts
> Have followed; for such loss, I would believe,
> Abundant recompense.
>
> (83–8)

The gain is one of reconstructing the past, renovation; it lives on, *changed*.

Nature and its objects can haunt. Things, times and experiences evoke harmonies and associations other than what they are: things are in motion, just as the beauty of things harmonises in the scene before Wordsworth. Involved is the creative power of the mind and of intelligent perception, a reciprocity between the poet's self and Nature, the other which stimulates him to all this feeling and discovery. Wordsworth calls this the sublime: the otherness, the independence of the object world, its fundamental mystery which can never be captured (it is 'heavy' and 'unintelligible'), yet which at the same time is sensible, perceived and thought. Haunting; evocation; the ineffable remainder even after scrupulous description; mystery; independence: these are the life of things, and discovered in experiential loss or ruin. We have called this **heterogeneity**.

1841 Paris – the rue Morgue

> Examining the whole neighbourhood, as well as the house, with a minuteness of attention for which I could see no possible object . . . he then asked me, suddenly, if I had observed anything peculiar at the scene of the atrocity.
>
> (Edgar Allen Poe 1980 [1841]: 119)

It was in the 1830s and 1840s that Edgar Allen Poe perfected his gothic genre of horror and invented the detective story. Death abounds. Morbidity and a fascination with the particulars of things accompanies an acute sensitivity to the materiality of the human body, and to bodies of evidence.

The story *Murders in the rue Morgue* (1980 [1841]) introduces the detective C. Auguste Dupin. He is fascinated by an extraordinarily violent double murder, whose horror mystifies the police, which seems to have been committed without any apparent motive in an upper storey of a Paris apartment, and in a room whose door was found locked from the inside. Dupin collects evidence, visits the scene of crime and, through what Poe terms '**ratiocination**', determines the murderer to be an escaped orang-utang. Beyond simple ingenuity this reasoning is not, as is often believed, a process of deduction, but one of **speculative reasoning**, as Charles Pierce called it – **abduction** (Sebeok and Umiker-Sebeok 1983). It depends upon leaps of the imagination linking details with potentially relevant contexts, stringing together scenarios to be tested against the world. Dupin connects traces of hair with the locked door, with a severed head, a body thrust up a chimney and bruises upon a throat, with voices heard by witnesses after the crime, with an animal he identifies in the pages of the natural historian Cuvier. He supposes that it could only have been an exotic ape; an advertisement in the newspaper announcing the finding of an orang-utang in the Bois de Boulogne brings its owner to Dupin's apartment, and with him confirmation that the crime has been solved.

Dupin is marginal, neither state police nor independent man of means. He is steeped in books and learning, yet his gaze is fixed upon the particulars of the world around. He operates in a film-noir netherworld of shuttered rooms, coming out only at night to wander the city streets where he might meet such horrors as these murders in the rue Morgue, where he might exercise his fascination with the surreal connections necessary to solve the strangeness of some crimes.

Six years earlier was published Poe's strange (and ludicrous) story, Berenicë, about another man's fascination with the world around him (1980 [1835]). 'This monomania, if I must so term it, consisted in a morbid irritability of those properties of the mind in meta-physical science termed the **attentive**' (1980: 20). The subject of the story attends obsessively to the thing-ness of things. His cousin Berenicë is dying of a consumptive, wasting disease which erodes her beauty:

> The eyes were lifeless, and lustreless, and seemingly pupilless, and I shrank involun-tarily from their glassy stare to the contemplation of the thin and shrunken lips. They parted; and in a smile of peculiar meaning, *the teeth* of the changed Berenicë disclosed themselves slowly to my view. Would to God that I had never beheld them, or that, having done so, I had died!
>
> (1980: 23)

His cousin expires; his fascination continues. He is found to have disinterred her body, out of his senses, and extracted her teeth. She is found to have been buried alive.

It was in the 1840s that photography began to spread as medium of record of the ineffable texture of things.

1881 David Davies

David Davies died here at Esgair Fraith – 'Speckled Ridge' – in 1942. He was 95 years old. For the last sixteen years of his life he had lived alone. Towards the end, he had begun to smell a bit, as old men inevitably do – of pigs, sweat, leather, piss – even though he con-tinued to order his life as she would have wanted. He washed in an enamel bowl on the table and shaved in a fragment of broken mirror on the window sill. And to the end, he worked – as a blacksmith and finally as a cobbler. There, where memory says the bellows once stood, where you can still find pieces of discarded shoe-leather, rusty hob-nails . . .

He had been, was, a 'pioneer'. He brought his family here in 1881. He was already 34. He came with all the energies and enthusiasms of a middle-aged man, fuelled by years of frustration and disappointment: 'If not now, then never.' 'To begin again, to wipe the slate clean.' 'A second chance, to get it right this time.' And his traces are all around us. It's he who built these walls, who roofed those sheds, who improved that land, who extended this house, who was proud enough to erect a date stone in the year of my grandma's birth – 1902.

In later years, idly scratching a pig's ear with a hazel twig, he remembered the shock of his first visit: how squalid the yard, a few chickens scratching in the dirt; how derelict the few buildings, their thatched roofs decaying and rotten. He remembered: how worn she had looked, aged beyond her years, although she was only 27; how defiantly she had described herself as 'Rachel Jones, Head, Single, Farmer, 35 acres' on the title deeds; how awful had been the squint in the child's eyes, the turn in her lip.

He remembered the rumours: that they had disguised the birth, pretending the child was a god-daughter, then later a niece, feigning difficulty with the language to the census recorders; that this Rachel Anne was in fact daughter to Rachel, herself daughter to John Jones, first occupant of Esgair Fraith; that she was the result of 'courting in bed', the old Welsh custom which lingered in the backward uplands; that after custom she had placed the wood of nine different trees under her pillow to make him come; that John Jones, Moelfryn had arrived with a ladder, crawled in through the bedroom window and lain with her; that she was 15 years old. And he remembered too hints of something more terrible, whispers of less than natural union. For truly she was a strange-looking child.

He had listened to the story of her father, already by this time half mythical: how he had dressed as a woman, had blackened his face, had gone with others to terrify incomers, to fire muskets in the night, to chant outside the Englishman's door, to smash the toll-gate outside Cwmann; how he had gone with others to build houses overnight, to get the roof on and a fire going by dawn, after custom, as proof of ownership; to squat the land, further down; how he had stood here on this bare hillside and looked at his hands and had seen the deep score-marks of the threads; how he had realised that the enclosure of this common would give him one last chance – official; how he would become John Jones, Esgair Fraith.

He had listened, from courtesy. But by now they were both wandering: she ever backwards, telling a life-story; he forwards, laying his plans. In fact, he remembered this John Jones, weaver, a 'big man' in God, who had heeded the word 'Escape for thy life; look not behind thee, neither stay thou in all the plain; escape to the mountain, lest thou be consumed'; who had dragged his family to the mountain-top, to this place beside Nant Clwedog-isaf; who had not realised that it was already too late – that the woollen industry had already fled to the burgeoning cities of Northern England, that the best places had already gone, the other Joneses already breaking the ground at Moelfryn, marking out their circle of fields; who had hacked and blasted stone from the quarry with dangerous abandon, who had built house, water mill, weaving sheds; who enclosed a few fields for livestock, though he was never a farmer. And Jacob said unto his brethren: 'Gather stones; and they gathered stones and made an heap: and they did eat there upon the heap.'

By now he was no longer listening though she rambled on: how they had all slaved at the looms, pulling threads, counting threads – five red, five black, five red; how the windows were always too small, a choice between wind and light; how the older children had escaped as soon as they could – to the coalfields of South Wales, to the opportunities of America; how her parents had died exhausted knitting socks; how the only things that had prospered were the trees – beech and sycamore, hazel and ash. These he would keep. And he would plant more. Of course, he got it cheap. And the Rachels disappeared, washed away, the only two ever to be born at Esgair Fraith.

It was to be his site of perfection though no plans or drawings ever guided him, only the logic of practice. Here the yard . . . there the wagon sheds and stables . . . here the machinery for cutting chaff, threshing corn . . . there the whim – a horse-operated turntable device which drove the machinery an aged cob trudging endlessly in circles . . . and there the stands for hay-ricks. One orchard and vegetable garden. One cottage garden. More trees. And lots and lots of gateways. His layout is littered with thresholds, with entrances and exits, openings and closings, insides and outsides, comings and goings, arrivals and departures . . . each one signalling greetings and farewells, beginnings and endings, visitations and withdrawals. He even built a junction! And for thirty years, it was all movement – horses, livestock, vehicles. And children. For they too went – Eleanor, Anne, David – to marriage, to war or perhaps to early deaths in the great flu of 1915.

And the pig idly turned its rump to the twig. Once he could have slit its throat catching the spurting blood in a tin bucket as the frothing squeal died, would have blanched the skin with boiling water in an oak trough, would have scrubbed off the bristles, would have stretched the back legs with a bar and hoisted it nose down over a beam, would have opened it from groin to neck in one slash, would have watched the glistening entrails spill out, would have eaten the brains first. But by this time, he kept them as companions. And age requires so little food.

Sometimes on the path to the 'Halfway' pub he would stop beside the piles of stones which the ancient Cambrians had built, or so they said, and look down on the farms of the hillside – Plas-newydd, Ddeunant, Bryn-meiog, Bryn glas, Blaen-y-waun, Pant-teg-isaf, Pant-meinog, Pant-y-ffin, Pen-cnwc and Meolfryn – on the lights of his constellation.

How he died, I've got no idea. In former times, they might have drawn his body up through the chimney, after custom. Most likely he would have been laid out on the night before the funeral, his neighbours sitting round. In 'Yr Hen Dy Fferm' – 'The Old Farmhouse' – D. J. Williams describes the watchnight service and the 'strange silence everywhere, even among the animals on the fold.' (Williams 1987)

1902 Grandma Pearson

Grandma Pearson – Lillian Toyne as was – was a farm maid, her father was foreman. In a family photograph of 1909 she stands, aged 7, hands clasped confidently. If you look closely you'll see she's wearing enormous boots. They belonged to her sister who in a fit of temper at this show of parental favouritism, ripped herself and another sister from the image. Gone forever . . . my family, minus two. Her father wears the dark suit of the nineteenth-century, Sunday best – a suit for all occasions. On his knee sits baby Jackie who in later life developed a terrible wasting illness. If you pressed his flesh it stayed there, the hand print remained.

At the age of 17, she 'laid out' her mother, washing, combing, dressing the body, in preparation for the gaze of others. Then later her father: shaving the face, scrubbing the hands. Just ten years ago, it was the turn of that same aged sister. 'But she died wi' 'er mouth open duck, and I couldn't shut it. I pushed and pushed. But Harold Cox managed it, so that's alright.' Harold Cox was her village undertaker. In the area where she lived, these are the omens of death: if a fire remains alight all through the night; if a dog howls at midnight; if two spoons are placed together in a cup; if you eat off a plate with another plate under it; if holly, used as decoration during Christmas-tide, is found to be shrunken and dried when taken down on Twelfth Night; if a white dove flies into a room; if a tallow candle, while alight, flickers and forms upon the side a mass called a 'winding sheet'. And if bees in a hive be not told of a death, another will follow in the same house shortly.

Her tiny house bore few possessions, a few favourite ornaments: plaster dogs, gifts from grandchildren. And photographs, ranked and revered like icons – husband, sons, grandsons. And a bed, a great mahogany bed, our family bed: site of birth and death, of sex and sickness. Of intimacy, nakedness, comfort, rest, dreams; of pillow-talk, adult matters, secrets, whispers, shared fears and of exhaustion, loneliness and 'listening to the night'. And my uncle sold it, secretly sold it, along with everything else. Not for me then the experiences Thomas Hardy conjures,

I see the hands of the generations
That owned each shiny familiar thing
In play on its knobs and indentations,
And with its ancient fashioning
Still dallying.

Figure 15
The Toyne family,
Grayingham,
Lincolnshire, 1909

THEATRE/ARCHAEOLOGY

Hands behind hands, growing paler and paler,
As in a mirror a candle-flame
Shows images of itself, each frailer
As it recedes

('Old Furniture', Hardy 1993: 115)

Her riches were in words, anecdotes, stories. Her daily practice was gossip. Through some extraordinary process involving the visitation of family and neighbours, glimpses of the street from behind her curtains, the daily perusal of the obituary column in the local newspaper and some almost mystical form of divination, she accumulated, processed and held together vast bodies of information. She knew who lived where, who was related to whom, what was happening over dozens of square miles, constantly up-dated and cross-referenced. A world picture, a world in which to live . . . and to die.

But as the end approached, her stories became fewer and fewer, until finally only one remained. And this she repeated over and over. She must have been about 5 years old, preparing the dinner for the harvesters returning from the fields. But the tap on the beer barrel was blocked. 'Well Lilian,' said her mother 'you'll just have to blow up it.' This she did, but it gushed back, giving her a mouthful of bitter ale. It was her first, and only, taste of alcohol.

In the area where she lived, these are the superstitions concerning death: the fastening of the doors of the room or the house hinders painfully the departure of the soul from the body; should a corpse lie in a village over Sunday night, there will be another death before the year is out; on no account should there be an odd number in the funeral party or soon the dead will call out for a companion; should anyone at a distance hail or try to attract your attention by waving a shovel, grab a handful of earth and immediately fling it in their direction or soon you too will be buried.

In the local nursing home in which she died, the village elders sit in a circle of armchairs. They rarely speak. After a lifetime together, there's nothing left to say. She came back from lunch one day, fell asleep and never woke up. She'd just had enough. And there's another gap in the circle.

A hundred years ago, she would have been carried to the grave by women, wearing long white dresses, white gloves and white calico veils. The coffin would have been borne underslung on white towels instead of 'the unsightly and dangerous practice of having them raised on men's shoulders'.

At the end, they just lifted the turf and popped her in on top of my grandfather, thirty-seven years separating them. Two skeletons and a few brass handles. For she, as with others of her generation, fearing the ignominy of the pauper's grave, had always saved just enough for her own funeral. But nothing more. Not even a headstone, no mark with our family name. No ostentation, please. We know our place, we Pearsons, even if it condemns us to eternal anonymity!

She left nothing because it was her philosophy to leave the world as naked as when she entered it. And yet her traces are everywhere: in the way I hold my knife; in the childhood prayer she taught which comes instantly to mind, 'Gentle Jesus, meek and mild, look upon a little child', in the silences of my stubbornness, in the shape of my ears. And in the stories I tell about her. And she thought I was my father whom she'd forgotten she had already lost.

We die in public and in private, quietly and violently, on the street, in deserted places, in bed. We spend a lifetime forgetting. And then close to the end, we remember. Grandma spoke dialect: 'Na me duck. Bye she's slaape. Put sneck on't doar.'

1912 George Shaw

We walked out, walked away, walked off – Augustus, George, John and me. Only George went back and he didn't last long. Cutting early docks and thistles on the dyke-side he was, down near Gander . . .

On the ship's manifest his occupation is given as farm labourer and that's what he was – ag. lab. – him and his. He was good with horses: rode side-saddle to the 'ings' every morning, clutching the heavy straw-stuffed collar; knew how to make a lazy 'jibber' shift. Shove a hot potato up its arse! In the photo, he is dressed in white – shirt, trousers, straw hat – with black neck-tie and square-toed boots; beard beneath his chin. He faces us, awkwardly, arms pressed to his sides, whilst the stallion – and stallion it certainly is! – stands in profile, placidly. It is a pose made by Lincolnshire farm-workers in their thousands, they and their beasts, neither quite sure why. Only the sugar-cane in the background is a give-away.

He knew how to swing, to lift, to push; to plough, to sow, to reap, to mow. So when it happened he was surprised rather than hurt, shocked at his own stupidly, shocked that an action he had done a million times – and in distant places – the slow arc of the scythe, had gone wrong, had turned against him: 'Oh, bugger.' Only then, 'Ow, oh God.'

They were all accident prone, or perhaps just a bit forgetful, him and his. Even his father-in-law, a Primitive Methodist minister with a stuck-on beard – who still believed Bishop Usher's calculation that God created the world, complete, in 4004 BC and who 'gained the confidence of both ministers and members in Snitterby Carrs' – had 'pain and sorrow arising out of the loss of one of his arms'. But whatever his lot 'he gave evidence of trust in God'. His granddaughter Lily had her arm off at the shoulder after being bitten by a snake and her daughter Annie had her hair shaved off after an accident with an exploding carbide lamp! Mind it's dangerous, the country. I saw Lellie Wilkinson after he'd been run over by a trailor, the scar tissue wrapped like twisted vines around his crushed legs; saw John Blanchard's fingers laying in the playground after he had tipped the old classroom fire-guard over onto the concrete whilst still gripping the brass surround; saw Snowy Lawman after he'd jumped onto an upturned pitch-fork in a haystack. I remember limbs mangled in harvesters, men suffocating in mud beneath overturned tractors . . . And a labourer falling into a pea-viner, which usually stripped the peas from the haulm and pod

Figure 16
George Shaw,
Queensland,
Australia, 1902

. . . and which did the same to him. And he thought of One-arm Charlie Foster and Peg-leg Reeson.

But it gushed from the start, the femoral artery severed: staining his whites – which he wore as a badge of exoticism: 'He'd been places, knew different habits'– the grassy bank, the muddy water. And they just couldn't staunch it, neither with chewed bread nor cow-muck. Even the string below his knees – which stopped rats running up his trouser legs – proved useless as a tourniquet. And he looked, in disbelief . . . He was 54 and this, he knew, was it.

Mind he'd seen it coming, the previous night. After a heavy day's scything he'd complained of 'heving the scythe point in 'is back' or having 'the hug', a kind of stitch which grips the groin and under the shoulder blade. Susannah had put a heated flat-iron on it – hot as hell – and it did the trick. But then someone put two spoons in the same teacup . . . And that very morning just as the steam packet was passing, another banker over the river in Kelsey Carrs had tried to attract his attention, God preserve us, by waving a shovel . . . So that then was that.

They'd married in Brigg at Christmas, 1879. They'd attended the Amateur Dramatic Company, whose efforts were much improved with the inclusion of Miss Cecilia Rorke of London, though the amateurs still did not put enough 'life into their agony' and who acted 'in a particularly cool and uninteresting manner'. And they'd heard the first rumours . . . rumours of a great adventure. Though they had no work to go to, they got free passage: him, Suzannah who was already pregnant with George Edward, William Herbert and Annie Alberta. He was 26, she 25 and both could read and write. They set sail on 5 June 1886 aboard the British India Steamship Company's S.S. Dacca which though designed for seventy-five first-class passengers and thirty-two second-class could take three hundred emigrants in the between decks on the outward journey: London–Java–Brisbane. The Dacca eventually sank in 1890 in the Red Sea with two hundred and fifty single girls aboard, though all were saved, saved to be servants and wives at some bleached and God-forsaken place in the outback. They landed at Bowen on 3 August; according to the disembarkation documents they 'Left with friends'. But they never got very far, overcome by the enormity of what they had done, of where they were.

At first he hauled timber: 'This is my team' the inscription on the photo of the six-horse wagon reads. In another picture, several teams stand at a long veranda; only the palm-trees are a give-away. Perhaps this is Goorganga Station, Proserpine where he worked for A. J. Cotton. At some point, he tried gold prospecting in Normanby. Not of course Normanby near Scunthorpe where Lord Sheffield laid out his parklands and gave a prize to the best team of plough jags. And not Normanby near Rasen where the bridge was so badly haunted that three parsons were sent for. 'They axed the spirit what she wanted an' she said "Life she wanted, life she'd ave!". So they gave her a live stag, an' she took it an' tore it limb from limb an' devoured it, an' whiles she was doin' it they pops 'er under an iron pot an' imprisoned her inside of it.' But the dusty holes of Normanby, Queensland.

The sugar only came later. The photo shows a corrugated shed, in a clearing: Kelsey Creek he called it, out of nostalgia or desperation or irony. The natives had long since skidaddled, or so they were told. Freddie, who as a child caught polio and thereafter wore a metal caliper and special platform boot, was born there on 17 November 1897 and baptised on 22 May 1898 in the Diocese of North Queensland. His baptism certificate shows the name William Robert crossed out and Frederick David Warren added. In later life he became a master carpenter and also something of a hermit. He lived in a caravan that he built himself, at the bottom of the garden. Amongst his few possessions were a paraffin lamp with a red, glass bowl, an early Phillips portable radio the size of a shoe-box and a bicycle with a petrol engine in the rear wheel, the sole product of some crazed inventor. Only starting was difficult as Freddie pedalled painfully to turn the motor.

Freddie also kept pigs. His great sow would farrow regularly and Nan would spend the next few days trying to save the inevitably short life of the runt. Pigs can smell death. Screaming accompanied slaughtering day from dawn, and as the great wooden trough was taken down from the barn ready for scalding and scrubbing they heard it. Some say that the village women would get together and in a private ritual eat the brains of the freshly slaughtered pig. I never saw it. Nasty thing, a pig bite: takes a lump of flesh clean out! And as Dot says: 'Once they've started, they may as well carry on!'

Freddie's shirts were a miracle. He always wore collarless, cotton shirts. But after a certain age, he refused to buy any new ones. So Nan had to cut more and more off the tails to patch collar, cuff and elbow. The result was a curious, if short, mosaic. In archaeology, any object of obscure purpose or design is conventionally referred to as a ritual object. Freddie's shirts were ritual objects! He once threw a whole bucket of wet chips into the hot fat. The explosion almost killed him. Coated the whole of the inside of the chip shop in potato! When he died, the women found ten-shilling notes stuffed into every cranny in the caravan: under the mattress, behind the tiny wardrobe, up the chimney of the stove . . . None of it legal tender.

His brother Alfred Melton – quarryman, railway shunter, Royal Marine, taxi driver, grocer, fish fryer who called his daughter Sheila – was also born there. Somewhere along the line they had three others, though Mary Jane and Charles Henry were to die young in the flu epidemic of 1917.

But they never stuck. It was always too humid, too big; too many options, too many possibilities. He was born in 1858 at Waithe Top just above the coastal marshes, above the dykes and banks and shifting sands and racing tides. And now he missed the cramped villages, the damp cottages. He missed the conformity of the enclosed landscape: straight hedges, straight roads, straight drains. And he missed the plough jagging and the ran-tanning.

And as the blood drained away, he remembered how they'd once ran-tanned a bad-tempered schoolmaster in Holton-le-Clay who'd thrashed a kid and then tied his thumbs to the clothes line. 'We got kettles an' cans, an' a great piece of sheet iron from the black-smith's shop – two of us 'eld this 'ere, an' three or four more got sticks an' 'ammers an' let drive at this sheet of iron. The Straw Man went in front – a large man 'e 'ad ter be, an' all covered in straw, an' a long straw tail 'angin off 'im. We went an' ran-tanned the school-master for three nights on end – we allus ran-tanned for three nights like that because then there was "no law". Third night, at the end, when we'd sung songs an' made a big din out-side 'is house for a long time, we all went to the bit of a green there was outside the Public 'ouse, an' we burnt the Straw man – only the straw offen the man, you know, but we called it Burnin the Straw Man!'

He remembered dragging the plough from door-to-door. 'Many an' manys the time I'se been round wi' the plough jags. I can't remember the play as we used ter do, but straw man was the first speaker, I remember. Carry this 'ere Straw Man for miles, we did – carried 'im right way into a house, an' set 'im down, tail and all, an' a' soon as 'e was set down 'e made a long speech, after which the play began. We never took a plough with us, but allus took Straw Man.'

He remembered too the reasons for leaving: the grinding poverty, the diseases of the damp, the children standing in the rain scaring crows from dawn to dusk. He remembered 'The shocking death of the opium-eater in Kirton in 1882 . . . one of the most shocking cases of depravity which has been brought to light in North Lincolnshire for some time has been disclosed in connection with the sad death of Ellen Charles. Although the family consisted of the husband Charles Charles, wife, daughter, three illegitimate grandchildren and a lodger, it appears that they had neither bed, bedstead, mattress nor bed linen of any kind in the house, and scarcely a particle of furniture of any kind. The old woman was found dead on Thursday morning yet no coffin was provided until Monday. In the mean-time the husband exhibited the utmost indifference; when the undertaker arrived the corpse was found on the bare floor surrounded by filth, the only covering being an old cloth.'

But return they did, all except Annie Alberta. She was 'a pioneer' who would eventually marry three times to a string of scrawny bushmen Jack Davies, Ernest Harris and Archibald Burns McDonald with whom she lived 'in sin' for twenty years. In the wedding photos they sit nervously: under lemon trees with step-children – 'Lily has got her mouth screwed up which spoils her. Lizzie and Jack look grand'; or in front of backdrops, fingering trilby brims, in white gloves, necks swivelling in collars. Annie always looks like she could eat them all. Lizzie in her confirmation whites, in her wedding whites . . . Lizzie who doesn't yet realise that the snake is waiting in the sugar.

They came home to the wetlands of the Ancholme valley: to sugar beet and spuds and mangold wurzels; to Brandywharf, to North Carr . . . to Hibaldstow Carr, where on a wet morning in April 1912 my great-grandfather, George Shaw, bled to death.

1937 cityscape

Major Green, arrested for murder, 15 January 1937. Arms resting, folded, on the desk, its contents visible below, out of focus. He looks out of shot distantly to the right, bareheaded and in a casual coat. A man in a pinstripe suit and hat looks at Green's hands . . . maybe. Two men in dark suits behind look out of shot to the right. A blurred face of a man, centred at the back, looks at the camera.

Wife of Major Green being escorted out of police station, 15 January 1937. Name not recorded, she is in a dark overcoat and hat, right arm extended, left over abdomen, she falls back against one of the two policemen, eyes half closed, she is shouting. The building angles back a little with her. The man behind in the pale hat and coat is carrying something . . . maybe he isn't a policeman.

Two photographs by Weegee (in Barth 1997: 92-3).

Weegee's on-camera flash captured it all starkly and in your face, and in a way which heightens the contrast between foreground and recedingly dark backgrounds and interiors. They are all so film-noir (Bergala 1997). His famous collection of photographs of New York, *Naked City* (1945) is an extraordinary and influential document of a city's life. In the collection of his photographs fragments seem to matter more than narrative connection, ambience more than story.

And in the photographs themselves there is an indeterminacy.

They look like random frames of a movie. The subjects include many backs of figures. Many are too close a shot. Many make reference to what is out of the shot – they witness a lack or absence. The long shots are missing crucial details, the flash bleaching them out, throwing backgrounds even deeper into shadow. And they are 'in your face' – many are about the brutality, the unseemliness of sordid urban crime. Weegee was fascinated by the forensic body. He wasn't a police photographer, but he recorded scenes of crime, working freelance at the edges.

It was not until the 1930s that crime reportage (the document) came to be centred upon the body – the dead body of the victim and the mug shot of the murderer, though the face of criminality had been the subject of much physiognomic and anthropological interest since the 1850s – those eyebrows joined in the middle. And the face of the criminal looks ordinary, suspiciously familiar; the criminal, the perpetrator, could be anyone. For crime is not written on our faces; it would seem the self has hidden interiors which leaves clues that need excavating. This modernist sensibility poses the question: Do we know even ourselves?

A chalk outline upon the ground. At the scene of a crime the body is a ghostly presence as it leaves traces and upon which traces are laid. Both victim and perpetrator. Here it is not an innocent repository of biological process. The mark on and of the body is always just that – an incidental detail as well as key to a past, a history, a memory. So in this indeterminacy and multiplicity of the trace – it could be anything – bodies go beyond the domain of signs, for at the heart is a nagging silence, a gap or lack. The latent criminality of modern urban space, its figures and artefacts, its scenography, is not about crime. It's about the way we look and see and understand aftermaths and traces, worlds of ruin and recollection.

Every answer and statement was filled with half-truths, half-lies and self-justifications . . . The truth about how she died is shrouded by the murky gloom of the world in which she lived. In a world of secrecy and deceit, questions from outside go unanswered. Sure, there were lies, contradictions, changes, additions. Is it ever any different? (Brith Gof: *From Memory* [*Body of Evidence*] 1995; text by Mike Pearson)

1942 the Royal Air Force

There is an archive of aerial photographs in Milton Keynes in England. They were taken by reconnaissance planes of the Royal Air Force during the Second World War of places all over Europe. The photographs were to survey, map and record, to prepare for military action. These photographs also record the end of traditional farming techniques and show many traces of ancient activity, signs in the earth of inhabitation now gone. For archaeologists this is an extraordinary resource – photographs of landscapes now so altered by half a century of agricultural activity, of a pace and intensity which has erased so much that may have taken thousands of years to shape. One helpful and efficient curator looks after the collection. But it is not enough; the photographs are in disrepair and we wonder how long they will last.

In 1942 an aircraft flew over Clywedog and photographed Esgair Fraith. There are, of course, no conifers in the photograph; and you cannot see David Davies. Perhaps he had already died, earlier that year. His triangular garden is there, and the sunlight catches on the roof of the biggest of his sheds.

1995 at ground level

The roof is no longer there, though there are some bits of corrugated iron. You walk up the track with a banked hedge to your left. A stream runs down most of the year; the whole place is sodden, in a gloom created by the grown-out sycamore hedges and the conifer plantation.

To the right the garden, still showing the signs of a lawn, and rhododendrons. And the sheds, or what were. You would think they had been abandoned centuries ago. Just by the entrance to the biggest, whose roof stands out in that aerial photo of 1942, are hundreds of rusting nails and bits of shoe-leather, ground into the earth, rotting. This was where David Davies did his cobbling and mending.

They buried Dai's sheep on the other side of the wall after the performance. And the date stone of 1904 is no longer there. We found it a couple of years ago and David, a friend, has it for safekeeping in his garden down the road.

What time is this place?

With others like Carlo Ginzburg (1989), we identify a forensic aesthetic, a conjectural pursuit of clues to events and worlds left behind. We have tried to explain how we see this as part of the archaeological component of our everyday lives – a melancholic aspect of our social fabric. So in telling an archaeology, in this theatre/archaeology, we make something of our contemporary historicity, our sense of time passing and pasts left in the present, our historical agency in the worlds we inhabit and look upon. Here we claim that this is encapsulated in the question of how to tell of a death.

This anthropological comment upon a style of reasoning in the social fabric of people and things has local historical roots. In the background are some connections, now two centuries old at least, involving experiences of cityscapes of the industrial world, conceptions of underworld and low life, crime and its documentation, the character of information about the comings and goings of people and their history, a romantic sensibility attuned to history, its material ruin and relevance to people's identity. As one of us has argued elsewhere (Shanks 1992a), the progress of science, the invention of photography, notions of the objective gaze, encounters with others and otherness, the bureaucracy of documentation, new public and private spaces in modernity are the true subjects of the history of archaeology, which is also our own.

1798, 1841, 1881, 1902, 1912, 1937, 1942, 1995. We can set dates and describe events, but archaeological time is of another order too. At the beginning of the chapter we shifted from the blank polar wastes of the Antarctic to what may be called a topology of archaeological time (and, of course, history and memory). This is a temporal landscape of that familiar grid or matrix of dates, places and events, but whose geometry is crumpled and folded back upon itself so that what was distanced in time and space is brought close. Michel Serres has played upon the words for time and weather being the same in French (*le temps*) and refers to this turbulent flux as temporal *chiffonage* – '*le temps ne coule pas; il percole* (time doesn't flow; it percolates)' (Serres and Latour 1995: 57-62). We have attempted to set off such percolation through the performative practice of the story-teller-guide.

AFTERWORD AND AKNOWLEDGEMENTS

A short genealogy:

At the first conference on 'Devising and Documentation', organised by the Centre for Performance Research in Cardiff in February 1993, a number of performance practitioners and companies were invited to give precise ten-minute reflections on particular aspects of their work. The chosen forms included lecture, demonstration, exposition, short performance. Several used video, slide and overhead projection. They were, by turn, polemical, anecdotal, autobiographical, descriptive, scripted, improvised. In each presentation, the remains of the past were used to create something in the present. And all these ways of remembering represented forms of documentation. This was a revelation for those delegates who had regarded the single viewpoint, real-time video-recording as the authentic record of performance. Julian Thomas also spoke on the nature of the archaeo-logical record, the vagaries of survival and how we make use of the traces of the past in the present. He suggested that we can neither create an authoritative record nor try to predetermine and control its interpretation. Perhaps the best we can ever do is to put exciting material into the world and then let it alight where it will, envisaging creative acts of interpretation at other times and in other places. An initial series of provocations towards a **theatre archaeology** were presented at the conference. Julian Thomas's responses to them completed a seminal piece published in *The Drama Review* (Pearson 1994a; Thomas 1994).

In the dialogue of a set of evolving relationships, articulated in a series of papers, presentations and practical projects manifest almost entirely within the discourse of archaeology, the deeper affinities of the two practices were further revealed. At the Theoretical Archaeology Group con-ference in Durham in December 1993, Julian Thomas organised a session entitled 'Performing Places' with papers addressing notions of space, place and site. Here performance theorists were present within an archaeological setting. Mike Pearson spoke on the genesis and formalisation of performance space. Heike Roms used Foucault's work on the panopticon to consider theatre as a 'spatial machinery of identity'. Clifford McLucas employed a complex interplay of video and slide projection, live action and his own paper pre-recorded on audio tape to examine the com-plexity of large-scale, site-specific performance. Thomas himself spoke on points of convergence between archaeology and performance. Mark Edmonds's paper considered body practices in neolithic flint mines whilst Michael Shanks and David Austin presented, as a heightened dialogue, an experiential view of life in and around a medieval Welsh castle.

Interdisciplinary approaches to performance and the past, and attendant projects such as the archaeology of the contemporary past (Schnapp 1997; Buchli and Lucas 2000) and archaeological sensibilities (Jonna Hansson and Fiona Campbell at Göteborg), have subsequently been elaborated at the conferences of the European Association of Archaeologists – Ljubljana, Slovenia (1994), Santiago de Compostela, Spain (1995), Riga, Latvia (1996) and Bournemouth, England (1999).

In parallel with his dialogue with Michael Shanks, Mike Pearson began the creation of a series of solo works which comprised a layering of narratives and within which historiography, oral history, memory and the art of the story-teller were welded together in a performed event. These included the trilogy *From Memory* (1991–5): *A Death in the Family*, an intimate reflection on a childhood in rural Lincolnshire and the death of his father; *Autopsy*, an account of the Welsh settlement of Patagonia and the slaying of Llwyd ap Iwan by Butch Cassidy and the Sundance Kid in 1910; *The Body of Evidence* (1995), speculations on the murder of Lynette White in Cardiff docklands in 1988. *Dead Men's Shoes* (1997) was about Scott's expedition to the South Pole in 1912. *The First Five Miles* . . . (1998) was on the enclosures of West Wales in the early nineteenth century. *The man who ate his boots* . . . (1998) comprised four interlocking narratives of moments of emigration in 1820, 1847, 1884 and 1968. And *Bubbling Tom* (2000) comprised a guided tour of the landscape of his childhood in the village of Hibaldstow, Lincolnshire.

Meanwhile Michael Shanks completed his narrative of design and mobility in the ancient Greek city-state (1999), part of a broader look at the disciplinary and cultural experiences of Classical Archaeology (1996). The latter continued that line of investigation represented by the book *Experiencing the Past* in exploring the cultural work, the performative behaviour that is archaeology (1994, 1995a, 1995b, 1995d, 1996, 1997a, 1997b, 1998, 2000a, 2000b, Shanks and Mackenzie 1994).

Shanks and Pearson have subsequently presented 'performed lectures' at the Centre for Performance Research conference 'Performance, Identity, Tourism', Aberystwyth, Wales (1996); at the Nordic Theoretical Archaeology Group conference in Göteborg, Sweden (1997) and at the 'Thinking through the Body' conference in Lampeter, Wales (1998). Their work on the ruined farm of Esgair Fraith was published in *Performance Research* (Pearson and Shanks 1997) under the title 'Performing a Visit: Archaeologies of the Contemporary Past'. In September 1998 Shanks and Pearson curated the Centre for Performance Research peripatetic conference entitled 'Performance, Places and Pasts', which guided academics, theorists and practitioners on a series of walks and visits to presentations and performances in the landscape of West Wales (see Savill 1998: 68–71). Amongst the presentations were Roger Owen's taped evocations of the landscape of his childhood set in three sheds on his family farm; Lisa Lewis's commemoration of her grand-father, given from the pulpit of the rural chapel where he once was a minister; and Eddie Ladd's tracing of the paths in the landscape, no longer visible, once used by dairy cattle, the whole conference invited to wear cow masks!

Shanks and Pearson's work together has been informed and energised by experiences of visiting (sites, colleagues, issues), and particularly of estrangement from the normative textures of intellectual discourse – exploring margins, negotiating relations between disciplinary cores and peripheries. In this, they owe a debt of gratitude to supporters and sceptics, friends and foes.

Acknowledgements from Mike Pearson.

Many of the notions expounded in this volume have informed, and been informed by, the generation of academic course material. My thanks inevitably go to my colleagues in the Department of Theatre, Film and Television Studies, especially Professor Ioan Williams, Dr Roger Owen, Lisa Lewis and Richard Gough of the Centre for Performance Research.

The undergraduate course in Performance Studies in the Department of Theatre, Film and Television Studies in the University of Wales Aberystwyth, discussed above, was informed by the invaluable advice of Professor Elin Diamond (Rutgers), Professor Joseph Roach (Yale), Professor Dwight Conquergood (Northwestern), Professor Mady Schutzman (CALARTS) and Dr Susanne Winnacker (Frankfurt), who attended the Performance Studies symposium in Aberystwyth in September 1998. Its development was inspired by the presence in Aberystwyth of Professor Peggy Phelan and other guests of the Centre for Performance Research (CPR), which is affiliated to the Department, and by the presence of the secretariat of Performance Studies international which organised its fifth conference, 'Here Be Dragons' in Aberystwyth in April 1999. Details of the course can be found on the web-site at http//:www.aber.ac.uk/~psswww

And there are others, for performance is always a social endeavour. For thirty years now I have been privileged to work with many individuals who have committed themselves to developing innovative means of theatrical production and exposition. They are numerous, but not legion. My thanks go to them all, particularly the members and former members of Brith Gof, without whom this volume would not have been possible. I'm sure they will understand if I mention by name Lis Hughes Jones whose remarkable work did so much to influence the nature of Welsh theatre in the 1980s, and my current collaborator Mike Brookes, who has supplied glimmers of light to illuminate the darkest of recent times.

Above all I am indebted to Heike Roms, not only for her constant support and encouragement but for her many observations and ideas which suffuse this volume without being fully credited (but see Roms 1993, 1997).

Acknowledgements from Michael Shanks.

My colleagues and friends at my previous institution, University of Wales Lampeter, helped me so much to realise the strengths of pluralist thought and the energy of theory. Too many really to list, I nevertheless want to mention David Austin, Yannis Hamilakis, Sarah Tarlow, Mark Pluccienik, Cornelius Holtorf, Quentin Drew. I know they will smile at this book.

Here at Stanford I am working with inspirational colleagues under a wonderfully open and experimental agenda, sharing hopes and plans with, among others, Ian Hodder (who introduced me to archaeology as an undergraduate and later supervised my doctoral work at Cambridge) and Ian Morris (with his tremendous and inclusive vision).

I thank the creative artists who have so changed my work and thinking. Helen Shanks, above all, with her superb work and outlook – cross media, deeply perceptive. The members of Brith Gof

– how lucky I have been since that day Mike Pearson came into my office at Lampeter, how much Cliff McLucas has offered in his extraordinary pieces.

Together we wish to mention the following.

Outside our institutions we both thank the many archaeologists who have taken our work seriously. Douglass Bailey at Cardiff, and John Barrett at Sheffield, always intelligently aware. At Göteborg Jonna Hansson and Fiona Campbell deserve special mention, further stretching the envelope in their own work, developing their own **archaeological sensibilities**, a new publishing initiative, and never allowing us to take ourselves too seriously. In Paris Laurent Olivier and Alain Schnapp have given great intellectual support and inspiration, particularly in relation to the project of archaeologies of the contemporary past (Schnapp 1997; Olivier 1999a, 1999b). Julian Thomas figures most significantly here too, with his own archaeological project now at Manchester, whose initial interest and responses stimulated this volume and who continues to inform our approaches (Thomas 1994).

Many of the basic tenets of theatre archaeology and its subsequent elaboration were developed in the context of conferences organised by the Centre for Performance Research at Aberystwyth, including those on 'Devising and Documentation', Cardiff, February 1993 and University of Lancaster, July 1994, on 'Performance, Identity, Tourism', Aberystwyth, September 1996 and on 'Performance, Places and Pasts', Aberystwyth, September 1998.

The book owes a debt to current Brith Gof artistic director Clifford McLucas for his championing of the work of Bernard Tschumi (1990, 1994a, 1994b, 1994c) and for developing approaches to site which inform this book (McLucas 2000, forthcoming). Joint thoughts with Mike Pearson can be found in McLucas and Pearson 1996 and 1999.

Walter Benjamin's essay 'The Storyteller' (1992: 83–107) informs and inspires much of the creative writing in this volume. His work generally has been an inspiration to us both (see particularly Shanks 1999).

Our remaining acknowledgements are arranged according to the sections of the book.

Theatre archaeology

The 'him' in the early part of this chapter is disabled performer Dave Levett. Since the early 1990s, Mike Pearson and Dave Levett have collaborated on a series of performances which have examined the expressive potential of different physicalities within the genre of physical theatre. Significantly, all four works have involved vigorous encounters between men. In *In Black and White* (1992), Dave worked both in his wheelchair and out, in a series of duets inspired by the photographs of Edweard Muybridge. In a subsequent series of performances – *D.O.A.* (1993), *Camlann* (1993) and *Arturius Rex* (1994), which paralleled material from various versions of the myth of King Arthur with contemporary events in Bosnia – Dave worked without his chair, developing a repertoire of lifts, carries, supports, encounters and close physical interactions with a wider group of colleagues from Brith Gof, notably Richard Morgan and John Rowley. Levett,

Morgan and Rowley were instrumental in devising the training technique named 'In All Languages', which was demonstrated at the CPR 'Past Masters: Antonin Artaud' conference, Aberystwyth 1996. For material on this work see Pearson (1998a) and Pearson and Levett (forthcoming). Also note Townsend (1998) on the representation of disability. Dave now lives his life as Lyn for most of the time.

On political ecology the work of Bruno Latour must be brought forward (1987, as well as citations made in the text). The argument here, and more generally in notions of heterogeneous networking, began development at a colloquium organised by Latour and held at the Schlumberger retreat at Les Treilles, Provence in June 1991, though the subject then was somewhat different – the social origins of technology/the technical origins of society (see Lemonnier 1993). Later developed in a course run by Shanks at the Archaeology Centre, University of Leiden in 1992, some of it has been published in the Finnish journal *Fennoscandia Archaeologica* (Shanks 1998).

Ideas of landscape in this chapter and that on theatre/archaeology began as archaeologist Andrew Fleming joined Lampeter from Sheffield in 1995 to help organise, with David Austin, a Masters and Ph.D. programme in landscape archaeology. It is worth mentioning how different to the United States are approaches to landscape in a distinctive British tradition (on this also below), and how influential have been the close links between Lampeter archaeologists and colleagues in the University Geography Department, creating an intellectual forum, at one time or another, of palaeo-environmentalists Martin Bell, Mike Walker, Astrid Casteldine and John Crowther, human geographers Chris Philo (now Glasgow), Paul Cloke, Catherine Nash (now Royal Holloway, London), Phil Crang (now Durham), Ulf Strohmeyer and Tim Cresswell, cartographer Trevor Harris, and archaeologists Julian Thomas (now Manchester), Chris Tilley (now University College, London). Drawing on this terrific expertise and collegiality, Michael Shanks ran a seminar in 1997 on landscape archaeology at Göteborg, where he holds a *Docentur*.

Our ideas on scenes of crime were fundamentally influenced by an exhibition of photography held at the San Francisco Museum of Modern Art in 1998 under the title *Police Pictures* (Phillips, Haworth-Booth and Squiers 1998). The exhibition carried as supplementary publication a haunting book by Luc Sante (1992), without which our ideas would simply not have matured.

In its examination of narrative, the chapter is inevitably informed by the work of John Berger (1975, 1984, 1985, 1989, 1990, 1992, 1995).

Theatre and archaeology

The conjunction of Kubrick, Tsukamoto, Theweleit and a Korinthian pot painter was first presented at a conference on ancient Korinth, held in Newcastle upon Tyne UK in 1992, and where it horrified many of the classicists in the audience.

The constituting features of the Greek city-state were questioned by Michael Shanks in an examination of some performative behaviours and their field of cultural referents recoverable from ancient artefacts and literatures (1992b, 1995a, 1995b). The insinuation is that the changes in the Greek Mediterranean of the first millennium BC, those usually connected in a narrative of the emergence of the *polis* (city-state) in the eighth century BC, were a lot to do with models of conduct and forms of gendered identity central to these performative behaviours (from ceramic design to soldiery to travel to political rhetoric). This argument was developed with further reflection upon the category of the cyborg and the necessary elision of people and things – society is simultaneously material artefact and socio-cultural relations. In understanding society, the separation of people and things is a false and disabling one (Shanks 1998). There were cyborgs in ancient Greece.

This chapter includes significant material on theatre space from Heike Roms's presentation at the Theoretical Archaeology Group conference, Durham December 1993, itself a reflection on Foucault (Roms 1993).

The particular commentary on visiting the past was first partly explored in a paper on critical romanticism presented at a Nordic TAG (Theoretical Archaeology Group) conference held in Helsinki in 1991, and later published with the helpful criticism of Kristian Kristiansen and colleagues associated with the Maison des Sciences de l'Homme in Paris (Shanks 1995d).

In a symmetrical look at the convergence of people and things in museums and theme parks, the phenomenon called 'heritage' has been subject to positive critique. With a focus upon the embodied experience of the past, the **consumption** of remains, material (ruin) and virtual (memory), mobilised in acts of cultural construction, was celebrated (Shanks 1992a, 1995d and the Pearson solo works). This contrasts with the conventional critiques of heritage as simply a reactionary, nostalgic and erosive **consumerism** (for example, Walsh 1992).

The section on choreographing the prehistoric body takes us both back to our first experiences in archaeology in the late 1960s and 1970s (Shanks and Tilley 1982). It is endebted to the innovative work of British prehistorians John Barrett (1988, 1991, 1994; Barrett *et al.* 1991); Richard Bradley (1993, 1998); Colin Richards (1988, 1992, 1996); Julian Thomas (1991a, 1991b, 1996, 1999); Christopher Tilley (1994); Mike Parker Pearson (1993) and Alistair Whittle (1988). They have set the agenda for a sophisticated social archaeology. Versions of the material included on neolithic architectures were presented at 'The Connected Body?' conference, Amsterdam School of the Arts, Amsterdam August 1995 (Pearson 1996d) and at the CPR 'Giving Voice: Archaeology of the Voice' conference, Aberystwyth April 1997.

Extended definitions of what constitutes performative behaviour and an application of aspects of performance theory, such as a comparison between the functioning of the theatrical object or 'prop' in performance and artefacts within burial contexts, helped illuminate performative aspects of the prehistoric funeral, in a chapter for a volume entitled *The Archaeology of Prestige and Wealth* edited by another archaeological collaborator Douglass Bailey (Pearson 1998b).

Theatre/archaeology

As the relationship developed, experimental performance practices began to indicate provocative models for the presentation of archaeological material. In acknowledging the performative nature of the lecture, it was possible to reassess and to recast it as a multimedia exposition carrying different orders of information or narrative within its various media; or as a performance-like activity including the manual examination of artefacts, improvised discussion and the speculative re-enactment of past behaviours and events; or as a mode of story-telling which includes the subjective experience of the archaeologist as well as the exposition of data. Here both Pearson and Shanks have also been involved in curricular and pedagogic experiment, designing course materials, teaching and learning environments for performance studies and archaeology (www. stanford,edu/~mshanks; www.aber.ac.uk/~psswww).

In several works Shanks has presented new formulations of an archaeological poetics, creative acts of interpretive construction using rhetorical and narrative devices of parataxis and hypotaxis (1992b, 1995c, 1995d, 1999). The book *Art and the Greek City State* (1999) presented an assemblage of fragments, a new historiographical arrangement of evidences surrounding, and subverting, a political narrative of the city-state.

Commencing at the European Association of Archaeologists conference in Santiago, Spain in 1994 Pearson and Shanks have devised forms of performance/lecture, both at site and in the lecture theatre, which include personal reflection and video and computer-generated projection to examine the phenomenology of place and the complexity of memory.

In retrospect, this chapter reflects many of the notions of Homi K. Bhahba (1994): ambivalence, liminality, hybridity, mimicry and performativity. It also draws upon the work of Paul Carter, a speaker at the 'Performance, Places and Pasts' conference held in Aberystwyth in September 1998 and curated by us both. He describes the imperial project as imagining an empty stage upon which theatre of history is enacted, with 'naming' of place as a form of appropriation (1987, 1996).

The chapter includes performance scripts drawn from Brith Gof's *Patagonia* (Pearson 1996a), and Pearson/Brookes *Dead Men's Shoes* and *The Man Who Ate His Boots* . . . As will be noted from uncredited quotations littered through the textual fragments, their composition was much influenced by the work of Gaston Bachelard (1964), Pierre Bourdieu (1977) and Walter Benjamin (1992). The text for *Dead Men's Shoes* inevitably draws upon Scott's account of the *Discovery* expedition (1953); Apsley Cherry-Garrard's classic *The Worst Journey in the World* (1994) and the work of Roland Huntford (1985) and Francis Spufford (1996).

For the social history of Esgair Fraith, we are delighted to acknowledge the research of Professor David Austin at Lampeter on our behalf and the material supplied to the Department of Extra-Mural Studies, University of Wales Aberystwyth 'Exploring Ceredigion' course, 1995. The various writings on folk customs are informed by Owen (1978) and Rudkin (1987).

Versions of *Deep Maps*, the Pearson/Shanks joint work on Esgair Fraith and basis for the sedimentary map with which the chapter ends, were presented at the CPR 'Performance, Identity, Tourism' conference, Aberystwyth, September 1996; at the Nordic Theoretical Archaeology Group conference, University of Göteborg, Sweden, April 1997 and at the Department of Archaeology, University of Sheffield, May 1998 (see also Pearson and Shanks 1997).

In **theatre/archaeology** knowledge is conceived as an historical process and achievement, though there is, concomitantly, no possible final account of things. There are always other ways of telling and reality itself is plural. Pluralism and multivocality, and related issues of relativism, were explored and defined in an experiment in multi-authored, co-operative theory (Lampeter Archaeology Workshop 1997). Pluralism and the active construction of knowledge were key themes in Shanks's study of the discipline and discourse of classical archaeology (1996) – interests constituting the classical archaeological imagination were unpacked. These included tourism and visiting (after the aristocratic grand tour of the eighteenth century), the character of the collecting connoisseur, and myths of European identity. These have begun to be explored in fieldwork in Sicily, in the documentation of an archaeological expedition to investigate an ancient city, another effort to retrieve and work upon archaeological remains. This and the performed lectures, with their rhetoric of assemblage, have involved Shanks in experiments in multimedia composition and authorship (www.stanford.edu/~mshanks).

The project *Footloose* is inspired by the work of Laurent Olivier. A version of *The Body of Evidence*, which included thoughts on the forensic gaze, was presented by both Pearson and Shanks at 'The Body in Archaeology' conference, University of Wales, Lampeter, June 1998.

Finally, we thank the Pantyfedwen Fund and the Department of Archaeology of the University of Wales Lampeter and Stanford University for material and financial support.

PERFORMANCES

Brith Gof: prehistory and links

During the 1970s Cardiff Laboratory Theatre, with whom Mike Pearson worked, developed a relationship with Eugenio Barba's Odin Teatret which resulted in that company touring Wales in 1980: Barba's endeavours in 'theatre anthropology' inevitably resonate in this volume. The booklet *Glimpses of the Map* (1979) on the early work of Cardiff Lab is available from CPR (Unit 6, Science Park, Aberystwyth SY23 2AH, Wales). In 1980 Mike Pearson trained in *Noh* theatre with Kanze Hideo in Tokyo, Japan. In the 1980s and 1990s, Brith Gof collaborated with a number of companies worldwide including Theatr Osmego Dnia (Poland), Test Department (London), Sand and Bricks (Hong Kong) and La Fura dels Baus (Catalonia).

Brith Gof

Artistic Directors Mike Pearson (1981-97) and Clifford McLucas (1991 to date).

Detailed material on the work of Brith Gof can be found in three academic theses by Savill (1993), Houston (1998) and Koch (1998); see also Savill 1990 and 1997. The booklets *Brith Gof 1981–85: A Welsh Theatre Company* (1985), *Brith Gof: A Welsh Theatre Company* (1988) and Y Llyfyr Glas (The Blue Book) (1995) are available direct from the company (c/o Chapter Arts Centre, Market Road, Cardiff, UK CF5 1QE). A documentary work on the company prepared by Clifford McLucas is forthcoming. A complete list of the performances of Brith Gof, with other material, can be found at www.BrithGof.org

Selected works mentioned in the text:

Gododdin (1988–9)
Collaboration with Test Department
Large-scale, site-specific performance
Cardiff, Wales (1988); Polverigi , Italy (1989); Hamburg, Germany (1989); Leeuwarden, Netherlands (1989); Glasgow, Scotland (1989)

Los Angeles (1990–2)
Site-specific performance and touring production
Premiere: Rhymney, Wales

From Memory (A Death in the Family and Autopsy) (1991)
Solo performance
Premiere: Welsh Folk Museum, Cardiff, Wales

Patagonia (1992)
Touring production
Premiere: Taliesin Arts Centre, Swansea, Wales

In Black and White (1992)
Collaboration with disabled performer Dave Levett
Premiere: Chapter Arts Centre, Cardiff

Der Gefesselte (The Bound Man) (1992)
Collaboration with German saxophonist Peter Brötzmann
Premiere: Westwerk Gallery, Hamburg, Germany

Haearn (Iron) (1992)
Large scale, site-specific performance
Premiere: British Coal Works, Tredegar

D.O.A. (1993)
Collaboration with disabled performer Dave Levett
Touring production
Premiere: Chapter Arts Centre, Cardiff

Camlann (1993)
Site-specific performance
Cardiff, Wales and Recklinghausen, Germany

Angelus (1994)
Collaboration with German saxophonist Peter Brötzmann
Premiere: Westwerk Gallery, Hamburg, Germany

Arturius Rex (1994)
Site-specific performance
Premiere: Cardiff, Wales

From Memory (The Body of Evidence) (1995)
Solo performance
Premiere: Welsh Folk Museum

Tri Bywyd (Three Lives) (1995)
Large-scale, site-specific performance
Clwedog Plantation, Lampeter, Wales

Prydain: The Impossibility of Britishness (1996)
Large-scale, site-specific performance
Cardiff, Wales and Glasgow, Scotland

Pearson/Brookes

Mike Pearson and Mike Brookes (1997 to date)

Dead Men's Shoes (1997)
Solo performance
Premiere: Welsh Industrial and Maritime Museum, Cardiff

The First Five Miles . . . (1998)
Solo performance and simultaneous live radio broadcast
Trefenter, West Wales

The Man Who Ate His Boots . . . (1998)
Solo performance
Premiere: Aberystwyth, Wales

BIBLIOGRAPHY

Abbott, E. A. 1998. *Flatland*. London: Penguin Books.

Adorno, T. and M. Horkheimer. 1979. *Dialectic of Enlightenment*. London: Verso.

Althusser, L. 1971. 'Ideology and Ideological State Apparatuses', in *Lenin and Philosophy and Other Essays*. London: New Left Books.

Althusser, L. 1977. *For Marx*. London: Verso.

Althusser, L. and B. Etienne. 1970. *Reading Capital*. London: New Left Books.

Amyx, D. A. 1988. *Corinthian Vase Painting in the Archaic Period*. Berkeley: University of California Press.

Anderson, B. 1991. *Imagined Communities*. London: Verso.

Anderson, P. 1980. *Arguments within English Marxism*. London: Verso.

Andrews, M. 1999. *Landscape and Western Art*. Oxford: Oxford University Press.

Antonaccio, C. M. 1994. 'Placing the Past: The Bronze Age in the Cultic Topography of Early Greece', in *Placing the Gods: Sanctuaries and Sacred Space in Ancient Greece*. Edited by S. E. Alcock and R. Osborne. Oxford: Clarendon Press.

Appadurai, A. Editor. 1986. *The Social Life of Things: Commodities in Cultural Perspective*. Cambridge: Cambridge University Press.

Arato, A. and E. Gebhardt. Editors. 1978. *The Essential Frankfurt School Reader*. Oxford: Blackwell.

Ashcroft, B., G. Griffiths and H. Tiffin. 1998. *Key Concepts in Post-colonial Studies*. London/New York: Routledge.

Aubrey, J. 1980-2. *Monumenta Britannica (edited by R. Legg and J. Fowles)*. Milbourne Port: Dorset Publishing.

Augé, M. 1995. *Non-Places: Introduction to an Anthropology of Supermodernity*. London/New York: Verso.

Austin, A. A. and P. Vidal-Naquet. 1977. *Economic and Social History of Ancient Greece: An Introduction*. Berkeley: University of California Press.

Bachelard, G. 1964. *The Poetics Of Space*. New York: Orion Press.

Bahn, P. G. Editor. 1998. *Tombs, Graves and Mummies*. London: Phoenix Illustrated.

Bapty, I. and T. Yates. Editors. 1990. *Archaeology after Structuralism*. London: Routledge.

Barba, E. 1982. 'Theatre Anthropology'. *The Drama Review* 26:5-32.

Barba, E. and N. Savarese. 1991. *A Dictionary of Theatre Anthropology: The Secret Art of the Performer*. London: Routledge.

Barrell, J. 1972. *The Idea of Landscape and the Sense of Place 1730–1840*. London: Cambridge University Press.

Barrett, J. C. 1988. 'The Living, the Dead, and the Ancestors: Neolithic and Early Bronze Age Mortuary Practices,' in *The Archaeology of Context in the Neolithic and Bronze Age: Recent Trends*. Edited by J. C. Barrett and I. A. Kinnes, pp. 30–41. Sheffield: Department of Archaeology and Prehistory.

Barrett, J. C. 1991. 'Towards an Archaeology of Ritual', in *Sacred and Profane*, *Oxford University Committee for Archaeology Monograph*. Edited by P. Garwood, D. Jennings, R. Skeates and J. Toms, pp. 1-9. Oxford: Oxford University Committee for Archaeology.

Barrett, J. C. 1994. *Fragments from Antiquity: An Archaeology of Social Life in Britain, 2900–1200 BC*. Oxford: Blackwell.

Barrett, J. C., R. J. Bradley and M. Green. 1991. *Landscape, Monuments and Society: The Prehistory of Cranbourne Chase*. Cambridge: Cambridge University Press.

Barth, M. Editor. 1997. *Weegee's World*. Boston: Little, Brown and Company.

Barthes, R. 1977. *Image Music Text*. London: Fontana.

Barthes, R. 1982. *Camera Lucida*. London: Jonathan Cape.

Barthes, R. 1986. 'The Death of the Author', in *The Rustle of Language*. Oxford: Blackwell.

Bauman, Z. 1995. *Life in Fragments: Essays in Postmodern Morality*. Oxford: Blackwell.

Bender, B. Editor. 1993. *Landscape: Politics and Perspectives*. Oxford: Berg.

Bender, B. 1998. *Stonehenge: Making Space*. Oxford: Berg.

Benjamin, W. 1970a. 'On some Motifs in Baudelaire', in *Illuminations*. London: Jonathan Cape.

Benjamin, W. 1970b. 'The Work of Art in the Age of Mechanical Reproduction', in *Illuminations*. London: Jonathan Cape.

Benjamin, W. 1992. *Illuminations*. London: Fontana Press.

Benjamin, W. 1999. *The Arcades Project*. Cambridge, MA and London: Harvard Belknap.

Benson, J. L. 1989. *Earlier Corinthian Workshops: A Study of Corinthian Geometric and Protocorinthian Stylistic Groups*. Amsterdam: Allard Pierson.

Bergala, A. 1997. 'Weegee and Film Noir', in *Weegee's World*. Edited by M. Barth. Boston: Little, Brown and Company.

Berger, J. 1972. *Ways of Seeing*. Harmondsworth: Penguin.

Berger, J. (with Jean Mohr). 1975. *A Seventh Man*. London: Writers and Readers.

Berger, J. 1979. *Pig Earth*. London: Writers and Readers.

Berger, J. 1984. *And our Faces, my Heart, Brief as Photos*. New York: Pantheon Books.

Berger, J. 1985. *The White Bird: Writings by John Berger*. London: Chatto and Windus.

Berger, J. 1989. *Once in Europa*. London: Granta Books.

Berger, J. 1990. *Lilac and Flag*. London: Granta Books.

Berger, J. 1992. *Keeping a Rendezvous*. London: Granta Books.

Berger, J. 1995. *To The Wedding*. London: Bloomsbury.

Berger, J. and J. Mohr. 1982. *Another Way of Telling*. London: Writers and Readers.

Berger, J., S. Blomberg, C. Fox, M. Dibb and R. Hollis. 1972. *Ways of Seeing*. London and Harmondsworth: BBC and Penguin.

Bergquist, B. 1990. 'Sympotic Space: A Functional Aspect of Greek Dining-rooms', in *Sympotica: A Symposium on the Symposion*. Edited by O. Murray. Oxford: Clarendon Press.

Bhabha, H. K. Editor. 1990a. *Nation and Narration*. London: Routledge.

Bhahba, H. K. 1990b. 'DissemiNation: Time, Narrative, and the Margins of the Modern World', in *Nation and Narration*. Edited by H. K. Bhahba. London: Routledge.

Bhabha, H. K. 1994. *The Location of Culture*. London: Routledge.

Bijker, W. and J. Law. Editors. 1992. *Shaping Technology/Building Society*. Cambridge, MA: MIT Press.

Biner, P. 1972. *The Living Theatre*. New York: Avon Books.

Binford, L. 1972. *An Archaeological Perspective*. New York: Seminar Press.

Binford, L. 1977. 'General Introduction', in *For Theory Building in Archaeology*. Edited by L. Binford. London: Academic Press.

Binford, L. 1981. *Bones: Ancient Men and Modern Myths*. London: Academic Press.

Binford, L. 1983a. *In Pursuit of the Past*. London: Thames and Hudson.

Binford, L. 1983b. *Working at Archaeology*. London: Academic Press.

Black, M. 1962. *Models and Metaphors: Studies in Language and Philosophy*. Ithaca: Cornell University Press.

Borges, J. L. 1970. *Labyrinths*. Harmondsworth: Penguin Books.

Bourdieu, P. 1977. *Outline of a Theory of Practice*. Cambridge: Cambridge University Press.

Bradley, R. 1993. *Altering The Earth*. Vol. 8. Edinburgh: Society of Antiquaries of Scotland.

Bradley, R. 1998. *The Significance of Monuments: On the Shaping of Human Experience in Neolithic and Bronze Age Europe*. London: Routledge.

Buchli, V. and G. Lucas. Editors. 2000. *Archaeology of the Contemporary Past*. London: Routledge.

Buck-Morss, S. 1991. *The Dialectics of Seeing. Walter Benjamin and the Arcades Project*. Cambridge, MA: The MIT Press.

Burke, E. 1998. *A Philosophical Enquiry into the Origin of Our Ideas of the Sublime and Beautiful and Other Pre-revolutionary Writings*. London: Penguin Books.

Burl, A. 1991. *Prehistoric Henges*. Princes Risborough: Shire.

Butler, J. 1990. *Gender Trouble: Feminism and the Subversion of Identity*. New York/London: Routledge.

Butler, J. 1994. *Bodies that Matter*. London/New York: Routledge.

Butler, J. 1997. *Excitable Speech: A Politics of the Performative*. New York/London: Routledge.

Byrne, R. and A. Whiten. Editors. 1988. *Machiavellian Intelligence: Social Expertise and the Evolution of Expertise in Monkeys, Apes and Humans*. Oxford: Clarendon.

Campbell, D. A. Editor. 1982–93. *Greek Lyric. Five Volumes. Loeb Classical Library*. Cambridge, MA: Harvard University Press.

Carman, J. 1996. *Valuing Ancient Things: Archaeology and Law*. London: Leicester University Press/Cassell.

Carter, P. 1987. *The Road to Botany Bay. An Essay in Spatial History*. London: Faber and Faber.

Carter, P. 1996. *The Lie of the Land*. London: Faber and Faber.

Chaikin, J. 1972. *The Presence of the Actor. Notes on the Open Theater, Disguises, Acting, and Repression*. New York: Atheneum.

Chapman, R. and K. Randsborg. 1981. 'Approaches to the Archaeology of Death', in *The Archaeology of Death*. Edited by R. Chapman, I. Kinnes and K. Randsborg. Cambridge: Cambridge University Press.

Chatterjee, P. 1993. *The Nation and its Fragments: Colonial and Postcolonial Histories*. Princeton: Princeton University Press.

Cherry-Garrard, A. 1994. *The Worst Journey in the World*. London: Picador.

Chippindale, C. 1994. *Stonehenge Complete*, Second edition. London: Thames and Hudson.

Chippindale, C., P. Devereux, P. Fowler, R. Jones and T. Sebastian. 1990. *Who Own's Stonehenge?* London: Batsford.

Clare, J. 1967. 'Emmonsails Heath in Winter', in *Selected Poems and Prose of John Clare*. Edited by E. Robinson and G. Summerfields. London: Oxford University Press, pp. 138–9.

Clarke, D. 1968. *Analytical Archaeology*, First edition. London: Methuen.

Clarke, D. 1973. 'Archaeology: The Loss of Innocence'. *Antiquity* 47: 6–18.

Clarke, D. Editor. 1977. *Spatial Archaeology*. London: Academic Press.

Cleere, H. Editor. 1984. *Approaches to the Archaeological Heritage: A Comparative Study of World Cultural Resource Management Systems*. Cambridge: Cambridge University Press.

Clifford, J. 1988. *The Predicament of Culture: Twentieth Century Ethnography, Literature and Art*. Cambridge, MA: Harvard University Press.

Cloke, P., P. Crang and M. Goodwin. Editors. 1999. *Introducing Human Geographies*. London: Arnold.

Cloke, P., C. Philo and D. Sadler. 1991. *Approaching Human Geography: An Introduction to Contemporary Theoretical Debates*. London: Paul Chapman.

Cloke, P., M. Doel, D. Matless, M. Phillips and N. Thrift 1994. *Writing the Rural: Five Cultural Geographies*. London: Paul Chapman.

Coldstream, J. N. 1977. *Geometric Greece*. London: Benn.

Collins, H. and T. Pinch. 1993. *The Golem: What Everyone Should Know about Science*. Cambridge: Cambridge University Press.

Collins, H. and T. Pinch. 1998. *The Golem at Large: What You Should Know about Technology.* Cambridge: Cambridge University Press.

Connerton, P. Editor. 1976. *Critical Sociology.* Harmondsworth: Penguin.

Connor, W. R. 1988. 'Early Greek Land Warfare as Symbolic Expression'. *Past and Present* 119:3–29.

Constantine, D. 1984. *Early Greek Travellers and the Hellenic Ideal.* Cambridge: Cambridge University Press.

Corbin, A. 1995. *Time, Desire and Horror: Towards a History of the Senses.* Oxford: Blackwell Polity.

Cosgrove, D. and S. Daniels. Editors. 1988. *The Iconography of Landscape: Essays on the Symbolic Representation, Design and Use of Past Environments.* Cambridge: Cambridge University Press.

Courbin, P. 1957. 'Une Tombe Géométrique d'Argos'. *Bulletin de Correspondance Hellénique* 81:322–86.

Cresswell, T. 1997. 'Imagining the Nomad: Mobility and the Postmodern Primitive', in *Space and Social Theory: Interpreting Modernity and Postmodernity.* Edited by G. Benko and U. Strohmeyer, pp. 360–79. Oxford: Blackwell.

Cronyn, J. 1990. *Elements of Archaeological Conservation.* London: Routledge.

Cumberland, G. 1996. *An Attempt to Describe Hafod.* Aberystwyth, Wales: Hafod Trust.

Curti, L. and I. Chambers. Editors. 1996. *The Post-colonial Question: Common Skies, Divided Horizons.* London: Routledge.

Daniels, S. 1993. *Fields of Vision: Landscape Imagery and National Identity in England and the United States.* Oxford: Blackwell Polity.

Davies, M. Editor. 1991. *Poetarum Melicorum Graecorum Fragmenta (Volume 1).* Oxford: Clarendon Press.

De Certeau, M. 1988. Trans. S. Rendall. *The Practice of Everyday Life.* London: University of California Press.

De Polignac, F. 1984. *La Naissance de la Cité Grecque.* Paris: Editions La Découverte.

De Polignac, F. 1994. 'Mediation, Competition and Sovereignty: The Evolution of Rural Sanctuaries in Geometric Greece', in *Placing the Gods: Sanctuaries and Sacred Space in Ancient Greece.* Edited by S. E. Alcock and R. Osborne. Oxford: Clarendon Press.

Deilaki, E. 1973. 'Archaiotites kai mnimeia Argolidos-Korinthias 1971-2'. *Arkhaiologikon Deltion* 28:80–122.

Deleuze, G. and F. Guattari. 1988. *A Thousand Plateaux. Capitalism and Schizophrenia.* London: Athlone Press.

Detienne, M. 1979. *Dionysos Slain.* Baltimore: Johns Hopkins University Press.

Diamond, E. 1995. 'The Shudder of Catharsis', in *Performativity and Performance.* Edited by A. Parker and E. K. Sedgwick. New York: Routledge: 152–72.

Diamond, E. 1996. 'Introduction', in *Performance and Cultural Politics.* Edited by E. Diamond. London/New York: Routledge: 1–12.

Díaz-Andreu, M. and T. Champion. Editors. 1996. *Nationalism and Archaeology in Europe.* London: University College London Press.

Diller, E. and R. Scofidio. 1992. 'Case No. 00-17163', in *Incorporations, Zone 6.* Edited by J. Crary and S. Kwinter, pp. 344–61. New York: Urzone Inc.

Dilnot, C. 1994. 'The Enigma of Things'. *Kunst Journaal* 5:21–32.

Douglas, M. 1966. *Purity and Danger.* London: Routledge and Kegan Paul.

Dreyfus, H. L. 1991. *Being in the World: A Commentary on Heidegger's Being and Time.* Cambridge, MA: MIT Press.

Dul, J. and B. A. Weerdemeester. 1993. *Ergonomics for Beginners.* London: Taylor and Francis.

Eagleton, T. 1983. *Literary Theory: An Introduction.* Oxford: Blackwell.

Eco, U. 1977. 'Semiotics of Theatrical Performance'. *The Drama Review* 21: 107–17.

Edensor, T. 1998. 'The Culture of the Indian Street', in *Images of the Street: Planning, Identity, and Control in Public Spaces.* Edited by N. R. Fyfe, pp. 205–221. London/New York: Routledge.

Edmonds, M. 1999. *Ancestral Geographies of the Neolithic: Landscape, Monuments and Memory.* London/New York: Routledge.

Elam, K. 1980. *The Semiotics of Theatre and Drama.* London: Methuen.

Elliott, B. Editor. 1988. *Technology and Social Process*. Edinburgh: Edinburgh University Press.

Fabian, J. 1983. *Time and the Other: How Anthropology Makes its Object*. New York: Columbia University Press.

Fairbrother, T. Editor. 1991. *Robert Wilson's Vision*. Boston, MA: Museum of Fine Arts.

Featherstone, M. Editor. 1990. *Global Culture: Nationalism, Globalisation and Modernity*. London: Sage.

Featherstone, M., S. Lash and R. Robertson. Editors. 1995. *Global Modernities*. London: Sage.

Finnegan, R. 1992. *Oral Traditions and the Verbal Arts: A Guide to Research Practices*. London/New York: Routledge.

Fischer-Lichte, E. 1995. 'Theatricality: A Key Concept in Theatre and Cultural Studies'. *Theatre Research International* 20:85–9.

Foucault, M. 1986a. 'Of Other Places'. *Diacritics* 16:22–7.

Foucault, M. 1986b. 'What is an Author?', in *The Foucault Reader*. Edited by P. Rabinow. Harmondsworth: Penguin.

Foucault, M. 1989. *The Order of Things. An Archaeology of the Human Sciences*. London: Tavistock/Routledge.

Fränkel, H. 1975. *Early Greek Poetry and Philosophy*. Oxford: Blackwell.

Friedman, A. 1992. 'Architecture, Authority and the Gaze: Planning and Representation in the Early Modern Country House'. *Assemblage 18*: 40–61.

Friedman, J. and M. Rowlands. 1978. *The Evolution of Social Systems*. London: Duckworth.

Fritz, J. 1978. 'Palacopsychology Today: Ideational Systems and Human Adaptation in Prehistory', in *Social Archaeology: Beyond Subsistence and Dating*. Edited by C. Redman. London: Academic Press.

Frontisi-Ducroux, F. 1984. 'Au Miroir du Masque', in *La Cité des Images*. Paris: Nathan.

Fuller, P. 1980. *Seeing Berger: A Reevaluation*. London: Writers and Readers.

Fuller, S. 1993. *Philosophy of Science and its Discontents*, Second edition. New York: Guilford.

Fuller, S. 1997. *Science*. Buckingham: Open University Press.

Fyfe, N. R. 1998. *Images of the Street*. London: Routledge.

Gernet, L. 1968. 'Frairies Antiques', in *Anthropologie de la Grèce Antique*. Edited by L. Gernet. Paris: Maspero.

Gero, J. and M. Conkey. Editors. 1991. *Engendering Archaeology: Women and Prehistory*. Oxford: Blackwell.

Giddens, A. 1979. *Central Problems in Social Theory*. London: Macmillan.

Giddens, A. 1984. *The Constitution of Society: Outline of the Theory of Structuration*. Cambridge: Blackwell Polity.

Giddens, A. 1987. 'Erving Goffman as a Systematic Social Theorist', in *Social Theory and Modern Sociology*, pp. 109–39. Cambridge: Polity Press.

Gilpin, W. 1782. *Observations on the River Wye and Several Parts of South Wales etc. Relative Chiefly to Picturesque Beauty Made in the Summer of the Year 1770*. London.

Gilpin, W. 1792. *Three Essays: On Picturesque Travel; and On Sketching landscape: to which is Added a Poem, On Landscape Painting*. London.

Ginzburg, C. 1989. *Clues, Myths and the Historical Method*. Baltimore: Johns Hopkins University Press.

Girard, R. 1977. *Violence and the Sacred*. Baltimore: Johns Hopkins University Press.

Godelier, M. 1973. *Rationality and Irrationality in Economics*. New York: Monthly Review Press.

Godelier, M. 1977. *Perspectives in Marxist Anthropology*. Cambridge: Cambridge University Press.

Goffman, E. 1971a. *The Presentation of Self in Everyday Life*. Harmondsworth: Pelican Books.

Goffman, E. 1971b. *Relations in Public*. Harmondsworth: Penguin Books.

Goldberg, R. 1988. *Performance Art. From Futurism to the Present. World of Art*. London: Thames and Hudson.

Gosden, C. 2000. 'Postcolonial Archaeology: Issues of Culture, Identity and Knowledge', in *Archaeological Theory Today: Breaking the Boundaries*. Edited by I. Hodder. Oxford: Blackwell Polity.

Gouldner, A. 1973. *For Sociology*. New York: Allen Lane.

Gouldner, A. 1976. *The Dialectic of Ideology and Technology*. London: Macmillan.

Goya, F. 1967. *The Disasters of War*. Toronto, Canada: Dover.

Greenaway, P. 1991. *The Physical Self*. Rotterdam: Museum Boymans-van Beuningen.

Greenaway, P. 1992. *100 Objects to Represent the World*. Stuttgart: Hatje.

Greenaway, P. 1993. *Some Organising Principles*. Swansea, Wales: Glynn Vivian Art Gallery/Wales Film Council.

Greenaway, P. 1997. *Flying over Water*. London: Merrill Holberton.

Gregory, D. 1989. 'Presences and Absences: Time–Space Relations and Structuration Theory', in *Social Theory of Modern Societies: Anthony Giddens and his Critics*. Edited by D. Held and J. B. Thompson, pp.185–214. Cambridge: Cambridge University Press.

Gregory, D. 1993. 'Interventions in the Historical Geography of Modernity: Social Theory, Spatiality and the Politics of Representation', in *Place/Culture/Representation*. Edited by J. Duncan and D. Ley. pp.272–313 London/New York: Routledge.

Grinsell, L. V. 1936. *The Ancient Burial Mounds of England*. London: Methuen.

Grotowski, J. 1969. *Towards a Poor Theatre*. London: Methuen.

Haas, J. Editor. 1990. *The Anthropology of War*. Cambridge: Cambridge University Press.

Hall, E. T. 1966. *The Hidden Dimension*. New York: Doubleday.

Hall, S., D. Hobson, A. Lowe and P. Willis. Editors. 1980. *Culture, Media, Language*. London: Hutchinson.

Hammond, J. 1973. 'A Potted History of the Fringe'. *Theatre Quarterly* III:37–46.

Hanson, V. 1990. *The Western Way of War: Infantry Battle in Classical Greece*. London: Hodder and Stoughton.

Hanson, V. Editor. 1991. *Hoplites: The Classical Greek Battle Experience*. London: Routledge.

Haraway, D. 1991. *Simians, Cyborgs and Women: The Reinvention of Nature*. London: Free Association.

Hardy, T. 1993. *Selected Poems*. London: Penguin Books.

Harré, R. 1979. *Social Being*. Oxford: Blackwell.

Harris, M. 1968. *The Rise of Anthropological Theory*. New York: Cornell University Press.

Hartley, P. 1999. *Interpersonal Communication*. London/New York: Routledge.

Harvey, D. 1969. *Explanation in Geography*. London: Arnold.

Hasford, G. 1980. *The Short-timers*. New York: Bantam.

Heat-Moon, W. L. 1991. *PrairyErth*. London: Andre Deutsch.

Heathfield, A. Editor. 1997. *Shattered Anatomies*. Bristol: Arnolfini Live.

Hebdige, D. 1979. *Subculture: The Meaning of Style*. London: Methuen.

Held, D. 1980. *Introduction to Critical Theory: Horkheimer to Habermas*. London: Hutchinson.

Henderson, J. 1994. '*Timeo Danaos*: Amazons in Early Greek Art and Pottery', in *Art and Text in Ancient Greek Culture*. Edited by S. Goldhill and R. Osborne. Cambridge: Cambridge University Press.

Hernandez, A. 1995. *Landscapes for the Homeless*. Hannover, Germany: Sprengel Museum.

Hesse, M. 1970. *Models and Analogies in Science*. Notre Dame, IN: University of Notre Dame Press.

Hewison, R. 1987. *The Heritage Industry: Britain in a Climate of Decline*. London: Methuen.

Higgs, E. Editor. 1972. *Papers in Economic Prehistory*. Cambridge: Cambridge University Press.

Higgs, E. Editor. 1975. *Palaeoeconomy*. Cambridge: Cambridge University Press.

Hindess, B. and P. Hirst. 1975. *Pre-capitalist Modes of Production*. London: Macmillan.

Hobsbawm, E. 1990. *Nations and Nationalism Since 1780*. Cambridge: Cambridge University Press.

Hobsbawm, E. and T. Ranger. Editors. 1983. *The Invention of Tradition*. Cambridge: Cambridge University Press.

Hodder, I. Editor. 1978. *The Spatial Organisation of Culture*. London: Duckworth.

Hodder, I. 1982a. *The Present Past: An Introduction to Anthropology for Archaeologists*. London: Batsford.

Hodder, I. 1982b. *Symbols in Action*. Cambridge: Cambridge University Press.

Hodder, I. 1989. 'This is Not an Article about Material Culture as Text'. *Journal of Anthropological Archaeology* 8:250–69.

Hodder, I. and C. Orton. 1976. *Spatial Analysis and Archaeology*. Cambridge: Cambridge University Press.

Hodder, I., M. Shanks, A. Alexandri, V. Buchli, J. Carman, J. Last and G. Lucas. Editors. 1995. *Interpreting Archaeology: Finding Meaning in the Past*. London: Routledge.

Horne, D. 1984. *The Great Museum: The Re-presentation of History*. London: Pluto Press.

Hoskins, W. G. 1955. *The Making of the English Landscape*. London: Hodder and Stoughton.

Houston, A. 1998. 'Postmodern Dramaturgy in Contemporary British Theatre: Three Companies'. Ph.D. thesis, University of Canterbury.

Hunter, M. 1975. *John Aubrey and the Realm of Learning*. London: Duckworth.

Huntford, R. 1985. *The Last Place on Earth*. London: Pan.

Hurwitt, J. M. 1985. *The Art and Culture of Early Greece 1100–480 BC*. Ithaca: Cornell University Press.

Jameson, F. 1991. *Postmoderism, or, The Cultural Logic of Late Capitalism*. London and New York: Verso.

Jarman, A. O. H. Editor. 1988. *Aneirin: Y Gododdin*. Llandysul, Wales: Gomer Press.

Jarman, M. R., G. N. Bailey and H. N. Jarman. Editors. 1982. *Early European Agriculture: Its Foundations and Development*. Cambridge: Cambridge University Press.

Johansen, H. and B. Olsen. 1992. 'Hermeneutics and Archaeology: On the Philosophy of Contextual Archaeology'. *American Antiquity* 57:419–36.

Johansen, K. F. 1923. *Les Vases Sicyoniens*. Paris: Champion.

Johnson, M. 1989. 'Conceptions of Agency in Archaeological Interpretation'. *Journal of Anthropological Archaeology* 8:189–211.

Johnston, R., D. Gregory and D. Smith. Editors. 1994. *A Dictionary of Human Geography*. Oxford: Blackwell.

Jones, D. G. 1986. 'Rhydcymerau', in *Welsh Verse*. Edited by T. Conran, pp. 285–6. Bridgend, Wales: Poetry Wales Press.

Kahn, J. S. and J. R. Llobera. Editors. 1981. *The Anthropology of Precapitalist Societies*. London: Macmillan.

Kastner, J. and B. Wallis. Editors. 1998. *Land and Environmental Art*. London: Phaidon.

Kaye, N. 1996. *Art into Theatre: Performance Interviews and Documents*. Amsterdam: Harwood Academic.

Kaye, N. 2000. *Site Specifics: Performance, Place and Documentation*. London: Routledge.

Keegan, J. 1976. *The Face of Battle*. London.

Keegan, J. 1993. *A History of Warfare*. London: Hutchinson.

Kenfield, J. F. 1973. 'The Sculptural Significance of Early Greek Armour'. *Opuscula Romana* 9:149–56.

Knorr-Cetina, K. 1981. *The Manufacture of Knowledge: An Essay on the Constructivist and Contextual Nature of Science*. Oxford: Pergamon Press.

Knorr-Cetina, K. 1999. *Epistemic Cultures: How the Sciences Make Knowledge*. Cambridge, MA: Harvard University Press.

Koch, J. 1998. 'Brith Gof. Ein walisisches Theaterexperiment'. Magister Artium thesis, Ruhr-Universität Bochum.

Kohl, P. L. and C. Fawcett. Editors. 1995. *Nationalism, Politics and the Practice of Archaeology*. Cambridge: Cambridge University Press.

Kopytoff, I. 1986. 'The Cultural Biography of Things: Commoditisation as a Process', in *The Social Life of Things: Commodities in Cultural Perspective*. Edited by A. Appadurai. Cambridge: Cambridge University Press.

Korshak, Y. 1987. *Frontal Faces in Attic Vase Painting of the Archaic Period*. Chicago: Ares.

Kroeber, A. L. and C. Kluckhohn. 1952. *Culture: A Critical Review of Concepts and Definitions*. Cambridge, MA: Peabody Museum.

Kron, U. 1988. 'Kultmahle im Heraion von Samos archaischer Zeit', in *Early Greek Cult Practice*. Edited by R. Hägg, N. Marinatos and G. Nordquist. Stockholm: Skrifter Utgivna av Svenska Institutet i Athen.

Kuhn, H. 1986. *The Conservation and Restoration of Works of Art and Antiquities*. London: Butterworth.

Kunze, E. 1991. Beinschienen. *Olympische Forschungen* 21.

Kunzru, H. 1996. 'The Unlikely Cyborg: An Interview with Donna Haraway'. *Wired* 2: 12 (UK).

Lacan, J. 1977. 'The Mirror Phase as Formative of the Function of the I as Revealed in Psychoanalytic Experience', in *Écrits: A Selection*. London: Tavistock.

Laclau, E. and C. Mouffe. 1985. *Hegemony and Socialist Strategy*. London: Verso.

Laing, R. D. 1965. *The Divided Self. An Existential Study in Sanity and Madness*. Harmondsworth: Penguin Books.

Laing, R. D. 1971. *Self and Others*. Harmondsworth: Penguin Books.

Lampeter Archaeology Workshop. 1997. Relativism, Objectivity and the Politics of the Past. *Archaeological Dialogues* 4:164–75.

Langmuir, E. 1997. *Landscape*. London: National Gallery Publications.

Larraine, J. 1979. *The Concept of Ideology*. London: Hutchinson.

Larraine, J. 1983. *Marxism and Ideology*. London: Macmillan.

Latour, B. 1987. *Science in Action: How to Follow Scientists and Engineers Through Society*. Milton Keynes: Open University Press.

Latour, B. 1989. 'Clothing the Naked Truth', in *Dismantling Truth: Reality in the Postmodern World*. Edited by H. Lawson and L. Appignanesi. New York: St Martin's Press.

Latour, B. 1993. *We Have Never Been Modern*. London: Harvester Wheatsheaf.

Lattimore, R. 1960. *Greek Lyrics, Translated*, Second edition. Chicago: University of Chicago Press.

Law, J. 1987. 'Technology and Heterogeneous Engineering: The Case of Portugese Expansion', in *The Social Construction of Technological Systems*. Edited by W. E. Bijker, T. P. Hughes and T. Pinch. Cambridge, MA: MIT Press.

Law, J. 1991a. 'Monsters, Machines and Sociotechnical Relations', in *A Sociology of Monsters: Essays on Power, Technology and Domination*. Edited by J. Law. London: Routledge.

Law, J. Editor. 1991b. *A Sociology of Monsters: Essays on Power, Technology and Domination*. London: Routledge.

Leach, E. 1976. *Culture and Communication*. Cambridge: Cambridge University Press.

Leighly, J. Editor. 1963. *Land and Life: Selections from the Writings of Carl Ortwin Sauer*. Berkeley: University of California Press.

Lemonnier, P. Editor. 1993. *Technological Choices*. London: Routledge.

Lewis, J. 1999. *Interpreting Pollack*. London: Tate Gallery.

Lewis, S. 1983. 'The Caernarfon Court Speech', in *Presenting Saunders Lewis*. Edited by A. R. Jones and G. Thomas. pp.115–26 Cardiff: University of Wales Press.

Lewis Jones, B. 1985. 'Cynefin – The Word and the Concept'. *Nature in Wales* :121–2.

Lichtenstein, R. and I. Sinclair. 1999. *Rodinsky's Room*. London: Granta Books.

Lillesand, T. W. and R. W. Kiefer. 1994. *Remote Sensing and Image Interpretation*, Third edition. New York: Wiley.

Lipe, W. 1977. 'A Conservation Guide for American Archaeology', in *Conservation Archaeology: A Guide for Cultural Resource Management Studies*. Edited by M. B. Schiffer and G. Gummerman. London: Academic Press.

Lipe, W. 1984. 'Value and Meaning in Cultural Resources', in *Approaches to the Archaeological Heritage: A Comparative Study of World Cultural Resource Management Systems*. Edited by H. Cleere. Cambridge: Cambridge University Press.

Loraux, N. 1975. 'HBH et ANDREIA: deux versions de la mort du combattant athénien'. *Ancient Society* 6:1–31.

Loraux, N. 1986. *The Invention of Athens*. Cambridge, MA: Harvard University Press.

Lowenthal, D. and H. Prince 1964. 'English Landscape Tastes'. *Geographical Review* 54:309–46.

Lowenthal, D. 1985. *The Past is a Foreign Country*. Cambridge: Cambridge University Press.

Lowenthal, D. 1991a. 'British National Identity and the English Landscape'. *Rural History* 2:205-30.

Lowenthal, D. 1991b. 'The Value of Age and Decay'. Paper delivered in Oxford University: Department of Building Pathology.

Lowenthal, D. and M. Binney. Editors. 1981. *Our Past Before Us: Why Do We Save It?* London: Temple Smith.

McGlew, J. F. 1993. *Tyranny and Political Culture in Ancient Greece*. Ithaca: Cornell University Press.

Mackenzie, D. and J. Wajcman. Editors. 1985. *The Social Shaping of Technology: How the Refridgerator Got its Hum*. Milton Keynes: Open University Press.

McLucas, C. 1993. Untitled paper presented to the 'Devising and Documentation' Conference, Centre for Performance Research Cardiff, February 1993.

McLucas, C. 2000. 'Ten Feet and Three-quarters of an Inch of Theatre: A Documentation of Tri Bywyd – a Site-Specific Theatre Work', in *site-specific art performance, place and documentation*. Edited by N. Kaye. London: Routledge.

McLucas, C. forthcoming. *The Host and the Ghost: Site Specific Theatre in the Work of Brith Gof.*

McLucas, C. and M. Pearson. 1996. 'Clifford McLucas and Mike Pearson (Brith Gof)', in *Art into Theatre: Performance Interviews and Documents*. Edited by N. Kaye, pp. 209–34. Amsterdam: Harwood Academic Publishers.

McLucas, C. and M. Pearson. 1999. 'Clifford McLucas and Mike Pearson', in *On Directing: Interviews with Directors*. Edited by G. Giannachi and M. Luckhurst, pp. 78–89. London: Faber and Faber.

Marcuse, H. 1955. *Reason and Revolution: Hegel and the Rise of Social Theory*, Second edition. London: Routledge and Kegan Paul.

Mason, P. 1987. 'Third Person/Second Sex: Patterns of Sexual Asymmetry in the Theogony of Hesiodos', in *Sexual Asymmetry: Studies in Ancient Society*. Edited by J. Blok and P. Mason. Amsterdam: Grieben.

Mauss, M. 1973. Techniques of the Body. *Economy and Society* 2:70–88.

Melrose, S. 1994. *A Semiotics of the Dramatic Text*. Basingstoke, Hants: The Macmillan Press.

Mercer, R. J. 1990. *Causewayed Enclosures*. *Shire Archaeology*. Princes Risborough: Shire.

Merleau-Ponty, M. 1962. *Phenomenology of Perception*. London: Routledge and Kegan Paul.

Molloy, P. 1983. *And They Blessed Rebecca*. Llandysul, Wales: Gomer Press.

Morgan, C. 1990. *Athletes and Oracles: The Transformation of Olympia and Delphi in the Eighth Century BC*. Cambridge: Cambridge University Press.

Morgan, C. 1993. 'The Origins of Pan-Hellenism', in *Greek Sanctuaries: New Approaches*. Edited by N. Marinatos and R. Hägg. London: Routledge.

Morgan, C. 1994. 'The Evolution of a Sacral "Landscape": Isthmia, Perachora, and the Early Corinthian State', in *Placing the Gods: Sanctuaries and Scared Space in Ancient Greece*. Edited by S. E. Alcock and R. Osborne, pp. 105–42. Oxford: Clarendon Press.

Morris, I. 1987. *Burial and Ancient Society: The Rise of the Greek City State*. Cambridge: Cambridge University Press.

Morris, I. 1994. 'Archaeologies of Greece', in *Classical Greece: Ancient History and Modern Archaeologies*. Edited by I. Morris. Cambridge: Cambridge University Press.

Morrison, B. 1993. *And When Did You Last See Your Father?* London: Granta Books.

Müller, H. 1990. *Germania*. New York: Semiotext[e].

Mumford, L. 1961. *The City in History: Its Origins, its Transformations, and its Prospects*. London: Secker and Warburg.

Mumford. L. 1966. *The Myth of the Machine: Technics and Human Development*. New York: Harcourt, Brace and World.

Murray, O. 1993. *Early Greece*, Second edition. London: Fontana.

Nagy, G. 1979. *The Best of the Achaeans: Concepts of the Hero in Archaic Greek Poetry*. Baltimore: Johns Hopkins University Press.

Nicholas, J. 1975. *Waldo Williams*. Cardiff: University of Wales Press.

Nora, P. 1989. 'Between Memory and History: Le Lieux de Memoire'. *Representations* 26:7–25.

Nora, P. 1997. *Realms of Memory: The Construction of the French Past: Traditions (European Perspectives) Vol. 2*. New York: Columbia University Press.

Norman, D. 1988. *The Psychology of Everyday Things*. New York: Basic Books.

Olivier, L. 1994. 'Archaeology as Mediation with the Past'. European Association of Archaeologists Annual Meeting, Ljubljana, Slovenia, 1994.

Olivier, L. 1999a. 'L'archéologie et la Construction du Présent'. *European Journal of Archaeology* 2:269–80.

Olivier, L. 1999b. 'Photographie, Archéologie et Mémoire'. *European Journal of Archaeology* 2:107–15.

Olivier, L. and A. Coudart. 1995. 'French Tradition and the Central Place of History in the Human Sciences: Preamble to a Dialogue between Robinson Crusoe and his Man Friday', in *Theory in Archaeology: A World Perspective*. Edited by P. Ucko. London: Routledge.

Ollman, B. 1971. *Alienation: Marx's Conception of Man in Capitalist Society*. Cambridge: Cambridge University Press.

Ondaatje, M. 1984. *Coming through Slaughter*. London: Picador.

Ondaatje, M. 1989. *The Collected Works of Billy the Kid*. London: Pan.

Orwell, G. 1990. *1984*. London: Penguin Books.

O'Shea, J. M. 1984. *Mortuary Variability: An Archaeological Investigation*. London: Academic Press.

Out, T. 1971. 'Guide to Underground Theatre'. *Theatre Quarterly* 1:61–5.

Owen, T. M. 1978. *Welsh Folk Customs*. Cardiff: National Museum of Wales.

Page, D. L. Editor. 1962. *Poetae Melici Graeci*. Oxford: Oxford University Press.

Parker, C., Medvedow, J. and Ferguson, B. Editors. 2000. *Cornelia Parker*. London: Institute of Contemporary Arts.

Parker-Pearson, M. 1993. *Bronze Age Britain*. London: Batsford.

Parry-Williams, T. H. 1974. 'Bro/Locality', in *Poetry of Wales 1930–1970*. Edited by R. G. Jones. Llandysul, Wales: Gwasg Gomer.

Pasolli, R. 1970. *A Book on the Open Theater*. New York: Avon.

Pavis, P. 1996. *L'Analyse des Spectacles*. Paris: Editions Nathan.

Payne, H. G. G. 1931. *Necrocorinthia: A Study of Korinthian Art in the Archaic Period*. Oxford: Clarendon Press.

Payne, H. G. G. 1933. *Protokorinthische Vasenmalerei*. Berlin: Keller.

Pearce, S. 1992. *Museum Objects and Collections: A Cultural Study*. Leicester: Leicester University Press.

Pearce, S. 1997. *Collecting in Contemporary Practice*. London: AltaMira Sage.

Pearson, M. 1993. 'Welsh Heterotopias'. *New Welsh Review* 21:19–21.

Pearson, M. 1994a. 'The Script's *Not* the Thing'. *New Welsh Review* 27:67–71.

Pearson, M. (with Julian Thomas) 1994b. 'Theatre/Archaeology'. *The Drama Review* 38–4:133–61.

Pearson, M. 1995. 'From Memory or Other Ways of Telling'. *New Welsh Review* 30:77–83.

Pearson, M. 1996a. 'The Dream in the Desert'. *Performance Research* 1:5–15.

Pearson, M. 1996b. 'The Temper of the Times'. *Performance Research* 1:94.

Pearson, M. 1996c. 'Reflexions sur l'Ethnoscenologie', in *La Scene et la Terre: Questions D'Ethnoscenologie*. Edited by C. Khaznadar, pp. 55–64. Paris: Babel/Maison des Culture du Monde.

Pearson, M. 1996d. 'Dem Bones, Dem Bones: The Body in the Neolithic', in *The Connected Body?: An Interdisciplinary Approach to the Body and Performance, Amsterdam Readings on the Arts and Art Education*. Edited by R. Allsopp and S. deLahunta, pp. 86–93. Amsterdam: Amsterdam School of the Arts.

Pearson, M. 1997a. 'Special Worlds, Secret Maps. A Poetics of Performance', in *Staging Wales*. Edited by A.-M. Taylor, pp. 85–99. Cardiff: University of Wales Press.

Pearson, M. 1997b. 'The Past was not Silent'. *New Welsh Review* 37:68–70.

Pearson, M. 1998a. 'My Balls/Your Chin'. *Performance Research* 3:35–41.

Pearson, M. 1998b. 'Performance as Valuation: Early Bronze Age Burial as Theatrical Complexity', in *The*

Archaeology of Prestige and Wealth, vol. 730. Edited by D. Bailey, pp. 32-41. Oxford: BAR International Series.

Pearson, M. and L. Levett. forthcoming. 'Devices and Desires'. *Contemporary Theatre Review.*

Pearson, M. and M. Shanks. 1997. 'Performing a Visit: Archaeologies of the Contemporary Past'. *Performance Research* 2:41–53.

Pearson, M., L. Lewis and R. Owen. 1999. 'An Optic to Examine Experience'. *New Welsh Review* 45:74-75.

Peate, I. C. 1972. *Tradition and Folk Life. A Welsh View.* London: Faber and Faber.

Peirce, C. 1958. Collected Papers; vol. 7. Cambridge, MA: Harvard University Press.

Perec, G. 1997. *Species of Spaces and Other Places.* London: Penguin Books.

Pheasant, S. 1986. *Bodyspace: Anthropometry, Ergonomics and Design.* London: Taylor and Francis.

Phillips, D. Z. 1995. *J.R. Jones.* Cardiff: University of Wales Press.

Phillips, R. 1997. *Mapping Men & Empire: A Geography of Adventure.* London/New York: Routledge.

Phillips, S. S., M. Haworth-Booth and C. Squiers. 1998. *Police Pictures: The Photograph as Evidence.* San Francisco: San Francisco Museum of Modern Art/Chronicle Books.

Pickering, A. Editor. 1992. *Science as Practice and Culture.* Chicago: University of Chicago Press.

Piggott, S. 1976. *Ruins in a Landscape: Essays in Antiquarianism.* Edinburgh: Edinburgh University Press.

Plenderleith, H. J. and A. E. A. Werner. 1972. *The Conservation of Antiquities and Works of Art: Treatment, Repair and Restoration.* Oxford: Oxford University Press.

Poe, E. A. 1980. *Selected Tales.* Oxford: Oxford University Press.

Pomian, K. 1987. *Collectionneurs, Amateurs et Curieux, Paris – Venise XVIème–XVIIIème Siècle.* Paris: Gallimard.

Pratt, M.-L. 1992. *Imperial Eyes: Travel Writing and Transculturation.* London: Routledge.

Pred, A. 1977. 'The Choreography of Existence: Comments on Hagerstrand's Time-Geography and its Usefulness'. *Economic Geography* 53:207–21.

Pred, A. 1990. *Lost Words and Lost Worlds: Modernity and the Language of Everyday Life in Late Nineteenth-Century Stockholm.* Cambridge: Cambridge University Press.

Pred, A. 1997. 'Re-Presenting the Extended Present Moment of Danger: A Mediation on Hypermodernity, Identity and the Montage Form', in *Space and Social Theory: Interpreting Modernity and Postmodernity.* Edited by G. Benko and U. Strohmayer, pp. 117–40. Oxford: Blackwell.

Purcell, N. 1990. 'Mobility and the Polis', in *The Greek City from Homer to Alexander.* Edited by O. Murray and S. Price. Oxford: Clarendon Press.

Pye, D. 1978. *The Nature and Aesthetics of Design.* London: Herbert Press.

Raab, L. and A. Goodyear. 1984. 'Middle-range Theory in Archaeology: A Critical Review of Origins and Applications'. *American Antiquity* 49:255–8.

Redman, C. L. 1999. *Human Impact on Ancient Environments.* Tucson: University of Arizona Press.

Reinelt, J. forthcoming. 'The Politics of Discourse: Performativity Meets Theatricality', unpublished manuscript.

Rendell, J. 1998. 'Displaying Sexuality: Gendered Identities and the Early Nineteenth-century Street', in *Images of the Street: Planning, Identity, and Control in Public Spaces.* Edited by N. R. Fyfe, pp. 75–91. London/New York: Routledge.

Renfrew, C. and P. Bahn. 1996. *Archaeology: Theories, Methods, and Practice*, Second edition. London: Thames and Hudson.

Richards, C. C. 1988. 'Altered Images: A Re-examination of Neolithic Mortuary Practices in Orkney', in *The Archaeology of Context in the Neolithic and Bronze Age: Recent Trends.* Edited by J. C. Barrett and I. A. Kinnes, pp. 42–56. Sheffield: Department of Archaeology and Prehistory.

Richards, C. C. 1992. 'Doorways into Another World: The Orkney-Cromarty Chambered Tombs', in *Vessels for the Ancestors: Essays on the Neolithic of Britain and Ireland.* Edited by A. Sheridan and N. Sharples, pp. 62–76. Edinburgh: Edinburgh University Press.

Richards, C. C. 1996. 'Henges and Water: Towards an Elemental Understanding of Monumentality and Landscape in Late Neolithic Britain'. *Journal of Material Culture*: 313–36.

Richter, G. M. A. 1970. *Kouroi: Archaic Greek Youths*. London: Phaidon.

Roach, J. 1996. *Cities of the Dead*. New York: Columbia University Press.

Roms, H. 1993. 'Theatre as the Spatial Machinery of Identities'. Paper presented to the 'Performing Places' Session at the Theoretical Archaeology Group Conference, University of Durham, December 1993.

Roms, H. 1997. 'Moving Landscapes: A Glance back at Recent Developments in Welsh Dance Theatre'. *Planet* 126:79–82.

Rostagno, A. with Beck, J. and Malina, J. 1970. *We, The Living Theatre*. New York: Ballantine.

Rowlands, M. 1989. 'Repetition and Exteriorisation in Narratives of Historical Origins'. *Critique of Anthropology* 8:43–62.

Rowlands, M. 1994. 'The Politics of Identity in Archaeology', in *Social Construction of the Past: Representation as Power*. Edited by G. Bond and A. Gilliam. London: Routledge.

Rudé, G. 1981. *The Crowd in History*. London: Lawrence and Wishart.

Rudkin, E. H. 1987. *Lincolnshire Folklore*. Burgh le Marsh, England: Robert Pacey.

Saferstein, R. 1998. *Criminalistics: An Introduction to Forensic Science*. Upper Saddle River, NJ: Prentice-Hall.

Sahlins, M. 1976. *Culture and Practical Reason*. Chicago: University of Chicago Press.

Salmon, J. 1977. 'Political Hoplites?' *Journal of Hellenic Studies* 97:84–101.

Sante, L. 1991. *Low Life*. New York: Farrar, Strauss and Giroux.

Savill, C. 1990. 'Dismantling the Wall'. *Planet* 79:20–8.

Savill, C. 1993. 'A Critical Study of the History of the Welsh Theatre Company Brith Gof'. M.Phil. thesis, University of Wales College Aberystwyth.

Savill, C. 1997. 'Brith Gof', in *Staging Wales*. Edited by A.-M. Taylor, pp.100–10. Cardiff: University of Wales Press.

Savill, C. 1998. 'Within a Sense of Place, there Lurks a Sense of Prejudice'. *New Welsh Review* 42:68-71.

Schechner, R. 1969. *Public Domain*. New York: Avon.

Schechner, R. 1973. *Environmental Theater*. New York: Hawthorn Books.

Schechner, R. 1977. *Essays on Performance Theory*. New York: Drama Book Specialists.

Schiffer, M. 1987. *Formation Processes of the Archaeological Record*. Albuquerque: University of New Mexico Press.

Schnapp, A. 1984. 'Eros en chasse', in *La Cité des Images*. Paris: Nathan.

Schnapp, A. 1996. *The Discovery of the Past: The Origins of Archaeology*. London: British Museum Press.

Schnapp, A. Editor. 1997. *Une Archéologie du Passé Récent*. Paris: Maison des Sciences de l'Homme.

Schutzman, M. 1998. 'A Fool's Discourse: The Buffoonery Syndrome', in *The Ends of Performance*. Edited by P. Phelan and J. Lane, pp.131–48. New York/London: New York University Press.

Scollar, I., A. Tabbagh, E. Hesse and I. Herzog. 1990. *Archaeological Prospecting and Remote Sensing*. Cambridge: Cambridge University Press.

Scott, R. F. 1953. *The Voyage of the 'Discovery'*. London: John Murray.

Sebeok, T. and J. Umiker-Sebeok. 1983. ' "You Know my Method": A Juxtaposition of Charles S Pierce and Sherlock Holmes', in *The Sign of Three: Dupin, Holmes, Pierce*. Edited by U. Eco and T. A. Sebeok. Bloomington: Indiana University Press.

Seddon, D. Editor. 1978. *Relations of Production: Marxist Approaches to Economic Anthropology*. London: Frank Cass.

Semin, D., T. Garb and D. Cuspit. Editors. 1997. *Christian Boltanski*. London: Phaidon.

Serres, M. and B. Latour. 1995. *Conversations on Science, Culture and Time*. Ann Arbor: University of Michigan Press.

Shanks, M. 1981. 'The Castle, Newcastle-upon-Tyne'. *Archaeologia Aeliana* 9 (5s): 75–89.

Shanks, M. 1990. 'Reading the Signs', in *Archaeology after Structuralism*. Edited by I. Bapty and T. Yates. London: Routledge.

Shanks, M. 1992a. *Experiencing the Past: On the Character of Archaeology*. London: Routledge.

Shanks, M. 1992b. 'Style and the Design of a Perfume Jar from an Archaic Greek City State'. *Journal of European Archaeology* 1:77–106.

Shanks, M. 1994. 'A Ruined Past: Experience and Reality'. *Archaeological Dialogues* 1:56–76.

Shanks, M. 1995a. 'Archaeological Experiences and a Critical Romanticism', in *The Archaeologist and their Reality: Proceedings of the 4th Nordic TAG Conference*. Edited by A. Siriiainen. Helsinki: Department of Archaeology.

Shanks, M. 1995b. 'The Archaeological Imagination: Creativity, Rhetoric and Archaeological Futures', in *Whither Archaeology: Archaeology in the End of the Millennium: Papers Dedicated to Evzen Neustupny*. Edited by M. Kuna and N. Venclovà. Prague: Institute of Archaeology.

Shanks, M. 1995c. 'Art and an archaeology of Embodiment: Some Aspects of Archaic Greece'. *Cambridge Archaeological Journal* 5:1–38.

Shanks, M. 1995d. 'The Forms of History', in *Interpreting Archaeology: Finding Meaning in the Past*. Edited by I. Hodder, M. Shanks, A. Alexandri, V. Buchli, J. Carman, J. Last and G. Lucas. London: Routledge.

Shanks, M. 1996. *Classical Archaeology: Experiences of the Discipline*. London: Routledge.

Shanks, M. 1997a. 'L'Archéologie et le Passé Contemporain: Un Paradigme', in *Une Archéologie du Passé Recent*. Edited by A. Schnapp. Paris: Maison des Sciences de l'Homme.

Shanks, M. 1997b. 'Photography and the Archaeological Image', in *The Cultural Life of Images: Visual Representation in Archaeology*. Edited by B. Molyneaux. London: Routledge.

Shanks, M. 1998. 'The Life of an Artefact'. *Fennoscandia Archaeologica* 15:15–42.

Shanks, M. 1999. *Art and the Early Greek State: An Interpretive Archaeology*. Cambridge: Cambridge University Press.

Shanks, M. 2000a. 'Archaeology/Politics', in *Blackwell Companion to Archaeology*. Edited by J. Bintliff. Oxford: Blackwell.

Shanks, M. 2000b. 'Culture/Archaeology: The Dispersion of a Discipline and its Objects', in *Archaeological Theory Today: Breaking the Boundaries*. Edited by I. Hodder. Oxford: Blackwell Polity.

Shanks, M. and I. Hodder. 1995. 'Processual, Postprocessual and Interpretive Archaeologies', in *Interpreting Archaeology: Finding Meaning in the Past*. Edited by I. Hodder, M. Shanks, A. Alexandri, V. Buchli, J. Carman, J. Last and G. Lucas, pp. 3–29. London: Routledge.

Shanks, M. and I. Mackenzie. 1994. 'Archaeology: Theories, Themes and Experience', in *Theoretical Archaeology: Progress or Posture?* Edited by I. Mackenzie. London: Avebury.

Shanks, M. and R. McGuire. 1996. 'The Craft of Archaeology'. *American Antiquity* 61:75–88.

Shanks, M. and C. Tilley. 1982. 'Ideology, Power and Ritual Communication: A Reinterpretation of Neolithic Mortuary Practice', in *Social Theory and Archaeology*. Edited by I. Hodder. Cambridge: Polity Press.

Shanks, M. and C. Tilley. 1987. *Social Theory and Archaeology*. Cambridge: Blackwell Polity.

Shanks, M. and C. Tilley. 1992. *ReConstructing Archaeology: Theory and Practice*, Second edition. London: Routledge.

Shapin, S. 1994. *A Social History of Truth: Civility and Science in Seventeenth Century England*. Chicago: University of Chicago Press.

Shapin, S. and S. Schaffer. 1985. *Leviathan and the Air Pump: Hobbes, Boyle and the Experimental Life*. Princeton: Princeton University Press.

Sherratt, A. and S. Sherratt. 1991. 'From Luxuries to Commodities: The Nature of Mediterranean Bronze Age Trading Systems', in *Bronze Age Trade in the Mediterranean*. Edited by N. H. Gale/Jonsered: Paul Åströms.

Sherratt, S. and A. Sherratt. 1993. 'The Growth of the Mediterranean Economy in the Early First Millennium BC'. *World Archaeology* 24:361–78.

Sinclair, I. 1997. *Lights Out for the Territory. 9 Secret Excursions in the Secret History of London*. London: Granta Books.

Skinner, Q. Editor. 1985. *The Return of Grand Theory in the Human Sciences*. Cambridge: Cambridge University Press.

Smiles, S. 1994. *The Image of Antiquity: Ancient Britain and the Romantic Imagination*. New Haven: Yale University Press.

Snodgrass, A. 1980. *Archaic Greece: The Age of Experiment*. London: Dent.

Snodgrass, A. 1991. 'Specialised sculpture avant la lettre'. *Classical Review* 43:376–7.

Spector, J. D. 1991. 'What this Awl Means: Toward a Feminist Archaeology', in *Engendering Archaeology: Women and Prehistory*. Edited by J. M. Gero and M. W. Conkey. Oxford: Blackwell.

Spivak, G. 1991. 'Identity and Alterity: An Interview'. *Arena*: 65–76.

Spolin, V. 1983. *Improvisations for the Theater*. Evanston, IL: Northestern University Press.

Spufford, F. 1996. *I May Be Some Time*. London: Faber and Faber.

Spybey, T. 1996. *Globalization and World Society*. Oxford: Blackwell Polity.

Steward, J. 1955. *Theories of Culture Change*. Urbana: University of Illinois Press.

Stewart, A. 1986. 'When is a Kouros not an Apollo? The Tenea "Apollo" revisited', in *Corinthiaca: Studies in Honour of Darrell A Amyx*. Edited by M. A. Del Chiaro. Columbia, MI: University of Missouri Press.

Stewart, A. 1990. *Greek Sculpture: An Exploration*. New Haven: Yale University Press.

Stoller, P. 1989. *The Taste of Ethnographic Things: The Senses in Anthropology*. Philadelphia: University of Pennsylvania Press.

Stoneman, P. 1998. *A Luminous Land: Artists Discover Greece*. Los Angeles: J. Paul Getty Museum.

Stoneman, R. 1987. *Land of Lost Gods: The Search for Classical Greece*. London: Hutchinson.

Stover, E. and G. Peress. 1998. *The Graves. Srebrenica and Vukovar*. Zurich/Berlin/New York: Scalo.

Strang, V. 1997. *Uncommon Ground: Cultural Landscapes and Environmental Values*. Oxford: Berg.

Strum, S. and B. Latour. 1987. 'The Meaning of Social: From Baboons to Humans'. *Information sur les Sciences Sociales/Social Science Information* 26:783–802.

Tarlow, S. 1998. 'Wormie Clay and Blessed Sleep: Death and Disgust in Later Historic Britain', in *The Familar Past? Archaeologies of Later Historical Britain*. Edited by S. Tarlow and S. West. London: Routledge.

Tarlow, S. 1999. *Bereavement and Commemoration: An Archaeology of Mortality*. Oxford: Blackwell.

Theweleit, K. 1987. *Male Fantasies. Volume One: Women, Floods, Bodies, History*. Cambridge: Blackwell Polity.

Theweleit, K. 1989. *Male Fantasies. Volume Two: Male Bodies: Psychoanalysing the White Terror*. Cambridge: Blackwell Polity.

Thomas, D. H. 1998. *Archaeology*. Fort Worth: Harcourt Brace.

Thomas, J. 1994. 'Theatre/Archaeology: A Response'. *The Drama Review* 38:133–61.

Thomas, J. C. 1996. *Time, Culture and Identity: An Interpretive Archaeology*. London: Routledge.

Thomas, J. S. 1991a. 'Reading the Body: Beaker Funerary Practice in Britain', in *Sacred and Profane*. Edited by P. Garwood, D. Jennings, R. Skeates and J. Toms, pp. 33–42. Oxford: Oxford University Committee for Archaeology.

Thomas, J. S. 1991b. *Rethinking the Neolithic*. Cambridge: Cambridge University Press.

Thomas, J. S. 1993. 'The Politics of Vision and the Archaeologies of Landscape', in *Landscape: Politics and Perspectives*. Edited by B. Bender, J. Gledhill and B. Kapferer, pp. 19–48. Providence, RI/Oxford: Berg.

Thomas, J. S. 1999. *Understanding the Neolithic*. London/New York: Routledge.

Thomas, J. S. and Whittle. A. W. R. 1986. 'Anatomy of a Tomb: West Kennet Revisited'. *Oxford Journal of Archaeology* 5:129–56.

Thomas, J. S. and C. Tilley. 1993. 'The Axe and the Torso: Symbolic Structures in Neolithic Brittany', in *Interpretative Archaeology*. Edited by C. Tilley, pp. 225-326. London: Berg.

Thomas, N. 1991. *The Welsh Extremist: Modern Welsh Politics, Literature and Society*. Talybont, Wales: Y Lolfa.

Thompson, E. P. 1978. *The Poverty of Theory*. London: Merlin.

Thorpe, A. 1998. *Ulverton*. London: Vintage.

Tilley, C. 1990a. 'Claude Lévi-Strauss: Structuralism and Beyond', in *Reading Material Culture*. Edited by C. Tilley. Oxford: Blackwell.

Tilley, C. Editor. 1990b. *Reading Material Culture: Structuralism, Hermeneutics and Poststructuralism*. Oxford: Blackwell.

Tilley, C. 1994. *A Phenomenology of Landscape. Places, Paths and Monuments*. London: Berg.

Time Out. 1971. 'Guide to Underground Theatre – Theatre Survey No. 1'. *Theatre Quarterly* 1–1:61–5.

Tomlinson, R. A. 1980. 'Two Notes on Possible Hestiatoria'. *Annual of the British School at Athens* 75:220–8.

Tomlinson, R. A. 1990. 'The Chronology of the Perakhora Hestiatorion and its Significance', in *Sympotica: a Symposium on the Symposion*. Edited by O. Murray. Oxford: Clarendon Press.

Townsend, C. 1998. *Vile Bodies. Photography and the Crisis of Looking*. Munich/New York: Prestel-Verlag.

Trigger, B. 1984. 'Alternative Archaeologies: Nationalist, Colonialist, Imperialist'. *Man* 19:355-70.

Tschumi, B. 1990. *Questions of Space: Lectures on Architecture*. London: Architectural Association.

Tschumi, B. 1994a. *Architecture and Disjunction*. Cambridge, MA: MIT Press.

Tschumi, B. 1994b. *The Manhatten Transcripts*. London: Academy Editions.

Tschumi, B. 1994c. *Event-Cities (Praxis)*. Cambridge, MA: MIT Press.

Tsigakou, F.-M. 1981. *The Rediscovery of Greece: Travellers and the Painters of the Romantic Era*. London: Thames and Hudson.

Tuan, Y.-F. 1976. 'Geopiety: A Theme in Man's Attachment to Nature and to Place', in *Geographies of the Mind: Essays in Historical Geography*. Edited by D. Lowenthal and M. J. Bowden. New York: Oxford University Press.

Turing, A. 1950. 'Computing Machinery and Intelligence'. *Mind* 59:433–61.

Turner, B. Editor. 1990. *Theories of Modernity and Postmodernity*. London: Sage.

Turner, G. 1996. *British Cultural Studies: An Introduction*, Second edition. London: Routledge.

Tylor, E. 1870. *Primitive Culture: Researches into the Development of Mythology, Philosophy, Religion, Language, Art, and Custom*. New York: Holt.

Ucko, P. and R. Layton. Editors. 1999. *The Archaeology and Anthropology of Landscape: Shaping Your Landscape*. London: Routledge.

van Gennep, A. 1960. *The Rites of Passage*. London: Routledge and Kegan Paul.

Vermeule, E. 1979. *Aspects of Death in Early Greek Art and Poetry*. Berkeley: University of California Press.

Vernant, J.-P. 1969. 'Le Mythe Hésiodique des Races: Essai d'Analyse Structurale', in *Mythe et Pensée chez les Grecs*. Paris: Maspero.

Vernant, J.-P. 1982. 'City-state Warfare', in *Myth and Society in Ancient Greece*. London: Methuen.

Vernant, J.-P. 1991a. 'A "Beautiful Death" and the Disfigured Corpse in Homeric epic', in *Mortals and Immortals: Collected Essays*. Princeton: Princeton University Press.

Vernant, J.-P. 1991b. 'Death in the Eyes: Gorgo, Figure of the Other', in *Mortals and Immortals: Collected Essays*. Princeton: Princeton University Press.

Vernant, J.-P. 1991c. '*Panta Kala*: From Homer to Simonides', in *Mortals and Immortals: Collected Essays*. Princeton: Princeton University Press.

Vernant, J.-P. and F. Frontisi-Ducroux. 1983. 'Figures du Masque en Grèce Ancienne'. *Journal de Psychologie* 1–2:56–75.

Vian, F. 1968. 'La Fonction Guerrière dans la Mythologie Grecque', in *Problèmes de la Guerre en Grèce Ancienne*. Edited by J.-P. Vernant. Paris: Mouton.

Wagstaff, J. M. Editor. 1987. *Landscape and Culture*. Oxford: Blackwell.

Waldman, M. 1972. *Waldman on Theater. The Photographs of Max Waldman*. New York: Anchor.

Wales, G. O. 1978. *The Journey through Wales and The Description of Wales*. London: Penguin Books.

Wallis, B. Editor. 1989. *Blasted Allegories: An Anthology of Writings by Contemporary Artists*. Cambridge, MA: MIT Press.

Walsh, K. 1992. *The Representation of the Past: Museums and Heritage in the Postmodern World*. London: Routledge.Weegee (A. Fellig). 1975. *Naked City*. New York: Da Capo.

Welton, D. Editor. 1999. *The Body*. Oxford: Blackwell.

West, M. L. Editor. 1992. *Iambi et Elegi Graeci*, Second edition. Oxford: Oxford University Press.

West, M. L. 1993. *Greek Lyric Poetry: Translated with Introduction and Notes*. Oxford: Clarendon Press.

Westwood, S. and J. Williams. Editors. 1997. *Imagining Cities: Scripts, Signs, Memory*. London/New York: Routledge.

White, L. 1959. *The Evolution of Culture*. New York: McGraw Hill.

Whittle, A. W. R. 1988. *Problems in Neolithic Archaeology*. Cambridge: Cambridge University Press.

Willey, G. 1953. *Prehistoric Settlement Patterns in the Virú Valley, Peru*. Washington, DC: US Government Print Office.

Williams, D. J. 1987. *The Old Farmhouse*. Carmarthen, Wales: The Golden Grove Book Company.

Williams, G. A. 1985. *When Was Wales? A History of the Welsh*. Harmondsworth: Penguin Books.

Williams, J. 1995. *Bloody Valentine. A Killing in Cardiff*. London: HarperCollins.

Williams, R. 1973. *The Country and the City*. London: Chatto and Windus.

Williams, W. 1991. *Dail Pren*. Llandysul, Wales: Gwasg Gomer.

Wishart, T. 1984. 'Sights and Sounds of 10th Century Coppergate'. *Popular Archaeology* 5:11–14.

Wordsworth, W. 1973. *Tintern Abbey*, in *Romantic Poetry and Prose*. Edited by H. Bloom and L. Trilling. Oxford: Oxford University Press.

Young, R. J. C. 1995. *Colonial Desire: Hybridity in Theory, Culture and Race*. London/New York: Routledge.

Zinserling, V. 1975. 'Zum Bedeutungsgehalt des archaischen Kuros'. *Eirene* 13:19–33.

INDEX

Note: Figures are indicated by italics.

auditoria 108–9,110–11
Augé, Marc 150
aura 95
Auschwitz 124
Austin, A. A. 81
Austin, David 179, 183
Australia 138
authenticity
    and dramatic re-enactment 116–19
    imagination and rupture 118–19
    and romantic fallacy 113–16
Avebury 38–9, 120

Bachelard, G. 141, 146,157, 161
backdrops 22–3
Bahn, P. 29, 34
Barba, Eugenio 187
Barrell, John 142–3
Barrett, J. C. 68–9,121–2, 125, 128
Barth, M. 176
Barthes, Roland 53, 159
Baudelaire, Charles 149
Bauman, Z. 20
Bender, Barbara 154
Benjamin, Walter XII, 1, 3, 33, 51, 52, 61, 68, 95,
    137, 148, 159
Berenicë 167
Berger, John 65, 147,151–2, 154
Bhabha, H. K. 15, 27–8,109, 185
Big Pit (Blaenafon) 118,127f
Black Gate (Newcastle uponTyne) 3
Blade Runner 96
Blake, William 106
Blindfold 8–9, 9f, 48f
body
    armour 79, 80f, 81
    Arturius Rex 134f
    Cusanu Esgyrn 126f
    death 77–8, 84–5 (see also mortuary rituals)
    eyes and gaze 73
    faces 75–6
    Der Gefesselte 48f, 94f
    gesture 16, 117, 120
    Gododdin 20f, 34f
    haptics 19, 120
    movement 16, 24, 121–2
    Pax 106f
    performance and meeting 18–20, 59
    performance and personal engagement 15–18,
        54
    posture 79–80
    proxemics 19, 120,127–8
    sensory experience 134, 135
    volume 16, 17
    walking 135–7, 138,156f
    warfare 79–80, 83–4
Boltanski, Christian 64

Borges, J. L. 26
Bourdieu, P. 141
Boyle, Robert 45–7,49–50
Brackenbury, Augustus 143,144, 145
Britannia 37
Brith Gof XI, XVII, 5, 63, 187
    Angelus 3, 4f,188
    Arturius Rex 35f, 106, 107f, 134f, 182, 188
    Camlann 20f, 21f, 105–6, 182, 188
    Cusanu Esgyrn 34f, 35f, 95f, 126f, 135f
    D.O.A. 48f, 95f, 182, 188
    From Memory (A Death in the Family and
        Autopsy) 66, 120, 180, 187
    From Memory (The Body of Evidence) 161, 177,
        180, 188
    Der Gefesselte 20f, 21f, 48f, 49f, 94f, 187, 188
    Gododdin (see Gododdin)
    Haearn 49f, 68, 106f, 188
    In Black and White 182, 188
    Los Angeles 13–14, 14f, 21f, 35f, 187
    Patagonia 108–9,132, 188
    Pax 95f, 106f, 157f
    Prydain: The Impossibility of Britishness 106, 188
    Tri Bywyd (Three Lives) 35f, 160–2, 188
Bronze Age 129
Brookes, Mike 13, 189
    see also Pearson/Brookes
Brötzmann, Peter 3, 4f, 20f, 48f, 49f, 94f, 188
Bubbling Tom 180
Buchli, V. 179
Bure, Johan 38
Burke, Edmund 15, 142
Burton, Robert 38
Butler, Judith 14, 69

Camden, William 37
Camlann 20f, 21f, 105–6, 182, 188
Campbell, D. A. 79
Campbell, Fiona 179
Cardiff Laboratory Theatre 5, 187
Carter, Paul 185
causewayed enclosures 122–3
Celtica 115–16, 117, 118
Centre for Performance Research (Cardiff) 8, 179
Ceredigion 142
Chatterjee, P. 36
Childe, Gordon 34, 100
cinema vocabulary 63
    see also movies
cityscape: walking 126f
    desire maps 147–8, 151
    flâneurs 149
    nomads 149
    ramblers 149–50
    urban time-spaces 150–1
    walkers 148–9
    see also Deep Maps: 1937 cityscape